Musings

Tales of Truth & Wisdom

by Linda M. Ford

fulcrum resources
Golden, Colorado

Library of Congress Cataloging-in-Publication Data

Ford, Linda M.

Musings : tales of truth and wisdom / by Linda M. Ford.

p. cm.

Includes bibliographical references and index.

ISBN 1-55591-980-4

1. Tales—Study and teaching. 2. Anthropology—Study and teaching.

I. Title

GR74.F67 2000

398.2—dc21 00-020361

Printed in the United States of America

0 9 8 7 6 5 4 3 2 1

Book design: Pauline Brown • Pebble Graphics • Denver, Colorado

Fulcrum Publishing

16100 Table Mountain Parkway, Suite 300

Golden, Colorado 80403

(800) 992-2908 • (303) 277-1623

www.fulcrum-resources.com

This book is dedicated with great love to my father, Clifford Ford, *who brought poetry into our family; to my mother,* Thelma Martin Ford, *for laughter and stories and more things than I can name; and to my talented sister,* Marti Ann Ford, *who inspired me to start writing.*

And *to the people of* Livingston *who will share the arrival of this book, for their love and for who they are.*

Contents

3
Resources

4
Room for Improvement

5
Beauty & Virtue

6
Wisdom & Foolishness

Introduction

The stories in this book were collected for several excellent reasons—but I would have collected them anyway, were there no good reason at all. The telling of stories seems to be a common thread in every human culture: tales about love, societal values, tricksters, heroes, and beliefs—myths that attempt to explain how and why things are and came to be.

A philosopher was once trying to interest his bored audience with his rational discourse. He then said, "Once upon a time Ceres journeyed in company with a swallow and an eel until they came to a river...." At these words, the entire company settled down and paid close attention to what the man had to say.

One version of the story says that the philosopher then proceeded to berate his audience for not listening to serious matters of importance but were instead more interested in idle tales. Personally, I think the philosopher was missing the point. Information isn't *everything*. Stories seem to bridge the gap between information and experience. And sometimes stories convey truth more effectively than does rational discourse.

I love stories, as my groaning file cabinets could attest, and *Musings: Tales of Truth & Wisdom* arose first from this love. Yet, equally important, this collection embraces human diversity. I believe that people have more things in common than they have differences, although our differences make us interesting.

As the book title indicates, these stories contain truth and wisdom. Truth is sometimes found in answers, but sometimes raising the question is part of wisdom.

This collection is divided into six general thematic sections. An index is provided for readers who are seeking stories concerning specific subjects and for cultural sources. Every story is provided with an endnote containing source and variant sources; some endnotes include additional storytelling or cultural information.

Readers may notice that the sources for many of these stories come from the nineteenth and twentieth centuries. This was a period of great interest in folktales and in folklore generally, so I found it to be an excellent period in which to focus my research. In some cases the older sources have been purposely chosen because they are closer to the original culture.

1

Community

Mountains cannot meet, but men can — Yiddish • The whole world is one city — Jewish • If you dig a pit for me, you dig one for yourself — Southern • When two partners have one mind, its sharpness cuts through metal — Japanese/Chinese • The heron and the oyster quarrel, and the fisherman gets the benefit — Japanese/Chinese • When you are in the town, if you observe that the people wear the hat on one side, wear yours likewise — Armenian • Silence gives consent — Yiddish • A house divided against itself cannot stand — Lincoln.
AESOP
BIDPAE
KRYLOV
SAXE

The Canoe and the Paddle

In this fable from Africa (Congo), Canoe and Paddle argue about which is more valuable.

One day Canoe said to Paddle, "I am more important than you!"

"No!" exclaimed Paddle. "You are not more important. Let us call each other equals and live on friendly terms together."

"What!" Canoe gasped. "You and I equals? In what? Are you as big as I?"

"Of course I am not as big as you, and you are not as small as I am. You can do things that I can't, and I can accomplish tasks that you will never do," said Paddle. "But if you still think you are more important, we'll settle it this way. In a little while the people will come and load you with goods, and then you can go down the river by yourself. I am so small that you will surely not need me."

After a time, a man came and loaded Canoe full of goods; when he had finished, he said, "Come, Canoe, why aren't we starting down the river?" But Canoe only answered, "Wait a bit." The man kept asking the same question, and he always received the same answer.

Then the man left Canoe and went to call Paddle, but Paddle wouldn't come. At last Paddle said, "Call Canoe and we will settle this matter!"

The case was tried in court, and Paddle won the argument. The verdict was that Canoe and Paddle were to be regarded as equals—neither was more important than the other.[1]

The Trees and the Axe

This fable, very similar to "The Trees and the Woodsman," (Part 6) has a different ending. It is attributed to Phaedrus.

A woodsman came into the forest and asked the trees to give him a handle for his ax. It seemed like such a minor request that the larger trees at once agreed to it, and they decided that the plain, homely ash tree should be taken to furnish the handle.

No sooner had the ash been sacrificed than the woodsman fitted the handle onto his blade. Immediately, he began chopping on all sides, striking down the strongest trees in the forest. The oak saw the truth too late and whispered to the cedar: "If we had not sacrificed our humble neighbor, we might have yet stood for ages ourselves."

When the powerful surrender the rights of the powerless, they give a handle to be used against themselves.[2]

Connected

This story is loosely based on the Greek myth of Ariadne and Theseus.

Once upon a time a young man was called upon to become a hero. A terrible monster lived deep in a winding cave, and it was the task of this man to go alone into the darkness to fight and slay the beast. Many other heroes had tried the same feat, yet all had perished, for if the beast did not destroy them, they died of hunger, lost in the darkness.

Now, the man had a friend who wanted to help. She thought and she thought about what could be done, for she had no skill with a sword. Finally she seized upon a plan. At the entrance of the cave she gave him a great ball of string, while she held one end.

As the young hero walked forward to meet the beast, he knew he would not perish in the darkness. With the string to guide him, he would easily find his way back to the light. And he found new courage in his hand and in his heart, for he was still connected to one who was watching and waiting and hoping for him.[3]

The Bat, the Birds, and the Animals

This ancient fable may have been told first by Aesop or Phaedrus. Variants have been found in the folklore of several cultures, including the Native American Modocs and the Ibos of Nigeria, Africa. Aesop concluded that if you are neither one thing nor the other, you have no friends.

Once upon a time the birds and the animals declared war upon each other.

The birds collected their army together and saw the bat sitting on a tree branch. "Come with us," the birds called to him. "Help us in our war against the animals."

"No," replied the bat. "I certainly won't fight on your side. See my fur? I am an animal, not a bird."

Later, the animals passed by under his tree and called to the bat. "Come, join us in our war against the birds." The bat spread his wings and said, "Look at me. I am not an animal, but a bird, so I can't possibly fight on your side."

To the relief of everyone, the animals and birds made peace with each other before the war began. Each army held a great party to celebrate the peace.

The bat came first to the campfires of the birds and wanted to join in the fun, but they all turned against him and he had to fly away. He then went to the animals, but they refused to have anything to do with him either. Ever since, the bat has been an outcast, accepted by neither the birds nor the animals.[4]

The Ringdove and Her People

This story is from the Fables of Bidpai, a wisdom collection from India. A similar story comes from the Shan people who live along the border of India and China.

There was a place where the birds enjoyed gathering upon the wide branches of a certain tree. One day, a fowler came to the tree, spread his net on the ground, and scattered seeds over it. He then hid himself a short way off. A ringdove and a number of her friends came and settled on the ground to eat the seeds and were caught in the net.

The birds flapped their wings and frantically tried to escape the net. Only the ringdove kept her senses. "Don't tire yourselves," she told her companions. "It is no use fighting against the net. Don't think only about yourself and your personal safety. If we work together we can fly the net away."

Taking her advice, they lifted their wings and managed to rise into the air with the net, leaving the fowler far below.

The ringdove directed them to the home of her good friend, a rat, so that he might free them from the net. Upon reaching his hole, she called his name. He came out and started gnawing upon that part of the net where the ringdove was entangled. Yet she insisted he first rescue her companions.

"Why?" he asked.

"Well," she explained, "my friends are strangers to you, so you might want to free only me because they do not matter to you. But I am sure that if you let them out first, you will continue until I am also released."

The rat was deeply impressed by the ringdove's unselfish concern for her friends. He set to work with so much zeal that all of the birds were soon free.[5]

The Unselfish Wren and the Selfish Owl

Here follows an English tale of the wren's efforts to bring fire to the earth.

There was no fire on earth, and it was a cold and dreary place to live. Only in the heavens was there fire, but it would be a terrible and dangerous task for anyone to go there and bring it back to earth. The wren was weak and delicate, but she cheerfully volunteered for the dangerous mission. The brave little bird nearly lost her life in the task, for during her flight the fire scorched away all of her plumage.

Moved by such unselfish devotion, the other birds each presented the wren with one of their own feathers. These would cover her bare and shivering skin.

Only the owl stood aloof in philosophic disdain. He refused to honor, even with such a trifling gift, an act of heroism that he himself had not performed. This callous attitude made the other birds angry, and they came to dislike him so much that they refused from that time to admit him into their fellowship. Ever since, the owl has been compelled to keep away from other birds during the day, and only when night comes on does he dare to leave his gloomy hiding place.[6]

The Horse and the Ass

This fable has been attributed to Aesop.

A well-fed, lazy horse was traveling in the company of a heavily laden ass. Both belonged to the same master. The back of the ass was nearly breaking under his load, and he asked the horse, for the sake of common kindness, to take some portion of it. The horse indignantly refused. The poor ass struggled on a little further, then fell down and died.

The master then laid the whole of the burden upon the horse's back, and the skin of the ass besides. It was no consolation to the horse to realize it was his own fault, because if he had been willing to share part of the ass's load, he would not now have all of it.[7]

The Partridge and the Cocks

This fable has been attributed to Aesop.

A man captured a partridge and clipped his wings so he could not fly away. He placed the partridge in a little yard where he kept gamecocks, who were rude and impolite to the newcomer.

At first the partridge thought he was treated meanly because he was a stranger. However, he soon discovered that the gamecocks argued and fought with each other constantly, so he stopped being surprised that they did not respect him.[8]

Had It Not Been a Fable

In this story from the Ibo people of Nigeria, there are some similarities to Aesop's fable "The Body and Its Parts" (Part 1). The law of hospitality to strangers that figures in this story is an important part of many cultures worldwide. The original folklorist who collected this tale added that the Ibo, who first narrated the legend, said: "Just think of this story; it practically seems to be true—had it not been a fable."

There was once a very wonderful man. He formed the different parts of the body—the head, feet, hands, eyes, and other members, so they could live separate and to themselves. When the man had completed everything he placed them in a beautiful garden. He gave them certain laws to follow. The most important laws were that they should be generous in charity and that they should show kindness and hospitality to strangers.

One day their creator decided to test the loyalty of the citizens of the garden. He disguised himself as a terribly deformed leper and applied first to the eyes for help. But the eyes thought he looked repulsive, so they drove him away in disgust.

Next he appeared to the head and fared no better, for the nose thought his sores too odorous to get near. The feet and the hands also refused to assist him.

Finally, the leper went to the stomach. The stomach would have liked to turn his back on the unsightly leper with the smelly sores, but he remembered the commands of his creator. So he treated the beggar kindly.

The next day the man sent messengers carrying gifts to the citizens in the garden. To the eyes he sent blindness; to the head, headaches; to the feet, rheumatism; to the hands, paralysis; and to the stomach, pain. All the parts were commanded to come to him. When charged with ungenerous and disloyal conduct, only the stomach could plead "not guilty."

Because the stomach was the only righteous one among them, their creator decreed that every other member of the body would be a servant to the stomach. The head should carry its food, the eyes must constantly watch the way the body should take, the hands were to find and prepare its food, and the feet should carry it wherever it chose to go.

Now, some might say that the stomach was stupid, whereas others would say that the stomach was loyal and kind because it begged to be allowed to share the troubles of the others. The creator agreed to the stomach's request and said that its place would be in the front, a position that exposed it to many dangers.[9]

Neighbors

This Danish tale shows trolls with a different characterization than most cultures, with the implication being that the prejudice of humans inhibits friendly relations with the trolls.

Once upon a time a young couple settled down in a small cottage. It lay in the middle of some barren countryside that had a bad reputation because trolls were believed to live in that area. But the man and wife cared nothing for such rumors. "When you trust in God," they said, "and when you do what is just and right to all people, you don't have to live in fear."

Late one evening they heard a knock at the door. When the man opened it, a little man walked in and wished them good evening. He wore a red cap on his head and a leather apron in which was stuck a hammer, and he had a long beard, long hair, and a large hump on his back. They immediately knew he was a troll, although he seemed so good-natured and friendly they felt quite comfortable.

"I see you know what I am," said the troll. "We have a problem, my people do. This is one of the few places we can live in the world. We have heard that you have come to dwell here, and our king is afraid you will do us harm and try to destroy us. He has sent me to you to beg, as nicely as I can, to allow us to live in peace. You will never be annoyed by us or disturbed by us in anything you do."

"You may be easy about that, good troll," said the husband. "I have never injured any of God's creatures willingly, and the world is large enough for us all. I think we can manage to agree with each other and live in friendship."

"Well, thank God!" exclaimed the little man, dancing about the room in joy. "This is wonderful news, and in return we will do all the good we can. And now I must leave."

"Wait," said the wife, "won't you stay and have some supper with us?"

"No, thank you," said the troll. "Our king and people are impatient for me to return, and it would be mean to make them wait for the good news." He said good-bye and left.

The couple kept their promise, living in peace and friendship with the little people. The trolls felt free to borrow what they needed from the husband and wife, and they always returned it in good condition. In the spring, they collected the stones from the field so that the man would have an easier time plowing. At harvest, they picked up all the stray ears of corn so that nothing might be lost to the young couple. The farmer and his wife were very grateful for such good neighbors, and on holidays, the wife always placed a dish of something special out for the celebrations of the trolls.

When their first child was born, the wife was very ill and nearly died. Her husband stayed up all night to do what he could. Once he became drowsy, and when his eyes opened, he saw the trolls crowding the cottage, rocking the baby, cleaning the room, and giving his wife a special herb tea. From that night she began to regain her health.

After several years, the couple and their children were invited to a feast at the caverns of the trolls. Although it was supposed to be a happy occasion, they could see their friends were sad. The trolls finally explained: The countryside was growing crowded, and they had decided it would be best to move across the sea, where some of their people had already gone. But they had wanted to have this last dinner with their good friends.

It was a sad occasion when the neighbors said farewell. The woman made them special cakes, and the trolls handed them a small sack of stones. But when they were gone and the man poured out the bag's contents upon the table, he discovered it was full of gold pieces, a gift from the trolls who valued peace and friendship.[10]

The Fairies' Cauldron

The failure to live up to a bargain lies at the heart of this English tale.

Once upon a time there was a great stone lying along a hill in Surrey, England. If anyone went to this place to borrow a yoke of oxen, or money, or something else, they could have it for a year or longer, as long as they kept their promise to return it. People would go to the stone, knock at it, and declare what they wanted to borrow and when they would repay it. A fairy voice would answer and tell them when they should come and find what they wanted at the stone.

One day a great cauldron and trivet were borrowed in this way, but they were not returned according to promise. Even though the cauldron was carried later to the stone, it was not accepted. Ever since, the fairies have stopped lending things to humans.[11]

The Wren as Firebringer

The following is one of several versions of Breton and Norman legends of how the wren brought fire from heaven to the earth. Many cultures tell stories of the sacrificial actions of the one who brings fire for the use of humankind. A famous example is the Greek myth of Prometheus.

The wren succeeded in obtaining fire from heaven and set off on her downward flight to earth. Alas! Her wings began to burn, and she was obliged to trust her precious burden to the care of the robin. His plumage also burst into flames, traces of which he still bears on his breast. The lark next came to the rescue and finished bringing the prize in safety to humankind for their use. The world would have been a cold and terrible place without the cooperation of the birds.[12]

How the People Came to Know Medicine Plants

Stories of the importance of hospitality can be found in many cultures. In this case, the visitor wished to bring the good knowledge of medicine to those who rejected him. The tale comes from the Native American people known as the Tuscarora.

Many winters ago a poor, sickly old man came to a village. The old man stopped at each wigwam and asked for food and a place to sleep during the night. He looked so sick that many of the families refused to let him enter their wigwams. He went the whole length of the village and at last came to one with a bearskin hanging over it. A kind old woman came out of this wigwam and brought food to him, then spread out a bed for him. The old man felt very sick. He told her what plants to gather in the woods to make him well.

The woman gathered these plants and did as he told her with them; the sores on his feet were thus healed, and he was better very soon. She promised not to forget the secret of the healing plants. In a few days he had a fever; once more he told her what plants and leaves to gather. She did so, and it was not long before he was well. She promised again not to forget what she had learned.

Many times he fell sick, but always with a new sickness. Each time he told the woman what plants to find to heal him. The woman learned more about medicine than anyone else knew.

One morning the old man told her that he had come to her village for that very reason, to teach the people the secrets that she now knew. Yet no one had welcomed him except the bear clan. "I am going away now," he said. "I came to do them good. No one but you would show kindness to the stranger, so now all tribes shall come to the bear tribe for help in sickness. You will show them the plants that can heal their sick people."

When the old man was finished talking he went out of sight. No one has ever seen him since that morning.[13]

The Body and Its Parts

This fable may have been told by Aesop, but see the earlier variant from the Ibo of Nigeria in "Had It Not Been a Fable" (Part 1).

One day it occurred to the parts of the body that they were doing all the work and the stomach was getting all the food. They held a meeting, and after a long discussion they decided to go on strike until the stomach agreed to do its proper share of work. For a day or two, the hands refused to lift the food, the mouth refused to accept it, and the teeth would not chew it.

But then the parts found they were not in a very good condition. The hands could hardly move, the mouth was parched and dry, and the legs grew wobbly and were unable to hold up the body. It was then they realized that even the stomach, in its dull, quiet way, was doing important work and that everyone must work together or the body would go to pieces.[14]

The Old Man's Wisdom

This story has been attributed to Aesop.

An old man had several sons who argued with one another constantly, and though he often asked them to live together in peace, they paid no attention.

One day he called his sons around him and pulled out a bundle of sticks. He asked each of them in turn to break the bundle across. Each put out all his strength, but the bundle resisted their efforts.

Then the old man cut the cord binding the sticks together and told his sons to break them separately. This was done easily.

"See, my sons," exclaimed the old man. "See the power of unity! Joined together by brotherly love, you can stand against the troubles that come your way. Divided, you will be at the mercy of the world."[15]

The Lion and the Four Oxen

This fable has been attributed to Aesop.

Four oxen were such good friends that they always stayed close together when in the fields. A lion watched for many days, but as he was never able to find one apart from the rest, he was afraid to attack. Whenever he came near, they turned their tails toward each other, so he faced their horns from every direction.

But the lion was clever and whispered some things to the field mouse, who whispered lies to the oxen. "What do you mean, I'm too fat!" one ox said to another. "The mouse told me what you said." Another demanded, "Who are you to say you do more than I do to protect us?"

The argument became heated, and the oxen went in anger to different parts of the meadow. Thus the lion easily killed them.

United we stand, divided we fall.[16]

The Elves and the Envious Shoemaker

Envy interferes with true community, as illustrated by this tale from Japan, but the jealous man receives a somewhat humorous justice for his mean-spiritedness.

Once upon a time there was a man who was caught in the mountains in the darkness. He took shelter in the trunk of a hollow tree. In the middle of the night a large party of elves gathered at the place, and the man was frightened. After a while, however, the elves began to have a great feast and then to sing and dance. The man was caught up in the fun and forgot about his fright. He crept out of his hollow tree to join the party.

When it was nearly morning, the elves said to the man: "You're a jolly companion, and you must come out and have a dance with us again. You must promise to come."

Now, this man had a wen (a growth) on his face, and the elves admired it greatly, so they took the wen from him. "You may have it back," said the little people, "when you return."

The man left the mountains overjoyed at his pleasant night and having gotten rid of the wen in the bargain. He told the story to all of his friends, who congratulated him warmly on being cured of his wen. But there was a neighbor of his who grew envious. He also had a wen and could not see why it should have been his neighbor who had such good luck. He went to hunt for the hollow tree to pass the night.

Toward midnight the elves came and began feasting and dancing. As soon as the man saw this, he came out of his hollow tree and began dancing and singing as his neighbor had done.

The elves mistook him for their former visitor and were delighted to see him. "You're a good fellow," they said, "because you remembered your promise, so we will give you back your pledge."

One of the elves pulled the wen out of his pocket and stuck it onto the man's forehead on top of the other wen that he already had. The envious neighbor went home weeping. But it wouldn't have happened if he could have enjoyed the good luck of his neighbor without wanting it for himself.[17]

The Birds in the Snare

This version of a story found in several cultures is from Russia and gives a different conclusion than "The Ringdove and Her People" (Part 1).

A hunter set a snare by a lake and caught many birds in it. Recognizing their danger, the birds decided to work together and fly away with the net. The hunter followed.

A man saw the hunter. "Where on earth are you going?" he demanded. "You can't catch those birds on foot."

"If there was only one bird, I wouldn't catch it," replied the hunter. "Since there are many, I only need to wait until they forget their danger; then I will have them."

When evening came, each bird tried to fly off in its own direction—one to the forest, another to the swamp, a third to the field. They began arguing about which way was best. All fell with the net to the ground, and the hunter easily captured them.[18]

An Argument Between the Two Hands

This fable from the Congo in Africa applies to community, male/female, and cultural relations.

The husband-hand (right) said to the wife-hand (left), "All the meat is mine: Wife, I will not give you any more meat. You never kill any animals!"

"Oh, really!" said the wife-hand. "You think that you alone kill the animals and you alone will eat the meat? All right; go ahead and eat your meat. And cut up your meat alone; I will not hold it for you. Cut your own leaves for cooking it yourself; chop the wood for the fire by yourself. Do your own curing of the meat if you want to preserve it. I won't touch it. Then weave your own baskets to carry the meat home; pick up the meat, and put it into the basket. Do all these things alone. Remember, I shall not touch it at all, since you think that you are the only one who hunts for the animals!"

So the husband-hand tried, and tried, and tried; but it was no use. He was quite unable to hunt, or cut, or gather, or chop, or weave, or carry alone. At last he had to leave his meat in the forest, where it spoiled and could not be eaten. All this because he had no partner to help him.

When the husband-hand wanted to go to the forest to hunt again, he said, "This won't do; we must go together. In the future we will both kill the animal, and together we will cut up the meat and prepare the leaves, the fuel, and the fire for cooking it. Together we will preserve the parts we wish to keep, and together we will weave the baskets, pack in the meat, and carry it home."

They returned to the forest and hunted the animals together. And they found that by helping each other, they could easily accomplish all that the husband-hand had been unable to do alone.

After their return home, the affair was thoroughly investigated by the community. The verdict was that although the wife-hand won the argument, the husband-hand came off best in the whole case, because when he realized he couldn't do anything without a partner, he admitted the truth and asked the wife-hand's help.[19]

Planting for the Future

This story comes from the Middle East.

One day the caliph went riding and saw a very ancient gentleman planting a fig tree.

"Why are you planting that tree?" asked the caliph. "After all, at your age you can hardly hope to taste any of its fruit."

"Perhaps that is true," the old man replied. "If God wills, I may live to taste the fruit of this tree. But if not, my children will do so, in the same way I have eaten the fruit of trees planted by my father and great-grandfather."

The caliph asked, "How old are you?"

"One hundred and seven."

"A hundred and seven!" exclaimed the caliph. "Well, if you really do live to eat fruit from this tree, be sure to let me know."

Several years passed, and the caliph forgot his encounter with the old man. Then one day he was told that an aged man desired an audience, saying that by the caliph's own command he had brought him a basket of figs.

The caliph was surprised to find that this was the same gentleman he had once seen planting a sapling who had now brought him some of the finest fruit from that same tree. He received the ancient peasant graciously and gave him a gold coin for each fig, in honor of his long years and faithfulness both to the past and to the future.[20]

The Swan, the Pike, and the Crab

The following fable is adapted from Ivan Krylov of Russia.

A swan, a pike, and a crab once agreed to share the work and drag a loaded cart. The moment came for them to start. They sweated. They strained. They pulled with all their strength! But the cart stood still.

Was the load too heavy? No, indeed, for it was very light. But the swan pulled toward the clouds. The pike labored toward the river. And the crab kept backing away.

"Now which of them was right, which wrong, concerns us not; the cart is still upon the exact same spot!"[21]

The Boys and the Frogs

This is an English fable.

On the edge of a lake in which a large number of frogs lived, a group of boys stopped to play. They thought it great fun to cast many stones into the water, which the terrified frogs dodged as best they could. At length, one frog scraped up his courage and lifted his head above the surface of the lake. He called to the boys, "Alas, young fellows. Why do you learn so young the cruel habits of the human race? Please think about the fact that although this may be a game for you, it means death for us!"[22]

The Hoopoe and the Woodpecker

Germans tell this tale of service between friends.

The hoopoe bird was the friend and companion of the woodpecker. The two birds once resolved to leave their native land for foreign parts, but the sea lay in their path. They flew halfway across, and then the woodpecker fell fast asleep! To save his companion from drowning, the hoopoe cried, "Hoop-hoop!" This kept his drowsy friend awake so he could make the passage in safety.

Anxious to show his gratitude, the woodpecker bored a hole in a tree to serve as a nest for the hoopoe. This was the first time the woodpecker ever used his pecking powers.[23]

The Pity of the Robin for the Wren

Varied stories are told in England of how the wren brought fire from heaven for the sake of humankind. Here, her friends seek to help after her sacrifice.

When the wren brought down fire from heaven, she lost all her plumage because it was scorched away. With one accord, the other birds each gave her one of their own feathers. The robin, in his anxiety and trouble, came too close to the poor wren, who was in flames, and his plumage took fire also. The traces of it are still visible on his red breast.[24]

Why Tigers Never Attack People Unless They Are Provoked

Disparate individuals prove fast friends in this tale from Africa.

A man, hunting one day in the forest, met a tiger. At first each was afraid of the other, but after some talking they became quite friendly. They agreed to live together for a while. First the man would live with the tiger in his forest home for two weeks. Then the tiger would come and live in the man's house.

The tiger treated the man better than he had ever been treated in all his life. Then came the time for the tiger to return home with the man. As they were going, the tiger was somewhat afraid. He asked the man if he would be safe. "What if your friends do not like my face and kill me?" he asked. "You need fear nothing," said his host; "no one will touch you while I am there." The tiger came to the man's house and stayed for three weeks. He had brought his male cub with him, and the young tiger became good friends with the man's son.

Some months later the man's father died. When the tiger heard of his friend's loss, he and his cub set out at once to see him, bringing a large sum of money to help the man.

As the tiger traveled home again, two of the man's friends lay in hiding and shot him. Fortunately, he was not killed, but he was very much grieved as he thought these men might have shot him at his friend's request. He decided to find out if the man had been involved. He went to the place in the forest where he had first met his friend. There he lay down as if he were dead, after telling his cub to watch and see what would happen.

By and by the man came along. When he saw the tiger apparently lying dead, he became terribly upset. He began to cry and mourn, and sat there all night long with the tiger's cub, to watch that no harm should come to the body.

When morning came and the tiger was quite sure his friend had nothing at all to do with the shot, he was very glad. He stood, to the man's great astonishment, and explained why he had pretended to be dead. "Go home," said the tiger, "and remember me always. In the future for your sake I will never touch a man unless he meddles with me first."[25]

Two Friends

This story is adapted from a Greek myth.

Once upon a time two boys grew up as neighbors and became the best of friends. Pythias and Damon were as close as brothers, and in some ways closer.

A sad day came when Damon's father moved to another country, but the two young men promised never to forget their friendship. Many years later Pythias found an opportunity to visit Damon. Their reunion was joyful, and although they had changed in many ways, their friendship remained the same.

During his visit, Pythias happened to offend the king of the country. The king threw him into prison and sentenced him to die in thirty days. Pythias begged the king for permission to first return home to say farewell to his wife and children and to his aged parents. The king only laughed. "Do you expect me to believe you will return?"

Damon stepped forward. "I will take his place in prison."

"Remember," said the king, "if he does not return, you will be killed in his place."

Damon insisted on remaining in prison while Pythias journeyed to his homeland. In the days that followed, the king often visited Damon in prison to laugh at him for believing Pythias would return and face death when he could so easily let Damon die in his place.

Thirty days passed, and Damon was led to the place of execution. At the last minute Pythias rushed forward, his clothing torn and ragged. He had battled storms and all kinds of obstacles, yet he arrived in time to save his friend.

But Damon objected and said he was still willing to die for Pythias. Their first real argument might have begun at that moment, except the king stopped them. Although he was a king, no one had ever shown him half as much loyalty as Damon and Pythias showed for each other.

"Neither man shall die," the king declared. "Instead, may I ask to be included in their circle of friendship?"[26]

The Judge's Strategy

This story about justice comes from Turkey and has been used in one of the poems by John Godfrey Saxe.

A faithful widow's cottage stood next to the mansion of a great lord. He wanted that piece of land for a summer house and tried to buy it from her.

"No," she replied. "It was my husband's home, and I wish to live here in his honor and memory."

Angered, the lord ordered the cottage torn down and a grand summer house built in its place.

The widow went straight to the judge and asked for help. He, in turn, went to the lord, who sat relaxing in the garden of his summer house. "Great sir," said the judge, "may I ask for some of the earth beneath your feet, enough to fill this sack?"

"Certainly," said the lord, laughing at the joke, and the bag was quickly filled.

"Now," said the judge, "please lift and place the bag upon my back."

"I'm sorry," said the lord, "but I fear my back would break to lift such a load."

"In that case," asked the judge, "how do you think you will manage in the day of judgment, when you must bear the weight of all the widow's land?"

Then the lord was filled with sorrow and repented of his deeds. "The land belongs to the widow," he declared, "and because this house stands upon it, the building is also her own." So, from that day on, the poor widow lived in the grand summer house of the lord.[27]

The Mussel and the Bittern Refuse to Make Peace

This is a very early fable from China.

A mussel was sunning itself along the riverbank when a bittern happened along and pecked at it. The mussel snapped its shell shut tight and neatly captured the end of the bird's beak.

The bittern said, "If you don't let me go today, and if you don't let me go tomorrow, there will be a dead mussel."

The mussel answered, "If I don't come out today, and if I don't come out tomorrow, then there will surely be a dead bittern."

Just then a fisherman came by and easily captured both the bittern and the mussel, and he took them home for dinner.[28]

The Frogs and the Fighting Bulls

The victims of war are the focus of this fable by Aesop.

A frog peeped out of a lake and saw two bulls fighting in the meadow. "Oh, dear!" he said to his friends. "What will become of us?"

"What are you so worried about?" the other frogs asked. "The quarrels of the bulls have nothing to do with us. They are only proving who is strongest and who will lead the herd."

"True," answered the first frog, "and that's why I am afraid. The one who is beaten will hide here in the marshes and will trample us to death."

That is exactly what happened, and many frogs died as innocent bystanders to a war that had nothing to do with them.[29]

The Two Bald Men

This fable was adapted from a French story.

One day two men, who both happened to be bald, walked the same road. Each spied a gleam of ivory and sprang forward to claim it.

"It's mine," exclaimed the first man.

"No! I saw it first," insisted the second.

A quarrel followed, beginning with words and ending with blows. The winner finished by losing the last few hairs he possessed. But he had won! He rushed forward and grasped his prize—an ivory comb.[30]

Enemies No Longer

Although this story is about a Chinese emperor, its cultural source is not known.

A Chinese emperor was told his enemies had raised a rebellion in one of the distant provinces. Promising to destroy his enemies, he called upon his soldiers to go forth. They marched forward, and the rebels submitted upon their approach.

Everyone thought the emperor would now take revenge, but they were surprised to see the captives treated most kindly.

"What is this?" cried one of his officials. "You have failed to keep your promise. You gave your royal word that your enemies would be destroyed. But you have pardoned all of them and even treated some with affection."

"I promised," replied the emperor, "to destroy my enemies, and I have kept my word. Look, they aren't my enemies anymore; I have made them my friends."[31]

The Eagle, the Cat, and the Pig

Fear paralyzes in this story attributed to Phaedrus and Aesop, with a version by Tolstoy.

An eagle built her nest in the top branches of an old oak tree, a wild cat dwelled in a hole in about the middle, and in the hollow part at the bottom lived a pig with a litter of baby pigs.

They might have stayed there in peace, but the cat wanted to make trouble. One day she crept up to the eagle. "Neighbor," she said, "have you noticed what the pig is doing? I believe she is determined to root up this tree in which we live, and when it falls she will eat our children." This put the eagle in a great fright, and she dared not stir from her home for fear the tree might fall in her absence.

Then the cat went down to visit the pig. "Listen to me, my friend," she told the pig. "Last night I overheard the eagle promising her young ones that the next time you went out, they would have one of your dear little children for supper." The pig was greatly alarmed and did not dare leave her hollow.

The fear of the eagle and the pig became so great that they and their young ones actually starved to death.[32]

The Three Vases

This story has been attributed to Aesop.

A miserly old man gathered a large amount of gold during his lifetime. To keep it safe, he placed the money in three vases and buried them secretly. When he was about to die, he called his three sons to him and told them of the treasure they would inherit and where the vases were hidden, one for each of them. He was too weak to finish what he was saying and soon died.

Now, the three young men had never seen these vases and thought perhaps they would be of different sizes. Each claimed he had the right to the largest container of gold. Their argument became very loud, and they began to fight. They finished the fight bruised and bleeding.

When all was done and they had patched up their injuries, the brothers dug up the three vases and discovered that each was the same size and held exactly the same amount of gold.[33]

The Price of Revenge

This fable has been attributed to Aesop.

The horse was angry with the stag because they had argued about the meadow in which they ate. Their quarrel was silly, for there was plenty for both of them to eat, but the horse was furious and wanted revenge.

The horse went to the man and asked for his help against the stag, and the man agreed. But the man pointed out it would be necessary to put a saddle and bridle on the horse if they were to overcome the stag. The horse accepted the saddle and bridle, and they went forth to punish the other animal.

After this, the horse wanted to be rid of the saddle and bridle because they kept him from going where he wanted to go. But the man refused. The price of the horse's revenge was the loss of his freedom.[34]

The United Pheasants

This tale about revenge and its price comes from Tibet. A variant appears in Hindu fables.

In a time long ago lived two pheasants whose bodies had grown together in the egg. Their names were Dharmika and Adharmika. One day, while Adharmika was asleep, Dharmika saw a piece of fruit washed ashore by the waves. He ate it because the fruit would feed the body they shared.

When the other awakened, he smelled the fruit on Dharmika's breath. "Where did you get it?" he asked.

"I found the fruit," Dharmika replied, "while you were asleep, and I ate it without waking you, so it would feed our common body."

Adharmika grew angry. "You have not acted rightly," he declared. "I will have my revenge."

On another occasion, when Dharmika had gone to sleep, Adharmika saw a poisonous fruit that the waves had brought ashore. He ate it, and both of the birds sickened and died. Such was the price of revenge.[35]

The Two Rabbits

This is a Spanish fable.

A rabbit raced from a pack of hungry hounds and tried with all his speed and strength to reach his burrow. As he prepared to duck into safety he spied another rabbit, who asked what was amiss. "Nothing less than a pack of greyhounds," he gasped. "I've nearly been run to death."

"What? Where? Ah, yes, I hear the bark of the dogs upon your track. But, good sir, there's not a greyhound in the pack. I can see them now, and though the difference is small, all the dogs are beagles."

"That's nonsense. The dogs I saw were greyhounds. I'm not blind."

An argument commenced. It was ended by the dogs, who upon arriving were delighted to find two rabbits instead of the one they had expected.[36]

The Lily and the Rose

This English fable is adapted from a poem by William Cowper.

The peace of the garden was broken by two lovely rivals. Each wanted to be the most admired. Each wanted to be held above the other. The rose swelled red with rage and pointed to the words of poets to prove her importance. The lily spoke of her graceful height, her royal flower.

A peacemaker came along. She wisely spoke of the glorious color of one, the stately demeanor of the other. Each was beautiful unto itself. There was no need for petty jealousies, or to seek for flaws in another. Each should be grateful for the gifts already possessed; no rival's merit made theirs any less.[37]

The King and the Cottage

This story is adapted from a poem by John Godfrey Saxe.

A king wanted a new palace and traveled throughout his kingdom, seeking a piece of land where he would have a beautiful view from each of his windows. He finally found the perfect spot. But an old woman already lived there in her tiny cottage, and she refused to move. She had been born in that cottage, had lived in it with her husband, and planned to die in that same little home.

The nobles of the court laughed at the woman. "Let us knock her ugly cottage around her ugly ears," they declared. They believed the mighty king would seize her land as his due. After all, he was the king, wasn't he?

"Good woman," the king told her, "pay no attention to these people. The king is on your side. Your cottage is your castle, and you shall live here as long as you wish. It is true, I have the power to take it. But who could honor my power if I used it to hurt my citizens? And who could respect me or my power if I ignore the law?" So, the king decided to build his castle beside the widow's home. They stood side by side, the grand palace and the tiny cottage.

The nobles of the court said the king was sick in his mind, but the people of the country loved him even more.

The king ruled his nation with honor and justice. But there are always those who envy royalty. Two such men lived in the palace, and they secretly plotted to kill the king. They planned the murder behind the widow's cottage, and the widow overheard their plan. She went straight to the king and told him of the plot.

"I understand now," the king exclaimed. "In respecting the rights of others, people may guard their own. The widow's humble cottage has saved my throne."[38]

Which Son Should Rule?

This original story uses some motifs from the Magyars of Hungary in which several stories begin with a king throwing his silverware.

Once upon a time a king sat by the window of his palace and spent the day sighing. The citizens of his kingdom weren't very nice. If someone was hungry or hurt, no one stopped to help. They enjoyed war and taking the riches that other kingdoms had gathered. When they weren't at war, they fought each other. This had never much bothered the king before, but now he was growing old and realized he had not been a very good king.

The king had three sons, and he was very proud of each. They were strong, brave, and handsome, and it was the king's job to decide which one should become king after him. Because he hadn't been a very good king so far, he wanted to at least do this one thing correctly.

The sons of the king noticed that their father seemed unhappy, but they didn't know why. The youngest son said he would ask. He went to the room where the king was sitting. "Father, what is it that makes you sigh and be sad?" The king was in a bad mood and didn't like to be disturbed, so he threw his spoon at his son. Fortunately, the prince ducked out of the way, and the spoon stuck partway in the door. He told his brothers it was no use asking such a grouch about anything.

Next, the oldest son said he would go and ask the king. He fared no better than his brother, for his father threw a fork at him, which stuck halfway in the door. "Give up on him," the oldest son said. "He's the biggest crab I ever saw."

The middle son decided that he would try anyway. "My father," he asked, "what makes you so sad?" The king was angrier than ever because he'd been disturbed twice already that day. He took up his butter knife and threw it. Lucky for the prince, he ducked out of the way, and the knife stuck most of the way into the door.

Then the middle son pulled with all his might and removed the spoon, the fork, and the butter knife and brought them back to his father. It was growing close to dinnertime, and the prince knew the king would need his silverware to eat.

The king was left alone. After he finished dinner, he suddenly jumped up. "I have it!" He called his court together and told them his decision. "My middle son will become king." The father had decided this because if his son could be nice to such a grumpy old man, maybe he could teach the people.

The king retired early, and the middle prince received the throne. The father no longer sat at a window and sighed, and his son made a much better king than he had ever been.[39]

The Honesty of the King

The hero of this tale is Persian.

A Persian king went hunting and wanted to eat some of his catch before he returned to his palace. Several of his servants went to a neighboring village and seized a quantity of salt to season the food.

However, the king suspected how they had acted and ordered them to immediately go and pay for it. Then he turned to his attendants. "This is a small matter in itself," he said, "but a large one as it regards me, for a king should always be just. The king is an example to his subjects; if he serves in trifles, they might become wicked. If I cannot make all my people just in the smallest things, I can, at least, show them it is possible to be so."[40]

Catfish Defeats Moose

Respect for the small and humble is taught in this tale by the Native American tribe of Menomini.

Moose was walking along the riverbank when he saw a catfish. "Why are you lying there in the water?" he bellowed.

"I simply decided to come to this part of the river," answered Catfish. "But what business is it of yours? I was created to live in the water, and I have a perfect right to be here."

"Well, I'm going to kick you once and that will settle you."

Moose rushed into the water, but when he raised his leg to kick Catfish, the little fish turned belly up and pointed his horns at Moose. He cried, "Take that!"

Moose stamped on the catfish and drove the horn into his hoof. He then leaped out of the water in great pain and ran up into the woods, having learned that it is wrong to despise anyone, however small and humble they appear.[41]

The Great Tower

This story comes from Mexico and is reminiscent of the Hebrew tale about the Biblical Tower of Babel, wherein the inability to communicate also stymies construction. Another story from Mexico tells that the giant Xelhua tried to build a tower into the sky, but the gods became angry with his presumption and twice broke it down—leaving only its remains, said to be the pyramid of Cholula.

In the far east from the city of Palenque, near the place where the sun rises, a great company of people came together to build a tower. They wanted to build a structure that would rise up into the heavens. What a magnificent accomplishment that would be! But their plans failed because all the builders spoke different languages. One would ask for a stone, but another would bring a piece of wood. They talked and argued until they couldn't accomplish anything.[42]

A Great Sacrifice

This story comes from Mexico.

Nezahualcoyotl was a prince, the son of a good and kindly king. When war came to their land, his father hid Nezahualcoyotl in the forest and proudly gave himself up to save his son. Nezahualcoyotl, whose name means Hungry Coyote, wandered through the forest and was eventually captured by the enemies of his father. They decided to cut him into pieces at their next festival.

One of the prince's friends, Quetlamaca, heard about this terrible thing that would happen and decided to save Nezahualcoyotl's life. Quetlamaca tricked the guards at the prison so he could get in to see the prince. There he insisted on exchanging clothes with his friend and sent Nezahualcoyotl into freedom. Then Quetlamaca bravely faced the fate that had been ordered for the prince.

It took many years, but Nezahualcoyotl finally won back his kingdom. And the sacrifice of his father and his friend helped many people, for he was a great and honorable ruler. He had high ideals, built schools, and did many other things for the good of his people.[43]

Turtle and His Drum Escape Leopard

Envy destroys a long friendship in this story from the Bulus of Africa.

Turtle and Leopard were good friends and lived together. One day each decided to make himself a drum. They went to the forest and chopped down a tree. Then they cut two sections out of the trunk and hollowed out their drums.

When everything was finished, Turtle's drum made a better sound than Leopard's did. Leopard became very jealous of Turtle and tried to take his drum away from him. Turtle ran away through the forest, with Leopard leaping after him. When they reached a stream, Turtle jumped in with his drum. The tribe of Leopard had never learned to swim, so he never got the drum.

A friendship can be broken when one friend's heart becomes envious.[44]

Company in Grief

The need to share grief with others and find comfort in companionship is illustrated in this story from the Native American Tahltans.

A long time ago somewhere near the sea, there was a large village of people. The people became sick, and all died except one man. He went hunting and brought much meat to the village because he wanted to give a feast for the dead.

But there was no one left to attend the feast. He invited the ducks and other birds to the feast, but they didn't come. He called the trees and stumps, but they also gave no heed.

Then the man went to the glacier and invited the ice people. Early the next day the ice people came out of the glacier and went to the man's feast. Everyone ate until they were full. They thanked the man and said, "We are poor, lowly people, and yet you invited us to the feast. Thank you!"

The man answered, "I asked everyone to the feast, but no one responded. Then I tried you, and I am glad you came. We have eaten together, and now my heart is at rest. I shall sleep well tonight. Thank you!"[45]

How Suspicion Spoils Friendship

Two young friends are taught to be enemies by their parents in this Bulu story (Africa). The Bulus tell a similar tale involving a young snake and a young frog.

Two young animals named Young Leopard and Young Otter played in longtime friendship. They never thought of hurting each other and did not know that one could kill the other.

One day, Young Leopard and Young Otter each went to his own village to see their fathers. When Father Leopard heard about Young Leopard's friendship, he said, "Don't ever play with Young Otter again. Instead, seize him and bring him here."

Father Otter was also very upset when he heard about Young Otter's friendship. "If you ever allow Young Leopard near you again, make sure that it is on the riverbank, near the water."

The next morning, the playmates met again. Young Leopard said, "Come, let us play!"

Young Otter answered, "My father warned me about you."

Young Leopard jumped forward and tried to seize Young Otter, but he leapt into the river and disappeared.

This is what happens when two friends hear the things they should not know.[46]

How Pigeon Learned That No One Stands Alone

This story comes from the Bulu people of Africa.

Pigeon and Branch-of-Tree had been good friends for many years. Then one day Pigeon insulted Branch-of-Tree's wife.

Branch-of-Tree said to Pigeon, "Let us talk about this problem that has come between us. This way our friendship will not be broken."

"No," Pigeon proclaimed, "I'm satisfied the way things are." Then Pigeon flew away. From high in the air, he looked down upon Branch-of-Tree and laughed. "Who are you?" he jeered. "Why don't you follow me? See how you have to stay in your own place. I don't think I need your friendship at all!"

That day, whenever Pigeon passed nearby, he delivered even more insults, but Branch-of-Tree kept saying, "Come, let us mend our differences and be friends again!"

As the afternoon passed, Pigeon's flights by Branch-of-Tree became less frequent, and after a time he simply ignored his former friend. Yet every time Pigeon came in sight, Branch-of-Tree repeated, "Please, let us talk about this and become friends again!"

Pigeon flew slower and slower. His wings felt weak and tired. Finally he said to himself, "*This* time, when I get to Branch-of-Tree, I'll stop and rest and talk with him." He turned that direction and tried to pump his tired wings, but they felt heavy … very heavy. Before long he fell to the earth and flew no more.

Thus it happens when a person despises and forsakes a friend.[47]

The Tortoise, the Leopard, and the Python

This story comes from the Bulu people of Cameroon, West Africa.

Once upon a time Leopard came to Tortoise and said to him, "Catch Python for me!" Then Python came to Tortoise and said, "Catch Leopard for me!"

Tortoise felt very bad. He dug a pit and made a covering over the top to hide it. When Leopard came to see Tortoise, Tortoise said to him, "Please go that way!"

As Leopard walked over the pit, he fell into it, and Tortoise covered it up again. Then Python came to see Tortoise, and Tortoise said to her, "Please go that way!" As Python was crossing the pit, she fell into it.

Tortoise then said to Python and Leopard, "You are both now in the pit, so settle this matter between you and leave me out of it."

Leopard said to Python, "I have caught many beasts of the forest, but I have never managed to catch a python."

"I am like you," answered Python. "I have caught many beasts of the forest also, but have I ever managed to catch you?"

"No," replied Leopard. "We are both mighty beasts."

"Indeed, yes," Python agreed.

And because they each respected the other, they ended as friends.[48]

The Fox and the Goose

This story comes from
South Carolina, the United States.

One day a fox was going down the road and saw a goose. "Good morning, Goose," he said. The goose flew up on a tree limb before answering, "Good morning, Fox."

"You aren't afraid of me, are you?" inquired the fox. "Haven't you heard of the meeting at the hall the other night?"

"No, Fox. What happened?"

"Why, all the animals met to pass new laws," said the fox. "They decided that no animal must ever hurt any other animal. Come down and let me tell you about it. The hawk mustn't catch the chicken, and the dog mustn't chase the rabbit, and the lion mustn't hurt the lamb. No animal may hurt any other animal."

"Is that so?" replied the goose.

"Yes, we will all live as friends. Come on down and don't be afraid."

As the goose was about to fly down, way off in the woods they heard "Woo-wooh! Woo-woooof!" and the fox whirled around.

"Come on down, Goose," he urged over his shoulder.

The dogs got closer, and the fox started to slink away.

"Wait a minute, Fox," called the goose. "You aren't scared of the dogs, are you? Didn't all the animals pass a law at the meeting not to bother each other anymore?"

"Yes," replied the fox as he trotted away, "the animals passed the law, but some of the animals around here don't have much respect for the law."[49]

The Sunken City

Greed and callousness toward the poor bring disaster in this legend from Holland.

Many centuries ago, the town of Stavoren was one of the most important ports in Holland. Its merchants traded with all parts of the world, and they brought back their ships filled with rich cargoes. As the town became more and more prosperous, its merchants and investors lived with great extravagance. Among these, none was wealthier than Richberta. She owned a fleet of the finest ships of the city, and she loved to decorate her great mansion with riches brought from around the world.

Strangely, Richberta was not happy. She held many parties, each more extravagant than the last, not because she enjoyed providing hospitality but to make others envious.

During one party a stranger came, saying he had traveled a great distance just to see the treasures of which wondrous stories had been told. Flattered, Richberta told her servants to bring him to the feasting table. After a time, he began to talk about the distant country of his birth and about his life. He always seemed to draw a moral from his adventures. Mostly, he spoke of the passing nature of all things earthly. The guests listened carefully, but Richberta was angry and disappointed that he had not marveled at her wealth and the treasures of her mansion.

Finally, Richberta demanded, "Have you ever seen such splendor as you now behold? Do your eastern kings have such treasures as mine?"

"No," replied the man. "They have no pearls or rich embroideries to match yours. Nevertheless, there is one thing missing from your hoard, and that is the best and most valuable of all earthly gifts."

In vain, Richberta begged him to tell her what that most precious of things might be. After a time, he rose to leave, and Richberta never saw him again.

From that day forward, Richberta strove to discover the meaning of the stranger's words. She was rich and possessed greater treasures than any in Stavoren—and yet she lacked the most precious of earth's treasures! It galled her pride.

In her anxiety to gain the precious thing, whatever it might be, Richberta sent all her ships to sea. She told each captain not to return until he had found some treasure that she did not already possess.

One captain set forth with provisions for seven years, but during the first storm he found it necessary to throw most of the supplies overboard to save the ship. The remaining food was spoiled by the seawater and rotted until it was unfit to eat. The entire cargo of bread was cast into the sea.

The captain then watched his crew grow sick and hungry from the lack of bread, and this opened his eyes to the real meaning of the stranger's words to Richberta. The most valuable of all earthly treasures was not pearls from the sea, or gold and silver from the mountains, or the rich spices from the Indies. The most common of all earth's products, found in every country, upon which the lives of millions depended—this was the greatest treasure, and this was bread.

Having reached this conclusion, the captain set sail for a Baltic port, where he took on board a cargo of corn, and he returned immediately for Stavoren.

Richberta was pleased to see the ship return so soon, and she implored the captain to tell her what treasure he brought with him. The captain told of his adventures—the storm, the loss of their store of bread, and the suffering of the crew—and told how in this he had discovered the great treasure that the stranger had been unable to find at her table. It was bread, he said simply, and the cargo he brought was grain.

Fury rose in Richberta. She demanded, "Cast the grain into the sea!"

It was a cruel decision. Stavoren had its share of poor families, and they were suffering much at that time, many of them dying from sheer starvation. The cargo of grain would have provided bread for them through the entire winter, so the captain begged Richberta to reconsider her decision. He even sent the barefooted and hungry children of the city to her, thinking that their misery would move her heart. All was in vain. In front of the starving multitude, the precious cargo was cast into the sea.

"This deed will ruin you," the captain said sadly.

And so it proved true. Far down in the bottom of the sea, the grain germinated, and a forest of bare stalks grew until they reached the surface of the water. The shifting sand at the sea's bottom was bound together by the stalks into a mighty sandbar that rose above the surface. No longer could the ships enter the harbor, for it was blocked by the dike of sand. As time passed, all the wealth and commerce of the proud city were at an end. Richberta saw her ships wrecked one by one on the sandbar, and she ended her life by begging for bread. Only then did she understand the words of the old traveler.

Years later, the sea burst through the dike of grain and sand and buried Stavoren forever under the waves.[50]

The Bear and the Sky Drinkers

This story has been attributed to Aesop.

A bear who lived in Siberia decided he wanted to see the world. He traveled from forest to forest and from one kingdom to another. One day he came to a farmer's yard, where he saw a number of fowls standing to drink by the side of a pool. After every sip they turned up their heads toward the sky. The bear couldn't resist asking why they followed such a strange custom. They explained that this was their way of giving thanks to God for the blessings they received. In fact, this was an ancient religious custom, which they would never abandon because of their conscience and their piety.

The bear burst into laughter, imitated their gestures, and made fun of what he called a superstition. Jeering at them, he called the fowls sky drinkers.

A cock answered, "As you are a stranger, sir, perhaps you may be excused the indecency of your behavior. But I tell you that none but a bear would make fun of religious ceremonies in the presence of those who believe them to be important. As for your name-calling, we have no objection to being known as sky drinkers. This custom is part of our faith, and we will not abandon it because of your ridicule."[51]

The Chameleon

This English fable has also been attributed to Aesop.

Two travelers made their journey more interesting by a debate over the color of the chameleon. One of them insisted it was blue. He had seen it with his own eyes as it stood upon a branch against the sky. The other traveler contended it was green. He had watched the creature very closely upon the broad leaf of a fig tree. Both were quite sure they were right and the other wrong, and their discussion grew into an argument.

Luckily, they met a third person upon the road and agreed to have him decide. "Gentlemen," said the third with a self-satisfied smile, "you could not have chosen a better person to settle the issue. I happened to catch a chameleon last night. You are both mistaken; the creature is totally black."

"That's impossible!" they both exclaimed.

"No," said the umpire. "You will see what I mean here in this little white box." He took a box from his pocket and lifted the lid.

"What!" all the men gasped, because the tiny creature was as white as snow.

The three men looked confused, and the chameleon spoke. "You must learn restraint and moderation in your opinions. As it sometimes happens, in this case you are all right; you have simply looked upon the subject under different circumstances. In the future, please allow other people to have eyesight as much as yourself."[52]

Why the Crocodile Does Not Eat the Hen

In this story from the African Fjort, the crocodile learns a lesson about kinship with other animals.

There was a hen who used to go down to the river's edge every day to pick up bits of food. One day a crocodile came near and threatened to eat her, and she cried, "Oh, brother, don't!"

The crocodile was so surprised by this cry that he went away, wondering how he could be the hen's brother. But he returned again to the river another day, determined to make a meal from the hen.

Again the hen cried out, "Oh, brother, don't!"

"Bother the hen!" the crocodile growled, as he once more turned away. "How can I be her brother? We are so different. She lives in a town on the land, and I live in my town in the water."

The crocodile was determined to find out about the matter, and he decided to ask his creator, Nzambi, about it. As he traveled on his way, he met his friend, Lizard. "Oh, Lizard!" he said, "I am very troubled. A nice fat hen comes every day to the river to feed, and each day, as I am about to catch her for my own meal, she startles me by calling me 'brother.' I can't stand it any longer and must settle the business with Nzambi."

"Silly idiot!" said the lizard. "You should do nothing of the sort, or you will only lose the argument and show how ignorant you are. Don't you know, dear Crocodile, that the duck lives in the water and lays eggs? The turtle does the same, and I also lay eggs. The hen does the same, and so does your family, my silly friend. Therefore, we are all sisters and brothers."

Ever since, the crocodile does not bother the hen.[53]

As Cuban as Hatuey

This story tells about a man from Haiti who serves Cuba.

Hatuey was a man of Haiti who heard how the people of Cuba suffered under the invaders from across the seas. The first thing those pale-skinned men had done was kill two children to lay hands upon the gold jewelry the youngsters wore.

In his heart Hatuey had a great love for the people of Cuba and felt for them in their suffering. So he traveled to Cuba to help the people fight for their freedom. Yet the weapons of the Spanish were too powerful, and the Cubans were driven back into the mountains. Even so, Hatuey continued to fight fiercely.

Prisoners fell into the hands of the Europeans. Hatuey would have never surrendered to save his own life, but he heard that the enemy was torturing the captives, trying to force them to tell where the resistance fighters were hiding. Hatuey set forth to help them, and a last terrible battle was fought. The Europeans captured Hatuey. The conquerors gave him a mock trial, then sentenced him to be burned to death.

He was bound to the stake. Wood was piled around him. Until the last, Hatuey refused to honor the Spaniards, who had invaded with such greed in their hearts. The wood was set on fire.

Thus Hatuey gave his life for the cause of his adopted people. Today, when a stranger loves the land for which the Haitian chief fought, he is called "as Cuban as Hatuey."[54]

Coyote and the Fleas

In this story from the Maidu people native to North America, the coyote gets a just reward for his rudeness.

The coyote walked along a road one day and came to where a mole was working. He stood and watched the mole for a while, then stuck his foot down in front of the mole and kicked him out of the ground, laughing and saying, "Hello, cousin."

The mole had a little sack that he was carrying, and the coyote thought it had tobacco in it. He demanded, "Here, give me a smoke."

The mole replied, "No, I have no tobacco. I don't smoke." The coyote answered, "Why, yes, you have! You have some in that little sack. Give me some!"

"No," the mole repeated, "I have no tobacco."

"Let me look in the sack," said the coyote.

"No. It is my sack, and you can't look at it."

But the coyote grabbed the sack and opened it anyway—to find it full of fleas! They jumped all over the coyote and started to bite him. The coyote yelled, "Take it back, cousin, take it back!"

But the mole had run into his hole and disappeared, and the coyote was left to howl alone. After a while he looked around and said, "People can call me Coyote."[55]

2

Love & Family

Home is where the heart is — unknown • The apple does not fall far from the tree — German/Dutch • Chicks that go into the chicken-house see their mother — African/Vandau • A friend will be known in difficult days — Armenian • The elephant does not know his trunk is heavy; So a mother does not feel the weight of her babe — Africa • A stranger can't tell where the shoe pinches — Yiddish • The stirrup is father of the saddle—Yoruba • Absence makes the heart grow fonder — English.

Why the Moon Has One Eye

This tale of love and self-sacrifice is adapted from the Pueblo culture native to the southwestern United States.

Once upon a time the moon was the wife of the sun, and all of their children were strong and good. The sun guarded their children by day, and the moon guarded them by night. The moon had two eyes and saw everything brightly and clearly, like the sun did. The birds flew always, the flowers never shut, the young people danced and sang, and no one knew how to rest because there was never any darkness.

The Trues thought better. The endless light grew heavy to the earth's young eyes, so they decided to put out one of the sun's eyes so that there might be darkness part of the time. But when they told the sun and moon, the moon wept for her handsome young husband and also for her sons and daughters, because the sun looked after the children and found them food.

The moon begged the Trues to take her own eyes instead. The Trues agreed, but they took only one of her eyes. So the earth slept, and it was very good.

Then she—who first had the love of children and paid for them with pain, as mothers often pay—did not grow ugly by her sacrifice. No; she is lovelier than ever, for the Trues gave her the beauty that is only in the faces of mothers.[1]

Salty Love

Variations of this story appear in many sources, including Shakespeare and the English fairy tale "Cap o' Rushes."

One day a king thought up a silly idea and decided to ask his two daughters how much they loved him.

"Oh," said the older princess, "I love you more than all the jewels in your crown."

This sounded very extravagant to the king, and he was well pleased. Then he asked his second daughter the same question.

After giving the matter great thought, she said, "My father, I look upon you as I look upon the salt in my food."

Such a dull and commonplace answer displeased the king. After all, he could boast to his fellow kings about his elder daughter's words, but he thought they would laugh at him for being compared to a salt shaker. Deciding the younger princess did not really love him at all, he gave her rags to wear and drove her from the palace.

Now, true princesses rarely remain unnoticed. In the way such things happen, a prince of a neighboring kingdom happened to meet with the younger daughter. They fell in love even though she was dressed in rags and was, at that time, working on a farm looking after a gaggle of geese. Being a wiser man than her father, the prince knew love doesn't have to be dressed up in something fancy.

All the kings of nearby countries were invited to the marriage feast of the prince and his goose girl princess. When she learned her father would attend, the princess told the cooks to bake him some very special dishes, all without any salt. As for herself, she was dressed so splendidly that her father never recognized her.

If you have ever tasted bread without salt, you may well imagine how disappointing the king found his meal. He finally threw down his fork and wept.

"Now I know," he cried, "how much my daughter loved me."

Fortunately, the princess and her husband weren't the kind to hold a grudge, so they forgave the king, and everyone lived happily ever after.[2]

Morning Sunrise

This story is adapted from a folktale of Africa. A similar story hails from China and involves a wife whose first husband turns up alive after many years. Remarried, she cannot decide between her two spouses. She decides death is her only alternative, but when her first husband pleads for her corpse, she decides not to die after all but to rejoin him.

A man had a very beautiful daughter who was so lovely that people called her "Morning Sunrise." Three young men eagerly sought her hand in marriage, and she found it difficult to choose between them. Therefore, she and her father embarked upon an experiment to discover which of them would make the best husband.

Morning Sunrise lay down on her bed as if she were dead. Her father then sent news of her death to each of the men, asking them to help with her funeral.

The messenger came to the first man, who exclaimed, "What can this mean? The girl isn't my wife. I certainly will not give any money for her funeral. I'll stay right where I am."

The messenger came next to the second man. "Oh, dear, no," he exclaimed. "I won't go! I shall not pay any money for her funeral expenses. Her father didn't even tell me she was ill."

When he received the message, the third young man at once prepared to leave. "I must certainly go for the sake of Morning Sunrise," he said. "I loved her so much and wished her to be my wife. My heart is sad that she is gone." He took money with him and set out for her home.

When he saw the third young man coming, her father called for his daughter. "Morning Sunrise, rise from your bed. Your true husband is coming."

Very soon they were married. The third young man and his beautiful wife lived happily ever after.[3]

The Legend of the Swan

This was adapted from a tale told by the Ainu of Japan.
The original recorder of this story commented that the legend of the swan teaches us that while people are busy destroying each other, the angels are earnestly engaged in scheming for human preservation.

God first made the swan and kept it in Paradise to be an angel; then humans were created to dwell upon the earth. But after living a long while in the world, the people became wicked and did nothing but quarrel among themselves and fight and kill one another. After a time of great killing, only one boy escaped by hiding in the grasses. He was all alone and too small to find food to keep himself alive.

A girl came suddenly from somewhere and comforted him. She carried the boy away and built him a beautiful house. When the child became a man, he and the girl were married and they had a large family.

The girl was a swan and had left her home in Paradise to take care of the boy and bring humans back to that area. This was the desire of God, to save the people. While the girl was alive, she always cried and sorrowed for the people if any of them became ill or died.

And so it is to the present day: When the swan's cry is heard, it sounds like a person weeping.[4]

The Loving Heart

This story incorporates folk motifs from different sources.

Once there was a king who was loved by all the citizens of his kingdom. His small country lived in great peace and happiness. However, His Highness remained without a wife, and his people agreed he must marry so that they might be assured of just leadership for generations ahead.

Now, the king tried to find a bride, but he felt no love for any of the princesses he had met.

One day, the king was riding through the countryside when he came upon a young woman of his own kingdom. She lived in a small cottage with her mother, far away from the nearest village. Within a moment, he fell deeply in love. This woman was as beautiful as any princess the king had ever seen. In comparison, her mother was the ugliest hag he had ever met, with dark stringy hair and a great wart on the end of her nose.

Each morning the king visited the woman and tried in every way to win her affection. After a year and a day, he knelt upon his knees and begged her to marry him.

She said, "No."

The king doubled his efforts. He brought gifts and wrote letters and poetry. He spoke of his love and the splendor of his palace. After another year and a day, he knelt and begged her to become his wife.

She said, "No."

For another year and a day, His Highness sought to win her love. With his own hands he repaired the roof of her cottage and dug a new well when her old one went dry. He even cleaned the shed for her cow, a smelly job, but it showed how much he loved her. Finally he knelt once more upon his knees, begging her to marry him, and she only answered, "No."

"Why not?" he finally cried. "Why won't you marry me?"

"Don't you understand?" she answered. "See my mother." He looked at the terrible old hag and shuddered but said it did not matter. Her mother would be honored and welcomed at the palace. "You still don't understand," she said. "My mother is a witch."

"I don't care," said the king. "She is still welcome."

"Haven't you listened?" she asked. "If my mother is a witch, what do you think I am? A witch! My heart is frozen, and therefore I cannot love you, or anyone."

But the heart of the king was filled with so much love he still begged the woman to marry him. "Let my love be enough for both of us," he pleaded.

Finally, the witch grew tired of saying no and agreed to be his bride. The one condition she made was that he would never expect the love she would never feel in her frozen heart.

With great pomp and celebration, the king married the witch. He kept his promise and gave an honored place to her mother in the palace. A year later, a daughter was born, and he wept with joy—yet his wife had no tears to share, for she loved neither the king nor their baby girl. When a famine came to the people, the king wept with agony over their suffering. The witch watched with a dry face, for she loved neither the king nor his people. In better times, a son arrived, and the king again wept for joy. Yet the eyes of his queen held no tears because her frozen heart loved neither husband, children, nor their people.

After five years of this, the people grew angry. They hated having a witch queen who cared nothing for them or for their king. They entered the palace and dragged out the witch. She was tied to a stake, and the people surrounded her with a great pile of wood so they might burn her to death.

In anguish the king cried out for the people to stop because he loved his wife so dearly. The crowd shouted "No!" and moved closer with the flames.

Then the king cast himself upon the wood. "If you must burn someone," he said, "let her go and burn me instead."

The people stood in silence for a moment, and then someone gasped. The witch stood, tied above her husband. Tears poured down her face and dripped upon his hair. The beating of her melted heart was heard by all. She was a witch no more.[5]

The Czar, His Wife, and Their Premarital Agreement

This story is told in several cultures; this version came from Serbia.

Once upon a time, a czar married the daughter of a peasant because he admired her beauty and her wisdom. As part of their marriage agreement, he promised that if he should ever banish her from the palace, she could take with her the one thing she liked best. One day, the czar did indeed grow angry and commanded his wife to leave. That night she gave him a sleeping potion, and when he was asleep upon the couch, she had him carried to her father's cottage.

When he awakened, the czar was very angry at being kidnapped. But his wife produced their marriage agreement. "You said I could take the one thing I liked best, and that is what I have done. You are the only thing I care about."

With these words, the czar remembered how much he loved his wife and asked her forgiveness. He put his arms around her, and they returned to the palace to live happily ever after.[6]

True Love

This story incorporates various folk motifs.

Once upon a time there lived a king who was a good king and normal in every respect except one: He almost never slept in a bed. Because he enjoyed the forest after dark, he had formed the habit of walking in the nearby woods in the middle of the night. When he grew tired, he simply laid himself down under a tree and slept. In the morning, he returned to the palace and his kingly duties.

One dark midnight, just as he prepared for sleep, the king spied a light in the distance. Wondering who had dared invade the royal forest, he decided to quietly investigate. A great party was taking place! The people were beautiful and wore flowers in their hair. They danced lightly and laughed with voices like silver bells. By this, the king knew they were fairy folk and would run away if they knew he was present.

From a hiding place the king watched the wondrous scene, and his eyes were drawn to one woman who seemed to him more beautiful than all the rest. Truthfully, she was no more beautiful than anyone else, yet she seemed more lovely because, within a blink of an eye, he had fallen in love.

Every night for a year, the king returned to his hiding place in the forest and watched his beloved dance and sing. He delighted in her smiles and laughter, but sorrowed also, knowing she would only run away if she saw him. How could he win a fairy for his bride?

Finally he went to the wisest old man of his kingdom and explained the situation. The wise man told him that to make her his wife he must wait until nearly dawn. Then, just as the fairies were slipping away back to fairyland, he must grab hold of the one he loved. No matter how she struggled, he mustn't let her loose. Once dawn arrived, she would have to remain with him forever and become his wife. "But," said the wise man, "she will only care for you in return for true love."

"I can bear anything to win her for my bride!" the king exclaimed joyfully. "There is certainly no love truer than mine!"

The king did just as the old man told him. He watched from one hiding place and then another, trying to stay close to his beloved in order to catch her. On the first and second nights, he found himself too far away to make the attempt, but on the third he succeeded.

Before she could leave, the king lunged forward, seized her, and held on with all his might. Suddenly she turned into a great serpent! They wrestled from one side of the clearing to the other, and he was soon battered and bruised in the struggle. Unable to break his hold, she transformed herself into a lion and slashed and bit him in her desire to be free. The blood ran from the cuts in his arms and shoulders. When this failed, the fairy became red-hot coals and he clutched them in his hands though his flesh burned and the pain grew terrible. She became water and tried to slip through his fingers. But he knelt close to the ground and cupped the water in his scorched hands, allowing no drop to escape.

The sun finally peeked over the horizon, and the fairy returned to her own self. She knelt on the ground and wept because she could not return to her home in fairyland.

The king could bear struggle and pain and hardship for her, but his heart melted at the sight of her deep sorrow.

"I cannot make you stay," he said. "I love you too much to buy my happiness at the cost of your own." Turning away, he closed his eyes; he could not bear the pain of watching her leave him forever.

In a moment he felt a gentle hand upon his cheek. He turned to see the tears drying upon her face, and he found love in her eyes. "I choose to remain with you," she said. "I believe I will find my truest happiness in your heart."[7]

Her Husband's Face

This story comes from Armenia.

Long ago, the king of Armenia led a revolt against Persia. Cyrus, the king of Persia, quickly invaded Armenia and conquered it. The household of the Armenian king was taken captive, including the wife of his son, Tigranes.

Tigranes came to Cyrus to discuss the terms of peace. Finally Cyrus asked, "What will you do to regain your wife's freedom?"

"Cyrus," answered the prince, "to save her from slavery, I would give you my life."

King Cyrus was moved by this declaration and promptly set free the entire household of the Armenian king.

When the royal family had returned home after this interview with Cyrus, there was much talk at the Armenian court about Cyrus. One spoke of his wisdom, another of his patience and determination, another of his kindness in releasing them. Still others spoke of his magnificence as a king, the grandeur of his surroundings, and his handsome face.

Prince Tigranes turned to his wife and inquired, "Did you also think Cyrus was handsome?"

"I wouldn't know," she answered. "I never looked at him."

"What did you look upon?" he asked.

She replied, "I looked at him who said that to save me from slavery, he would give his own life."[8]

Brotherly Love

In this story from the Middle East, two brothers care more for each other than for themselves.

There once were two brothers who lived and worked together, sharing the produce of their fields.

One night they threshed their grain and divided it into equal heaps. Then they slept upon the threshing floor to prevent theft. During the night one of the brothers awoke and said to himself, "My brother is a married man with a wife and children to care for. Yet I am single. I surely do not need as much as my brother and do not need an equal portion." Quietly he rose from his bed and took seven measures from his heap and placed them on his brother's. Then he went back to sleep.

A short while later, the second brother awoke. He lay awhile in the darkness and considered the goodness of his wife and children. It seemed to him that he had great joys to which his brother was a stranger. He thought, "My brother has no one to care for him or share his burdens; he should really have more than an equal share." Quietly he rose from his bed and transferred seven measures from his own heap to his brother's portion.

In the morning each brother was amazed to find that their portions of grain were equal. They laughed when the story came out, but they knew their threshing floor had been made special by unselfish love.[9]

A Song in the Heart

A version of this story is told by Leo Tolstoy of Russia;
another variant is found in Ukrainian sources.

A tailor tried to manage his nine children after the death of his wife. The desperate man worked day and night to support his family and to care for them when he came home at night.

One Christmas Eve he had nothing to give them except a joyful Christmas song. So he stood them up in the order of size, like organ pipes in a row. They learned his happy song and filled the neighborhood with the sound of it.

A cranky old bachelor was disturbed by all the happy sound and came to the tailor's home to stop it. He decided, however, that he might solve his own unhappy condition if he were able to obtain a child for himself. He offered the tailor a large sum of money for one of the children, any one the tailor might choose, and promised to rear the child as a gentleman or, if a girl, as a fine lady.

The father looked over his noisy brood. First he considered his firstborn. No, he could not give up that one—there was something special about that child that made her indispensable to his love. In turn he considered the second and third and fourth and on up to the ninth, but there was not a child to spare because each was precious.

Then the neighbor offered a large sum of money if the family would only refrain from singing. The father thought this seemed more reasonable, so he accepted the money and put it away, planning how he would use it to benefit his children.

In the next few days, when the children started to hum or sing he always stopped them. "Remember," he said, "we have accepted a bargain for silence."

A great gloom settled over the family.

Finally the tailor saw there was only one thing to do; return the money and let the children sing again.

He took the money back for the sake of his nine children, none of whom could be spared, and all of whom must have a song in their hearts.[10]

The Matsuyama Mirror

This story of a mother's love, and how her daughter sought to follow her example of goodness, comes from Japan. One version of the tale includes a wicked stepmother, but the following seems to be the more common rendering.

A long, long time ago, there lived a young man and his wife. They had one child, a tiny daughter, whom they both loved with all their hearts.

One day the father went away on business to the city. When he returned he brought many gifts. One of these gifts was a mirror, the first ever seen in that area of the country. The wife was amazed to see her image reflected, and for several days she looked into the mirror often. She finally put it away, for she feared becoming vain and selfish by the sight of her own pretty face.

The years passed, and the wife never spoke of the mirror; as for her husband, he had forgotten all about it. So the daughter grew up and knew nothing of her own good looks or of the mirror that would have reflected them.

One day a great unhappiness came upon the family. The good, kind mother fell sick, and although her family waited upon her with loving care, she grew worse and worse, until at last she knew she would not live much longer.

The woman felt very sorrowful, grieving especially for her daughter, who would be left without a mother. After some thought, she called the girl to her and said, "My darling child, you know I am very sick. Soon I must die and leave you and your dear father alone. When I am gone, promise you will look into this mirror every night and every morning. There you will see me and know I am still watching over you." She took the mirror from its hiding place and gave it to her daughter, who promised to do as she had asked. The mother was now calm and contented when she died.

The daughter never forgot her mother's last request. Each morning and evening she took the mirror from its hiding place and gazed into it long and earnestly. There she saw the bright and smiling face of her lost mother—not pale and sickly as in her last days, but the beautiful young mother of long ago. Each night the face in the mirror seemed to tell the story of what that day had held; each morning it seemed to look encouragingly upon whatever might be in store for her. When it had been a happy day the face smiled back at her. When she was sad, the face seemed sad, too. The girl was especially careful never to do anything unkind because she knew how disappointed the face would appear. Day by day the daughter lived in her mother's sight and tried to please her as she had done in her lifetime.

The father saw that every night and morning without fail his daughter looked into the mirror and seemed to talk with it. Finally, he asked the reason for her strange behavior.

"Father," she said, "I look in the mirror every day to see my dear mother and to talk with her." Then she told him of her mother's dying wish and how she had tried to keep her promise.

The father could not find it in his heart to tell his daughter that the image she saw in the mirror was simply the reflection of her own sweet face, which through loving service was becoming more like her mother's every day.[11]

Gray Eagle and His Five Brothers

Brothers and sisters help and learn from each other in this Native American tale.

There were six falcons who were orphaned when their parent birds were shot on the same day. None except the eldest falcon were able to care for themselves. The eldest was Gray Eagle, and he went out to hunt for his brothers and sisters. While he was hunting one day, his wing was broken, and he was unable to fly back to the nest. His siblings searched for him, found him, and brought him home, but he urged them to leave him. Winter was coming, and they must travel south.

He told them, "It is better that I alone should die than for you all to suffer on my account."

They refused to leave, saying they would share his sufferings. Whether he lived or died, they would live or die with him. They found a hollow sycamore tree and carried him to it. Then they laid in provisions to carry them through the winter.

When spring came, Gray Eagle had recovered. He taught his siblings the art of hunting, and they all worked to replenish their stores. Only the youngest eagle, Peepi, had no luck. Each day he came home with an empty game bag and rumpled feathers. He explained that he always caught game, but it was taken by the white owl.

One day Gray Eagle went with him and saw that Peepi did indeed catch something to eat, after which the white owl came and took it from him. Gray Eagle fixed his talons in the owl and took him captive. Peepi felt very proud to finally be taking something home. He then tried to exact revenge upon the white owl by pecking at his eyes. Gray Eagle stopped him and urged his young brother not to show such a revengeful temper.

"Don't you know that we are to forgive our enemies?" Gray Eagle said, letting the white owl go free. To the owl he said, "In the future let this be a lesson. Do not play the tyrant over those who may chance to be weaker than yourself."

The love and harmony of Gray Eagle and his siblings continued. They never forgot each other, and on the fourth afternoon of each week (the anniversary of the day on which they had found the wounded Gray Eagle) they met in the hollow of the old sycamore tree to discuss family matters and advise each other.[12]

The Sacrifice of Tui-chongi

This myth tells of the self-sacrificial love of one sister for another. It is told by the Angami Nagas of Asia, who live in parts of Assam, Bengal, and Burma.

One day a girl named Tui-chongi went walking on the hills with her younger sister, Neungi. It was April, and the sun blazed down on them. Neungi began to cry for water. "How can I get you water on top of a hill?" asked Tui-chongi. "The springs are all dry."

"Water, water, or I will die," wailed the younger girl.

"Would you rather have water than me?" asked Tui-chongi.

"If I don't get water, I will die, and then what would I need you for?" answered the spoiled girl. So Tui-chongi, to satisfy her younger sister's thirst, changed herself into a river, and Neungi drank and was satisfied. Only then, when it was too late, she realized what she had done and sat down and wept for her sister.

The new river flowed down the hills and into the country of the Bengalis. The king of the Bengalis was curious and sent explorers to find out the source of the new river. The explorers found Neungi and brought her back to the palace, and she and the king decided to marry. But the king's sister was jealous of her sister-in-law, and when Neungi's son was born, she threw the baby into the new river and told everyone he had died.

Although Tui-chongi was now a river, and even though Neungi hadn't acted very nicely, she still loved her sister, so she took care of the child. She also loved the next six children of Neungi, who were thrown into her waters. When they were grown, she sent them to the king. They told their father their story, and Neungi and her husband were very glad. The king banished his evil sister, and he and his family lived happily ever after.[13]

Robin Redbreast

The Native American Chippewa tribe explains the robin's friendliness to humans in this story of excessive parental ambition. A similar tale is told by the Menomini.

There was once a man who was very ambitious for his son. When his time of fasting came, the man wanted the boy to go without food longer than anyone else. This way he believed his son would become a greater warrior than anyone else.

After the normal period for the fast had ended, the father came to the lodge where his son was lying weak from hunger.

"Is the time for the fast finished, Father?" asked the boy.

"Yes," answered the father, "but if you fast for a longer time, you will be a greater warrior."

So the boy stayed in the lodge and fasted as his father had asked. The father came back to the lodge and urged him to keep on for still longer.

But the next day when the father entered the hut, his son had changed into a robin. Before he flew away to the woods, he told his father not to be sad for him.

He said, "I shall be happier in my present state than I could have been as a man. I shall always be the friend of people and keep near their dwellings. I could not satisfy your pride as a warrior, but I will cheer you with my songs."[14]

The Three Crabs

Also attributed to Aesop, this fable can be found in Liberia.

One fine day the mother crab went walking with her two children. She told them, "Run on ahead, children, and have a good time playing! I will soon catch up with you."

"No," said the smaller child, "we came out to walk with you and do not wish to leave you."

"Besides," said the larger child, "don't you see, Mother, that we are made just like you and can go no faster than you?"[15]

The Story of the Crow and Her Ugly Fledglings

This tale comes from Romania, although many other cultures tell of how a mother may be biased in favor of her children.

Of all the birds, the crow is often considered the ugliest—especially the baby birds. A legend tells that some time after God had created all living beings, God wanted to look at the young birds and animals and give them suitable gifts and food.

The birds and animals came, one by one, and the heavenly court looked at them, patted some and stroked others, and was very pleased with every one of them. So God blessed them and gave them food by which to live. The last to come was the crow, bringing her little brood with her, very proud of them. But the heavenly court was very surprised and asked, "Can these be God's creatures? Where did you get them?"

The crow said proudly, "These are my very own children."

"Go and search the world," they told her, "and find another one more beautiful."

Annoyed, the crow went away and flew all over the earth to search for another young one that would be more beautiful than the ones she had brought to God. But no other young bird appeared so beautiful in her eyes as her own children. So she returned to God. "I have been all over the world," she said, "and I have searched high and low, but there are no birds more beautiful than my own."

God smiled. "Quite right, you are one of the true mothers; no other child is so beautiful in their eyes as their own."

Then God blessed the little crows and sent them away into the world with their own special gifts.[16]

The Sunshine

In this story from Denmark, a little girl brings light to her grandmother.

Once there was a little girl named Katharine who had an elderly grandmother—such a very, very old grandma, with white hair, and wrinkles all over her face. Katherine loved her and did everything she could to please her.

The grandmother's room was on the north side of the house, where no sunshine came. Kate often puzzled over how she could manage to bring some sunshine to her grandmother's room. She looked at the flowers in the open air. They seemed to gather the golden light, as did the trees and even the wings of the birds. It often seemed as though the sun clung to her own face and clothing and hair when she walked in the garden. Perhaps she could keep it with her and bring it into the room on the shady side of the house.

Every bright day she went to the garden to collect the sunshine and then ran as quickly as she could to her grandmother's room. But as soon as she walked inside the door, the rays were gone. At least, she couldn't see them, but her grandmother always said: "I am glad to see you; it is a bit dreary here, but when you come in, the bright sunshine peeps out of your eyes and cheers the room about me."

Katharine wondered at her grandma's words and checked the mirror to see whether the sunshine really did peep out of her eyes. She never saw any, but because her grandmother did, every day she brought the beautiful sunshine to the elderly woman, who then told her stories about kings and heroines until the little girl's eyes sparkled with joy.[17]

Hoopoes and Gratitude

This tale is derived from the folklore of ancient Egypt, whose people used the hoopoe bird to illustrate the quality of gratitude.

The hoopoe bird finally left his nest and soared into the world, independent at last. He flew over the golden sands, bathed in the Nile River, and eventually had a family of his own. But in visiting his parents one day, he saw that they were growing old and feeble.

The hoopoe had seen other birds and knew that they paid no attention to their aging parents. But somehow that didn't seem right to him. So he made a fresh new nest in the place where he'd been a fledgling and came every day to trim his parents' wings and bring them food.

After many days, he was overjoyed to see his parents growing new feathers, and after a time they were even able to look after themselves again.[18]

Clever Manka

This story is from Czechoslovakia.

One day the new burgomaster listened to a dispute between a poor shepherd and a greedy farmer. Being inexperienced, he was unsure how to decide and proposed that whoever made the best answer to a riddle would win the case. He asked, "What is the swiftest thing in the world? What is the sweetest thing? What is the richest? Bring your answers to me tomorrow."

The farmer went home in a temper, for he felt that the previous burgomaster would have decided in his favor immediately. He also did not know the answer to the riddle. But when he discussed the matter with his wife, she said, "Why, husband, I know the answers. Our gray mare must be the swiftest thing in the world. You know that nothing passes us on the road. As for the sweetest, did you ever taste honey any sweeter than ours? And I'm sure there's nothing richer than our chest of golden ducats we've saved for the last forty years."

The farmer was delighted.

The shepherd arrived home discouraged and sad. He had a daughter, a clever girl named Manka, who met him at the door and asked, "What is it, Father? What did the burgomaster say?"

"I'm afraid I've lost. The burgomaster set us a riddle, and I shall never guess it."

But when the shepherd gave her the riddle, Manka told him what to say.

When the shepherd reached the burgomaster's house, the farmer was already there rubbing his hands and beaming with self-importance. Again the riddle was asked, and the farmer gave the answer his wife had given him.

"Hmmmm," said the young burgomaster. "What answer does the shepherd make?"

The shepherd bowed politely and answered, "The swiftest thing in the world is thought, for it can run any distance in the twinkling of an eye. The sweetest thing of all is sleep, for when a man is tired and sad, what could be sweeter? The richest thing is the earth, for out of the earth comes all the other riches."

"Good!" the burgomaster cried. "Good!"

So the shepherd won the case, and when the burgomaster insisted on knowing who gave him the answers, he finally admitted it was his daughter. When the burgomaster found she was as beautiful as she was clever, a marriage was arranged. His only precondition was that Manka should never interfere with any of his cases. "If you ever give advice to anyone who comes to me for judgment," he said, "I'll turn you out of my house at once and send you home to your father."

They were married, and all went well until the day two farmers came to the burgomaster to settle a dispute. The mare of one had foaled in the marketplace, and the colt had run under the wagon of the other farmer, who then claimed it for himself.

The burgomaster was thinking of something else while the case was presented, and said carelessly: "The man who found the colt under his wagon is the owner."

The true owner of the colt stopped to tell Manka of the decision, who was upset with her husband for making so foolish a decision. She advised the farmer what to do but told him never to say it was she who had given the advice. So the farmer took a fishing net and began casting it into the road.

"What are you doing?" demanded the burgomaster when he saw the sight.

"Fishing."

"Fishing in a dusty road? Are you daft?"

"Well, it's just as easy to catch fish in a dusty road as for a wagon to give birth to a colt."

Then the burgomaster recognized the man and had to confess the truth of what he said. "Of course the colt is yours and must be returned to you," he said. "But who told you to do this? You surely didn't think of it yourself." The farmer tried not to say, but the burgomaster questioned him until he learned that Manka was at the bottom of it. Angry, the burgomaster went into the house and called his wife. "I told you what would happen if you interfered in my cases. You're going back to your old home. But you may take with you the one thing you like best in my house, for I won't have people saying I treated you badly."

Manka did not object but asked only that they might share a last meal together, then part as friends. Her husband agreed, and Manka served a fine supper of all his favorite dishes. The burgomaster opened his finest wine and pledged Manka's health. He ate so much that he grew drowsy and fell asleep in his chair. Then, without waking him, Manka had him carried to the wagon that was waiting to take her home to her father.

In the morning, the burgomaster found himself in the shepherd's cottage. "What does this mean?" he roared.

"Nothing, dear husband, nothing!" Manka answered. "You know you told me I might take with me the one thing I liked best, so of course I took you. That's all."

For a moment the burgomaster rubbed his eyes in amazement and finally laughed heartily to know he'd been outwitted.

"Manka," he said, "you're too clever for me. Come, my dear, let's go home."

So they climbed back into the wagon and drove home. The burgomaster never again scolded his wife. Instead, whenever a difficult case came to him, he always said, "I think we had better consult my wife. You know she's a very clever woman."[19]

The Old Man and His Son

This story comes from a Turkish fable that supplies the moral that your child will behave toward you as you behaved toward your parent.

A feeble elderly man gave his home to his son, but soon the helpless father found himself driven from the house and forced to take refuge in a hospital. One day he saw his son passing by and called out to him, "For the love of God, my son, at least send me a simple pair of sheets from that store of belongings for which I worked a lifetime."

The son promised to do as his father asked. When he arrived at home he said to his own son, "Take this pair of sheets and carry them to your grandfather at the hospital."

The boy left one of the sheets at home and brought the other to the hospital. Some time later his father happened to count the sheets.

"Why didn't you do as I told you and carry the two sheets to your grandfather?" he asked of his son.

The boy answered, "I decided that when my father becomes old and goes to the hospital, I shall need this sheet to send to him."[20]

The Father's Prophecy

This ironic story from Soviet Georgia (Gurian) shows that "dysfunctional families" weren't invented in the modern age.

A man had the habit of telling his son, while beating him, that he would never be any good. The boy grew tired of being abused and ran away from home. Ten years later he became very important and was appointed governor of the same area in which his father lived.

When he arrived at his post, the new governor told his general to find a certain man in a particular village and to bring the man to him. The general happened to arrive at night, dragged the old man out of bed, and took him to the governor.

The governor stretched himself to his tallest and ordered the man to look him in the face. "Do you know me?" he asked.

The old man stared. "Ah, Governor, you are certainly my son."

"Didn't you tell me when I was a boy that I would never be any good? Now look at me."

"Well," replied the father, "I wasn't wrong. You are only a governor. Besides, what man worthy of the name would send for his father in the way you have done? You may be a governor, but you aren't any good."[21]

How the Wicked Sons Were Duped

Variations of this theme can be found in many cultures; this one comes from Kashmir of the middle east.

A wealthy old man thought he was on the point of death, so he called for his sons and divided his property among them. As it turned out, he did not die but lived on for several years.

Oh, but these were miserable years for the man!

The old fellow had to put up with the worst indifference, and sometimes abuse, from his sons. Before, they had tried to please their father, hoping to receive a greater portion of his money. Now that they had received his property, they didn't care when he died, except the sooner the better because he was a needless trouble and expense. This gave terrible grief to their father.

One day he met a friend and told him all his troubles. The friend sympathized and thought of a solution. In a few days he visited and put down four heavy bags.

"Look here, friend," he said. "Your sons will hear about my visit and will ask you about it. You must tell them that I came to pay off a long-standing debt with you, and that you are now richer by several thousand gold pieces. Keep these bags in your own hands, and don't let your sons see inside for any reason as long as you are alive."

When the young men heard about their father's sudden wealth, they began to do everything they could to please him. Nothing was too good for the old man they had treated so badly before that time. They continued this until their father's death. At that point they grabbed the bags—and found only stones and gravel inside![22]

Murillo and His Slave

John Godfrey Saxe wrote a poem from the Spanish story about one of that country's artists.

It is said that the artist Murillo found in his studio one day a lovely sketch of Mary, the mother of Jesus. Yet all of his students denied the work was theirs. The painting had been done during the night, but Murillo declared there was no need for such a talent to hide his work in the darkness. The painting lacked polish, but its genius was clear.

"Sebastian!" Murillo turned to his slave. "Who cares for this room while I am in bed?"

"I do, sir," Sebastian replied.

"Then keep better watch," the master ordered. "If this painter returns and you let him slip away because you were sleeping, you shall be severely punished."

Now, while Sebastian slept, he dreamed of his painting. When he awakened, he worked again at the portrait he had earlier begun. He finished as daylight came. "Ah," the artist breathed and then discovered Murillo at his side.

"Who is your master?" Murillo demanded.

"It was you," Sebastian stammered.

"I don't mean that," said Murillo. "Tell me what painting teacher you have had."

"Yourself, Señor," the slave answered. "When you teach your other students, I listen to the daily lesson and have treasured every word."

Then Murillo turned to his students and asked whether they thought punishment or reward was appropriate. "Reward!" they all answered. "He's kind today," said one student to Sebastian. "Ask for your freedom."

The boy groaned and fell on his knees. "No! I ask instead for my father's freedom, not my own!"

"You shall have both," Murillo replied. "From this time forward you shall be a slave no more, but like a son to me. But it is not your talent that has won this double freedom, it is your heart."[23]

The Wind and the Sun

Aesop is believed to have first told this fable.

One day the sun and the wind argued about who was the stronger of the two. They saw a man traveling and agreed to settle their argument through him. The winner would be the one who could get him to remove his cloak.

The wind tried first. He sent a terrible blast of cold air that nearly tore the cloak from its fastenings, but the man seized the garment with a firm grip. The wind blew until he had no more strength to puff, but the man only huddled into the fabric and hurried along the road. In exhaustion, the wind finally gave up the struggle.

Then the sun came out, shining bright and warm. Before long, the man smiled and removed his cloak so he might enjoy the day now that it had grown lovely once more. The sun smiled, knowing that kindness achieves more than force.[24]

The Great Bell

This story of a daughter's love and self-sacrifice comes from China.

The emperor of China sat upon his great throne, surrounded by his servants and lords. He was very sad because he could think of nothing more to do for his country. Already he'd had the wise ones write a wonderful book of wisdom. He had built a beautiful capital city and protected his people with a wall. Bridges and watchtowers had been built. But he wanted to do one more wonderful thing for his people before he died.

"Why not have a bell made?" asked one of his officials. "The bell tower remains empty, and the people need a bell to sound out the hours of the day."

"A bell!" exclaimed the emperor. "That is just the thing, but it must be the most marvelous bell ever made."

"Yes, Your Majesty; it will be a gift the people will treasure."

"Yet who shall make this bell? It must be a talented man."

"How about Kwan-yu?" suggested the official. "He made the imperial cannon; he can also cast a giant bell. Surely he alone is worthy of the task, for only he can do it justice."

Kwan-yu was not so certain of his ability to make a bell. After all, a cannon is quite different. And what if he should fail? Wouldn't the emperor's anger fall against him?

There was no way to tell the emperor he did not wish to cast the bell, and when Kwan-yu was called before the throne he found that the task would be even greater than he had imagined. The bell must be heard for over thirty miles in every direction. It must include iron, gold, and brass to give depth and strength, and silver must be added to give the bell a sound of sweetness. How could these different metals be combined?

Kwan-yu set out to read every book he could find upon the subject of metals and the casting of bells. He offered generous wages to anyone who had experience with such work. The silver and the brass, the iron and the gold were gathered together. Every day the emperor sent a messenger to ask when the bell would be finished.

Finally, Kwan-yu set a day for the casting. The emperor himself stood by to watch. The metals were melted and poured into the great pottery mold. The breaths of everyone were hushed. Time passed while the mold cooled and the metals hardened. Then workers came with mallets to break the pottery mold away from the bell.

Alas! When the bell was revealed, it was nothing of beauty, only a sorry mass of metals that would not blend.

The emperor was disappointed. "Here is a mighty failure," he said, "although it is symbolic of this country. There are many different kinds of metal, and united in a proper way they would make a bell so beautiful and so pure of sound that the entire universe would stop to look and listen. But, divided, they make an ugly thing. Oh, my China! How many wars there are between the different peoples of the country, also making an ugly thing. If only all the people, great and small, different and alike, would unite, then this land would be a wondrous nation."

The people applauded at this speech, but Kwan-yu lay at the feet of his emperor. "Ah, Your Majesty!" he cried. "I am unworthy to do this task. Take my life, I beg you, as a punishment for my failure."

"Stand, Kwan-yu," said the emperor. "I would be a poor king indeed if I did not give you another opportunity to accomplish your task. Rise up and learn by your failure so that your next casting will be better."

The next day Kwan-yu began his task again. He studied everything he could, but his heart was heavy; he could not learn the reason for his failure and so he could not determine how to avoid the same disaster the second time. And every day, the imperial messenger came and inquired when the next casting would be done.

The second trial was made, and it was even more disastrous than the first. This time, the emperor was displeased. Kwan-yu must succeed or pay the price of his failure.

For a week after this, Kwan-yu lay ill, unable to bear the terrible worry. Of all those who attended him, the most faithful was his daughter, Ko-ai.

When Kwan-yu regained his health, he again started his preparations. But his heart was very heavy, for he could not determine why the castings had failed or how to make them succeed.

In terrible anguish for her father, Ko-ai traveled to the home of a learned magician. "Tell me," she begged, "how I can save my father, for the emperor has ordered his death if he fails a third time in the casting of the bell."

The magician asked her many questions, then studied a long time in his book of knowledge. Finally he turned to Ko-ai.

"Your father's failure was the only thing to expect," he explained. "When a man seeks to do the impossible, he can expect nothing except failure. Gold cannot unite with silver, nor brass with iron, nor any of them together."

"Then what can be done?" she cried.

"My books tell me that only the blood of one good and pure can unite the metals; one who gives up life willingly can make this impossible thing possible."

Ko-ai understood the answer, and her heart beat faster. She loved the world with all its beauties; she loved her birds and her friends; she had expected to marry soon, and then there would have been children to love and cherish. But she loved her father most of all.

The day came for the third attempt to cast the bell. The emperor took his place and waited with a stern face. He had twice excused Kwan-yu's failure and could not allow another to pass. Yet he really loved Kwan-yu and hoped there would be no need to punish him for a third disaster.

Kwan-yu himself had given up all thought of success, for he could see no sign that anything had changed from the first or second casting. He had settled his business affairs; he had already bought the tomb for his burial and made arrangements for his funeral. Kwan-yu was prepared to die.

Unnoticed, Ko-ai slipped along the wall from the spot where she had been standing with her mother and stood opposite the huge tank in which the molten metals bubbled and hissed, fiery red with a raging heat. At just the right moment, she sprang with a great leap into the boiling liquid, crying out with her clear, sweet voice, "For you, dear Father! It is the only way!"

In a moment she was gone. Not one thing remained except Ko-ai's slipper, which her father had sprung forward and caught as he tried to save her life.

This is the story of the great bell, for it is said that the sacrifice was complete and the metals joined together; the bell that Kwan-yu cast was more beautiful than any eye had ever before looked upon. When it was swung in the bell tower, a richer, sweeter sound could not be heard.

And the emperor understood, as he looked upon this bell, that it would teach his people the greatest lesson of all: love, self-sacrifice, and devotion.[25]

Love and Worry

This allegory was adapted from a poem by John Godfrey Saxe.

A young man was traveling when a stranger appeared before him and warned, "Your way is rough and full of danger. You've heard of me; my name is Worry. For your protection, I intend to dog your steps and watch you everywhere you go with careful and kindly intentions."

Worry was such a dismal-looking sort of fellow that the young man started off with faster footsteps, hoping to leave him behind. But Worry followed at a distance. Before long, the man met Pleasure, a dashing fellow, very fine and cheerful.

"Come! Follow me!" Pleasure cried, and for a while the man did, but it was such a crazy dance that he grew tired of it. And still Worry dogged his footsteps.

Then he met a beautiful maiden by a fountain and knew her immediately, for she was Love. "O Love!" he cried. "Please set me free from this terrible Worry."

"I'm sorry, I can't," she replied with a smile. "But don't be distressed. In my presence, even Worry has got a trick of smiling."[26]

The Bear Story

The Eskimos tell this tale of mother-love, jealousy, offered sacrifice, gratitude, and adoption.

Many moons ago, a woman of the Inuit people obtained a polar bear cub only two or three days old. Having long desired just such a pet, she loved it dearly, as though it were a son. She fed it and made a soft warm bed alongside her own and talked to it as a mother does to her child. She had no living relative, so she and the bear lived alone. She named the bear Kunikdjuaq.

Kunikdjuaq, as he grew up, began to hunt. He brought the food to his mother before eating any himself, and he received his share from her hands. Kunikdjuaq learned to be a better hunter than the rest of the Inuit, who became jealous of him. Despite his long years of faithful service, they decided to kill the bear.

On hearing this, the old woman was overwhelmed with grief and offered to give up her own life if they would spare Kunikdjuaq, who had so long supported her. They refused her offer. That night, the woman had a long talk with her son—now well grown in years—telling him that wicked men were about to kill him and that he must go away and not return. She also begged him not to go so far away that she could not come out and see him.

The bear gently placed one huge paw on her head and then threw both around her neck. "Good mother, Kunikdjuaq will always be on the lookout for you and serve you as best he can." He departed, and the children of the village grieved for his absence almost as much as the old woman did.

Not long after this, being in need of food, she walked out on the sea ice and recognized him as one of two bears who were lying down together. He ran to her, and she patted him on the head in her old familiar way. Then he brought her meat. She continued to come to him for a long long time, the faithful bear always serving her and receiving the same unbroken love of his youth.[27]

Each His Own Heart

In this story, adapted from a tale of the Batanga people of Africa, individuality, even within the family, is lifted up as a value.

A man had three sons. One day he called them together and suggested they marry, but the sons knew no one they wanted to wed in that town. So they set out on a journey together, saying they must marry three women who had the same father and mother. Before long they met three such sisters. But there was a terrible dispute, and one of the brothers was left behind while the other two brothers and the three sisters traveled on their way. The abandoned brother came before the king and brought suit against his brothers because they had married the sisters while he was still unmarried.

The king sent the brothers home to their family and told them they should settle the argument among themselves. But he also told them that even if they were all children of the same mother and father, each should have his own heart and do his own mind. So the third brother married the woman who wanted to marry him, and they lived happily after this.[28]

Brotherly Love

This story of a boy's love for his father and his brothers comes from China.

Many years ago there was a boy whose mother died when he was very young. His father soon married another woman, and two other sons were born. The stepmother loved her own sons and gave them the best of everything in the house; to her stepson she gave the worst.

It was the custom in China to make winter coats with a layer of cotton batting inside the lining. One winter the father bought enough cotton to make coats for his three sons and handed it to his wife. But she put all the cotton in the coats of her own sons. For her stepson she used old rotted fabric and put only the dried flowers of rushes in his jacket.

Neither the boy nor his father knew what the stepmother had done. The boy always felt cold without understanding why. One day, when there had been a great snowfall, the father took his eldest son out for a pleasure drive. It was too cold for a coat made only from dried rush flowers. The boy's body shook, his hands turned blue, and he couldn't hold the reins. After a while the reins fell to the ground and the horses galloped down the road, the carriage rocking to and fro.

The father thought it had happened because his son was lazy, so he took the whip and hit him with it lightly to gain his attention. The rush-flower coat was too fragile for even the lightest blow; the rotted fabric tore, and the father could see why his son was so cold. The father wept when he realized what had happened.

"This is my mistake," he cried. "I have made your life miserable because I married a second wife."

The father went home, proclaiming his intention to divorce his wife. The son knelt upon the ground and touched his hand to his full heart. He said, "We three brothers would still need a mother to bring us up, and so you would marry another woman if you divorce your wife. Then there would be three sons who might be cold because they all had a stepmother; if you do not divorce your wife, there will be only one son who is cold. Which way is better?"

His father understood his words and did not divorce his wife. But the stepmother overheard what the boy had said, and her heart was made gentle by his words. After this, she treated him as kindly as her own sons.[29]

The Feast of Tongues

It is believed that this is a fable by Aesop. Some traditions say this event actually happened and Aesop himself was the slave called upon to buy the best and worst food for his master, Xanthus.

The master invited a large group of people to dinner and asked his cook to prepare the finest food money could buy. When the first course was served, it was tongue soup and tongue appetizers. The cook served the second course—tongue salad—and the third course, roasted tongue with fine sauces.

The master grew angry and demanded an explanation of his cook. "Didn't I tell you to provide the finest food you could find?"

"But I did," the cook answered. "What is better than the tongue? It is the tool by which learning is expressed, contracts are made, and words of love are spoken. Nothing is equal to the tongue."

The master and his guests applauded the wisdom of the servant. The host then said to his company, "Please come to dinner tomorrow, and I will ask my cook to give us the worst meat he can find."

The guests assembled the next day and, once again, ate nothing but soup, appetizers, salad, and roast made from tongue.

"What is this?" inquired the master. "I asked for the worst meat you could find. Only yesterday you said this was the finest food available."

"Well," replied the cook, "what could be worse than the tongue? What other instrument tells lies, commits treason, creates injustice, and speaks unkind words to friends and loved ones?"

The master and his guests could only agree. The tongue can be the best—or the worst—thing imaginable.[30]

The White Heron

The heron is much loved in Korea,
for she is seen as the self-sacrificing friend of humankind.

Once upon a time, for a reason unknown, the ringing of the bell at a certain temple would save humanity from death. Desperately wanting to save her human friends, a white heron flew to the temple bell to ring it. Lacking a way to ring the clapper, she dashed herself against the bell frantically. Again and again she pecked, until her bill was quite worn away. But she never regretted this sacrifice in the service of those she loved.[31]

Golden Heart

This story is part of legends and tales connected with El Dorado and Atlantis and likely arose from several cultural influences. It has a possible link with the Mexican lore of Quetzalcoatl, who was said to have taught the people the ways of peace and virtue, then left, promising to return someday.

There was once a beautiful island in the east where the sun rises. On this island, called Atlantis, the winds were soft and warm and filled with the perfume of sweet flowers. The sun shone warm overhead, and at night the moon came out big and round like a silver ball. Some people called it the Happy Island because it was so beautiful and pleasant and safe. In the middle of the island was a wonderful city called the City of the Golden Gates. Indeed, the gates were golden and the people lived there in peace.

The king's son was a handsome youth known as Golden Heart because he was so gentle and kind. The people loved him dearly and often brought him gifts because they wanted Golden Heart to have everything his heart desired.

The royal gardens were Golden Heart's special care, and he raised many different trees, plants, and grains. There he learned which trees produced the best wood for building homes, what plants could help heal the sick, and which grains produced the finest foods. But he did not raise only useful things, but also scented flowers and other beautiful plants.

Honeybees and butterflies loved Golden Heart's garden. The bees built honeycombs and filled them with honey. The butterflies did little work, but Golden Heart watched as they changed from ugly grubs into caterpillars and finally into gorgeous butterflies with spotted wings. Golden Heart's father told his son that the butterfly was like a soul—the immortal part of ourselves. He wished his son to be as busy and useful as the honeybee and to do no more harm to other creatures than did the pretty butterfly.

One day, Golden Heart went into the splendid throne room where his father was meeting with his wise men. The wise men told the king of a strange and sad land over the sea, toward the setting sun, where the people did not live in peace.

"Your Highness," said the wise men, "send someone of your household to this sad place to teach them how to cultivate the land, build cities, and work together and help each other."

Golden Heart sprang forward. "Dear Father, let me go. I am able to sail the seas and am willing to devote my life to teaching these people to live as brothers and sisters of each other."

The king felt proud of his son, but he loved him so dearly that it was hard to think of letting him go. It was equally difficult to refuse such a noble request.

"Do you realize, my son," he asked, "that this will require a great deal of hardship and self-denial?"

"Yes, Father, but nothing in life comes without effort; knowing this makes us healthy, happy, and wise."

"Then go, my Golden Heart," answered the king, "and may you walk with my blessing."

For days after this, great preparations were made for the departure of the king's beloved son. At daybreak one morning, Golden Heart set sail in his snake-skin boat, and all the citizens of the country came with the king to throw flowers and emeralds into the sea, because they wished to show their love for Golden Heart. It was almost as hard for them to see him go as it was for his father, but they still blessed his journey. In doing so, they were sacrificing their future king for the good of a strange race of people who needed a teacher to show them how to live a better way. The king and his people knew they were giving the best they had, and they knew Golden Heart was giving up luxury and comfort because he would rather be useful.

It was a day of sorrow in Atlantis; it was also a day of joy and love.[32]

The Jewels of Cornelia

This story comes from the early days of Italian history, when Rome ruled the Western world.

Cornelia lived in Rome with her two sons. She was not very well off, for her husband was gone, yet she never seemed unhappy or discontented. Life to her seemed very worthwhile. Her joy was in her sons, who loved her greatly in return.

With a wise mother and brave hearts, the two boys grew into manhood and became great warriors. They fought for Rome and proved themselves so courageous that when they returned home, Rome honored them. A grand reception was given to welcome the heroes, and all the great men and women of Rome were invited. Even the emperor himself planned to attend!

The day of honor came, and the two young men proudly escorted their mother to the reception. Her eyes shone with love and pride.

Having sons who are heroes does not make a mother rich, and Cornelia was still poor. She came to the reception dressed only in a simple white robe; no jewels or gold hung about her neck or adorned her hair or arms. Cornelia looked very different from the fine Roman ladies surrounding her, for they shone with splendid golden chains and jewels.

One of the ladies wore such magnificent jewelry that she drew all the eyes in the room. But for Cornelia's sons, she could not compare with their mother.

Many women envied the beautiful lady with the marvelous adornments. "Ah," said one woman to her friend, with jealousy in her voice, "to have such magnificent adornment—this is my idea of happiness."

"But look at Cornelia, who has no jewels," remarked her friend.

"What need for that? Why waste time upon her, when I can see the brightest jewels of Rome?"

"Yet it seems to me that the lady in jewels is no happier than Cornelia," the friend persisted.

"But to have such gold and jewels, what a wonderful life that would be."

Later these same women approached the proud mother.

"You seem happy, Cornelia," said the one, "and I can certainly understand why, for your sons have won great honor."

"Yes, my happiness is complete," replied Cornelia.

"It is a wonderful gathering," the second friend remarked. "All of the brave and rich and powerful have attended, and I have never seen such wonderful jewels anywhere. Have you noticed?"

"Yes, they are quite lovely," Cornelia answered absently, for her eyes were upon her sons as they came near. Her smile flashed once more across the room.

The friend spoke again. "Don't you wish for jewels like that lady's over there? Don't you envy her?"

"Envy?" Cornelia asked, her eyes hardly leaving her sons. "What need do I have for envy, when I have far greater jewels than hers. See, here are my jewels!" Her arms wrapped around her two sons and held them close.[33]

The Husband Who Was to Mind the House

In this story from Norway, a husband learns to respect his wife when he learns that she can do his job quite well, whereas he makes a mess of the housework.

Once upon a time there was a man so mean and so cross that he never thought his wife did anything right in the house. One evening during hay-making time, he came home scolding and making a fuss.

"Dear husband, don't be so angry," said his wife. "If you are not satisfied with the way the house is run, let's change our work tomorrow. I'll go out with the mowers and mow, and you can mind the house at home."

The husband thought that was a fine idea. His wife would learn what a difficult job he had and how hard he had to work, and he would show her how things should be done at home. In any case, he needed the rest.

Early the next morning, the wife balanced a scythe on her shoulders and went into the hayfield with the mowers and began to mow. The husband stayed at home.

First, the husband decided it was time to churn the butter. After he had churned it for a while, he grew thirsty and went down to the cellar to tap a barrel of cider. Just when he was putting the plug back into the barrel, he heard a clattering overhead. The pig had come into the kitchen!

He leaped up the cellar steps with the barrel plug in his hand, determined to chase out the pig for fear it would upset the butter churn. He was too late, for the pig had already knocked the churn over and stood there grunting with pleasure as he drank the cream running all over the floor. At that, the husband grew wild with rage and quite forgot the cider barrel as he ran at the pig as hard as he could. He caught it too, just as it ran out of doors. Sadly, he gave it such a kick that piggy died on the spot.

Then all at once he remembered that he had the cider plug in his hand. When he got down to the cellar, every drop of cider had run out of the barrel and made an awful mess on the floor.

The man cleaned up the two messes and then went to the barn to milk the cow in hopes of getting enough cream to fill the churn again. He had churned awhile when he remembered that the milk cow was still shut up in its stall and had not been fed or had anything to drink all morning. But it was quite a distance to the meadow where the cow usually spent her day grazing. He had a better idea; he'd put her on top of the house! The house was roofed with sod, and a nice crop of grass was growing there. As the house lay close against a steep rock, he thought if he leaned a plank slantwise at the back, he would easily get the cow onto the roof.

There was another problem, however, because his tiny son was crawling around on the floor. He mumbled to himself, "If I leave the churn again, the child is sure to upset it, and we have no more cream."

So the man put the churn on his back and went out with it. Before he took the cow onto the roof, he decided he ought to give her water. As he stooped over at the edge of the well, all the cream ran out of the churn, over his shoulders and around his ears, and down into the well.

Stamping with anger, the man shoved the cow up onto the roof. It was getting time for the midday meal, and he had to hurry. But he was afraid the cow might stray off the edge of the roof and break her legs or her neck. So he climbed back onto the roof to tie a rope around her neck. He slipped the other end of it down the chimney and tied it around his waist.

He next rushed to grind the oatmeal and then realized he should have put the kettle of water on to boil first; dinner would be even later. There'd be no butter for the porridge, but he tried to scrape a bit of the cream out of the churn so at least there'd be something. While he was hard at it, the cow fell off the housetop. As she fell, she dragged the man up the chimney by the rope. He was stuck halfway up, and she hung halfway down.

By now, the wife had been working many hours and had mowed a great field of hay. She'd expected her husband to come and call the workers home for dinner, but the sun was well past its highest point and he still had not come. At last she decided she'd waited long enough and came home.

When she arrived at the house, she saw the poor cow swinging in the breeze, so she ran and cut the rope in two with her scythe. Of course, as soon as she did this her husband came tumbling down out of the chimney. When she came into the house, she found him standing on his head in the porridge pot!

After this, the husband could never find fault with the way his wife managed the home or the dairy or any of the other work she did on the farm. He was even heard to ask her advice on different matters. But he was never very fond of porridge after that.[34]

3 Resources

Necessity breaks iron — German • What good is a golden beaker when it is full of tears — Yiddish • Better return home and make
a net than stand on the bank and regard the fish with longing eyes — Japanese/Chinese • Spilled water cannot be gathered up again
— Japanese/Chinese • Without going you can get nowhere; without doing you can do nothing — Japanese/Chinese • It is easier
to know how to do than to do it — Japanese/Chinese • Clothes make the man — Dutch, Persian • Waste not, want not — unknown.
MOQUI
BILOXI
INDIA
APACHE

How the Birds Came to Have Feathers

Beauty is no substitute for comfort and usefulness in this Native American story.

A very long time ago the birds had no feathers. They shuddered when the winter wind brushed its icy fingers against their skin. In the summer they feared the fierce glare of the sun and hid in dark and hidden holes.

After many summers and winters of misery, the birds came together for a council meeting. One wise old bird told them, "All the animals have coverings of some kind. We must obtain coats to protect us from the changing seasons."

But this was easier said than done. There were coats to be had, but only after a long and weary journey. Who among the birds would go? Who was strong enough; who was brave enough?

For a very long moment there was utter silence.

Finally, Turkey Buzzard stepped forward. "I will go," he offered. "My wings are strong, and I am not afraid."

The birds applauded gladly and watched Turkey Buzzard rise into the air. Each of them wondered what sort of coat he would bring home for them. A few secretly wished they could pick their own, but not at the price of such a journey.

Mile after mile Turkey Buzzard traveled, beating his wings against the air. Finally he came to the place where the coats were kept.

What wonderful suits of clothing! What magnificent colors! Ruby reds and handsome greens, rich browns and sooty grays, and glowing blues. There were shimmering yellows, dazzling whites, and black ones like shining ebony.

What a choice to make! Turkey Buzzard decided to pick his own coat before anyone else's. After all, he had come so far and thought it was only right he should have first pick of the lovely array.

He slipped on a coat of blue, then yellow, red, and black. He even found some with many colors and strutted up and down, imagining how everyone would admire him more than any other bird. Of course, he must also fly a distance in each suit of clothing to see how it fitted. But this one was too heavy! Another did not hang right. Yet another slowed his wings. One by one he laid each brilliant coat aside, for they did not fit and he could not fly in them as he liked.

Finally, at the bottom of the pile, Turkey Buzzard found a dull brown suit that he had ignored because it was so plain. It fit perfectly. When he flew, it was so light and comfortable he could rise higher and higher and could race through the air faster than ever before.

"Well," said Turkey Buzzard to the sky, "so what if it is plain and rather ugly? This coat is the one I want."

So Turkey Buzzard gathered up the more elegant coats and flew home to the council house where the birds waited for him. Each of them chose the suit they liked best, and since that time, the birds have been well dressed.[1]

The Moqui Boy and the Eagle

Earth stewardship in respecting creation is illustrated by this tale from the Hopi (or Moqui) people native to North America.

A Moqui boy named Tai-oh had a captive eagle that he loved deeply. One day the boy's sister spoke unkindly to the eagle. "If you were not here," she said, "I would receive the rabbits he catches, instead of you." She continued to give him food, but the eagle refused to eat because he felt her words were unfair.

When the boy returned from his hunt, the bird told him what had happened. Then the eagle explained that he was lonely for his family and wished to visit them. He invited the boy to come with him to the beautiful sky-country where all eagles lived.

The eagle could fly, but Tai-oh had to climb a great many miles. Day after day he climbed, and day after day the clouds came closer. Finally Tai-oh reached the eagle's home and stayed in the great sky-country. He was surprised to find that the eagle citizens were very much like his own people. They only wore their feathers when they entered the world where humans lived.

Tai-oh enjoyed himself very much because the country of the eagles was so beautiful and the people were so friendly. However, after many months, one of the wise old eagle men came to Tai-oh. "Although we enjoy your presence in our country," he said, "I think you should return to your home. Your parents are grieving because they think you are dead." Tai-oh had not realized that he had been gone so long. He thanked the wise old eagle man.

"After this," the eagle told Tai-oh, "whenever you see an eagle caught and held captive, you must let it go free; for now you have been in our country and know that when we come home, we take off our feather-coats and are people like yourself."

Tai-oh was carried home by his friend, and they parted with much affection. This is why to this very day the Moqui will not keep an eagle captive.[2]

Why the Bat Has an Old Skin

Not properly caring for belongings and resources leads to their loss in this tale from the Jicarilla Apache people native to North America.

A bat once did a man a favor. In return, the man promised to give the bat a basket of beautiful feathers.

"Thank you," said the man when the bat had finished the job. "Here are your feathers. But remember, don't go out on the plains. There are many small birds there who might take your feathers from you."

"I'll remember and be careful," the bat promised.

The bat hurried away, glad she finally had beautiful feathers. She forgot all about the man's words and traveled out into the plains. The small birds swooped down upon the bat, grabbing one feather after another until they were all gone.

Sad at the loss of her feathers, the bat returned to the man. He gave her a new supply of feathers and warned her once more to be careful.

For a while, the bat was careful. But one day she wandered onto the plains. Swoosh! Grab! Snap! The small birds stole every feather she had.

"Oh, dear," she thought. "I must go back to the man."

"Why can't you be more careful?" the man demanded.

"I will, I will," the bat vowed.

The bat intended to take good care of her third batch of feathers, and for the rest of the day she kept her promise. But before long she had gone here and there and was enjoying herself so much she forgot about everything else. Once again, the small birds took away her feathers; once again, the bat returned to the man.

"Please fill my basket with feathers," the bat asked for the fourth time.

"No!" the man told her. "Because you are so careless, I won't give you a single feather more. The old skin on your basket will have to do."

"Very well," sighed the bat. "I suppose I deserve to lose them. I never could take care of those feathers."[3]

The Little People of the Senecas

The Seneca, part of the Iroquois federation of North American native people, tell this story of earth stewardship and the appropriate use of resources.

Two men went hunting and found a place where the deer came to eat the salt in the sand. They waited in the trees until many deer came. Then they started shooting their arrows at them.

The men had to throw away much meat in order to save the deerskins for leather. All the hunters could think about was getting more and more skins. There was more meat than even the wolves could eat. Finally, no more deer came.

The hunters made enormous rolls of deerskin and started the journey home. They soon grew hungry but found only acorns to eat. The wolves howled and followed, for they had gathered in great numbers to eat the deer meat and now there were no more deer. The hunters became very weak and said, "Our wigwams will see us no more. We shall starve, and the deerskins will never be used." They sat by a great rock and waited to die.

One of the hunters took a stick and hit a rock. Suddenly a little man appeared. "You are starving," said the man, "because you killed and did not eat. You fed the wolves; now the wolves may come to feed on you. The little people have driven the deer to another forest. There they can live and be found by other hunters who will use their gifts and not waste them. You were selfish and greedy. You wanted all the deerskins in the forest and were very foolish."

The hunters promised that in the future they would be wise and careful, so the little people agreed to feed them. The hunters fell into a strange sleep. When they awoke they were near their homes. Their skins were gone, but their lives were saved.[4]

Legend of the Starling

Concerns for ecology and pollution are raised in this ancient tale from the Ainu people of Japan.

Once upon a time, a man went to the river to fetch water, but when he began to dip it up he found that it was very dirty and not fit to use. He found a starling, covered with filth, washing in the river and making all the water dirty.

The man was angry and laid the matter before God in prayer.

God also became angry and came down from heaven.

"Why have you done this?" God asked the starling. "Why have you come and spoiled the water? Because you have done this, from now on you can't drink from the river, but only from the rain or dew that drops from the lichens on the tree."

From that time the starlings have never tasted river water.[5]

The Coyote and His Guest

Acting according to one's abilities, and not attempting what one is clearly unsuited for, is the point in this Native American story from British Columbia, Canada.

Coyote felt hungry and thought he would pay a visit to Tsalas, who lived in an underground lodge some distance away. Tsalas treated him kindly and said he would catch some fresh fish for him to eat. This was a special talent of the Tsalas bird. Tsalas went to the river, where he made a small hole in the ice, and started diving for fish. Coyote watched all his movements from the top of a ladder.

Before long, Tsalas had caught a good number of fish. He took them to his lodge and cooked some of them for Coyote. As he was leaving, Coyote invited the bird to visit him the next day.

The following morning, Tsalas traveled to Coyote's house, where he was offered old meat, but unlike Black Bear, the bird did not eat such food. Therefore, Coyote said he would get some fresh fish for him. Coyote left the house and, after making a hole in the ice, put his head down the hole to look for the fish before diving. Then he found he couldn't get his head out again!

Tsalas became curious at Coyote's long absence, so he went to look for his friend and found him with his head stuck in the icehole. He pulled Coyote out, more dead than alive.

"Poor fellow!" said the bird. "You are very foolish to try to do things that are beyond your powers." Tsalas then put his head down the hole and soon tossed plenty of fish out on the ice. He made a present of them to Coyote and went home.[6]

Heart and Mind Compete

This story was inspired by an Armenian tale.

One day Heart and Mind argued about which of them was more necessary to the world and to the happiness of each person. When they saw a woodcutter walking home from his day's labor, they agreed to make a test of this man.

Mind flew away from the woodcutter, leaving only Heart to direct his actions. As the man passed through the village, a poor woman came up and begged for something to feed her children. Overcome by pity and forgetting everything else, the man handed her not only the bread he carried but every coin he possessed. With gratitude, she left, and he went on alone. Then a hungry child asked for a gift, then another anxious mother. But he had nothing, for he already had given everything to the first woman. When he returned to his home, his children greeted him, asking what they would have for supper, but they had none because he had nothing left from his day's work.

The following morning, Heart left the man and Mind took possession. The woodcutter started for the forest but, passing through the town, he heard a man discussing his journeys in faraway lands. Eager for news, the woodcutter stopped to listen and ask questions. He meant only to stay a moment, but it was so interesting and his mind was so hungry to fill itself up that he spent the entire day there. In the evening he returned to his home empty-handed. His children went hungry once again.

Heart had another chance the next day. The woodcutter hurried to the forest, remembering the longing faces of his son and daughter. He raised his axe to chop down a tree when he noticed a bird sitting on one of its branches. He wept, thinking how he might have startled the bird into some injury. Going to another tree, then another, he chopped nothing, for one fed a squirrel and another was surrounded by lovely flowers he could not bear to trample. So it was throughout the day, and he again returned home with no bread for his children.

The following morning, with Mind as his companion, the woodcutter set out again. Passing a group of children, he observed that one held a puzzle. The cleverness of the puzzle intrigued him. He sat down immediately and spent the entire day studying how it was formed and how it might be solved. Walking home empty-handed, he met children in need and anxious mothers, but he had no more to give to them than to his own hungry children.

At this, Heart and Mind agreed to end their argument. Only when they worked together could the world survive and be happy.[7]

The Kingfisher and the Little Fish

Folk wisdom says, "A bird in the hand is worth two in the bush." In this fable attributed to Aesop, the value of a sure thing is asserted.

A kingfisher bird fished all day and caught only a little fish. "Please let me go," begged the fish. "I am much too small to be eaten right now. If you put me back in the river I shall soon grow; then you can make a good meal of me."

"No, no," said the kingfisher bird, "I am hungry and have you now, which is better than some imagined future meal. After all, I may not catch you later."[8]

The Ant and the Katydid

The stewardship of preparation is the focus in this fable variant from the Biloxi people native to North America. The story is probably originally the story of "The Ant and the Grasshopper," which has been attributed to both Aesop and La Fontaine.

The ancient of ants was building a house. She worked hard every day so that she could finish her home before winter arrived. The katydid and the locust never thought about the future; they just sang all the time and enjoyed the warm weather.

When it became very cold, the katydid and the locust came to the home of the ancient of ants and wanted to live there because they had no house of their own.

The ancient of ants scolded them. "After you grew up, all you did was sing and play. I don't have room in my house for you."

Then the katydid and the locust were ashamed, and when the winter became very cold, they died. And so it has been ever since. Katydids and locusts die every winter because all they do is sing during the warm weather. But because the ants work hard and plan ahead, they live in warm houses during the cold weather.[9]

The Farmer and His Sons

Hard work yields a treasure in this fable from Aesop.

A certain farmer, sick in bed and awaiting death, called his sons around him and gave into their care his fields and vineyards. He informed them that a treasure lay hidden somewhere on the farm no more than a foot below the surface.

The sons thought their father spoke of money that he had hidden. After he was dead and buried, they dug deep all over the farm but found nothing. Yet, the soil was so well tilled from all the digging that the next year's crops were especially abundant. In this way the sons learned what their father meant by telling them to dig for hidden treasure.[10]

The Goose Who Laid the Golden Eggs

This story has been attributed to Aesop.

One day a man found a golden egg in the nest of his goose. When he took up the glittering egg, he discovered it was genuine gold. Every morning the same thing happened, and he soon became rich by selling his eggs.

He became greedy and wanted to get all the gold the goose could give without waiting. So, he killed it and opened the goose—only to find nothing.[11]

The Bee and the Fly

This fable probably belongs to a later period than Aesop's.

One day a fly came near a beehive. One of the bees asked him what business he had coming so close. "We are the queens of the air," said the bee. "You have no right to intrude on our air space."

"I'm sure you have good reason to be angry with me," replied the fly. "Someone would have to be crazy to want anything to do with so quarrelsome a nation."

"Whhhhaaaat!" gasped the bee, enraged. "We have the best laws and the finest policy in the world. We eat the most fragrant flowers, and all our business is to make honey, which is the sweetest thing on earth. All you do is eat what people have thrown away."

"We live as we can," answered the fly. "Poverty isn't a crime, but I'm sure that malice and spite are. I agree, the honey you make is sweet, but your heart is all bitterness. To be revenged upon an enemy, you will destroy your own life. Take my word for it: It would be better to have fewer talents and to use them with more wisdom."[12]

The Miser

Variations on this fable can be found in collections attributed to Aesop.

A miser once buried all his money in the dirt at the foot of a tree. Every day he went and feasted upon the sight of his treasure. A thief watched him and came one night to carry off the gold. The next day the miser found his treasure gone and wept loud with his grief until all the neighbors gathered around him. He told of his golden treasure and how he visited it every day and now it was gone.

"Did you ever take any of it out to spend?" asked one person.

"No, of course not," the miser said. "I only came to look at it."

"Then come again and look at the hole," replied the neighbor, "and it will do you just as much good."

Wealth unused might as well not exist.[13]

The Gardener and His Employer

The dangers of extremism and the importance of moderation
are matters of stewardship in this story attributed to Aesop.

In the middle of a beautiful flower garden lay a large pond filled with golden fish. Aside from housing the fish, the water from this pond was intended for watering the garden.

The gardener was so anxious to care for the flowers that he almost emptied the pond, and there was barely enough water to keep the fish alive. His employer came to walk in the garden and saw this mismanagement. "Although I am very fond of flowers," he told the gardener, "I am also very fond of my pond and its fish."

The gardener obeyed his employer to such extremes that he gave no water to the flowers so he could make sure the fish had enough.

The employer again visited his garden and to his great distress saw his beautiful flowers all dead or wilted. "You fool," he said to the gardener. "In the future don't use so much water for the flowers that you kill the fish, and don't leave so much in the pond that you kill the garden!"[14]

The Silkworm and the Spider

This story has been attributed to Aesop.

One day a silkworm worked at producing silk fibers. Nearby was a spider swiftly weaving a web; she felt nothing but contempt for the silkworm whose work was lovely but slow. "What do you think of my web, my lady?" the spider cried. "See how large it is, and I only began it this morning; and it is so fine and transparent. You must admit that I work much faster than you."

"Yes," said the silkworm, "but your labors are designed to trap small creatures for you to feed upon. Besides, when people see your webs, they are quickly swept away as messy and unwanted. Mine are preserved with great care and in the end make a cloth highly treasured all over the world."[15]

The Nail

In this story from Germany, hurrying slowed everything.

A merchant had done a good day's business at a fair, disposed of all his goods, and filled his purse with coins. In a hurry to reach home by evening, he sprang upon his horse's back and rode away. At noon he ate in a small town, and as he was about to set out again, the stableboy who brought him the horse said, "Sir, a nail is missing in the shoe on the left hind foot of your animal."

"Let it wait," replied the merchant. "I am in a hurry, and no doubt the shoe will hold for the six hours I have yet to travel."

Late in the afternoon, he stopped to feed and water his horse. At this place also, the stable boy came and told him a nail was missing in one of the shoes and asked him whether he should have it replaced. "No, no, let it be!" answered the merchant. "It will last for a couple of hours, until I reach home. I am in a hurry."

He rode off, but his horse soon began to limp, and from limping began to stumble, and finally stopped altogether. So the merchant had to leave the horse on the road and walked home with his luggage on his shoulder. He arrived at last, late at night.

"And all this misfortune," he said to himself, "is due to the want of a nail. More haste, the less speed!"[16]

The Eclipse

This fable has been attributed to Aesop.

One day while the moon was under an eclipse, she complained to the sun. "My dearest friend," she said, "why don't you shine upon me as you used to do?" "I'm sorry," said the sun, "I certainly intended to shine upon you."

"Oh," said the moon, "now I understand. It's that dirty planet, the earth, who has gotten in between us."[17]

The Ship and the Sailors

This fable has been attributed to Aesop.

A ship moved very slowly toward its home port because there was so little wind. The sailors talked the captain into letting them throw out the ballast in the hope that once the ship was lightened she would move faster through the water.

Not long after this was done, a breeze came up; within a few hours it had become a furious wind. The ship had been relieved of the ballast that would have kept her steady in the storm; thus it keeled over, and everyone on board nearly drowned.[18]

The Monkey and the Peas

This version of the story was derived from Leo Tolstoy of Russia. Another version is told in India.

A monkey was carrying two handsful of peas. One little pea dropped out. He tried to pick it up and in doing so spilled twenty. He tried picking up the twenty and spilled them all. Then he lost his temper, scattered the peas in all directions, and ran away.[19]

The Dairy Cow

The importance of cultivating and using resources is illustrated in this fable by Tolstoy of Russia.

Every day a man's cow gave a pail of milk. The man decided to have a dinner party and invited several people. He decided not to milk the cow for ten days, figuring that on the tenth day the cow would give ten pails of milk. But the cow's milk had dried up, and she gave less milk than ever before.[20]

Why the Sky Is Far Away from the Earth

The people of the Santal Parganas of India call their creator Thakur Baba. They once believed Thakur Baba lived in the sky and that the sky was very close to the earth.

Years ago, the people of the Santal Parganas ate some of their meals on plates made of leaves. They knew they should throw away their dirty leaf plates properly, so there should not be garbage around the home. Such trashiness would offend the creator.

But sometimes people were careless. One day a family finished their meal and threw the dirty plates out the door. A great gust of wind carried the plates up to the sky, making Thakur Baba very unhappy.

This is why Thakur Baba decided the sky shouldn't be so close to human beings. Because humans made too much garbage, the creator lifted the sky far away from the earth.[21]

The Three Princes Named Brave, Smart, and Hugh

This story is adapted from various folk motifs.

Once upon a time, a king had three sons. The eldest was named Hugh after his father. The middle son was named Smart, and the youngest son was named Brave.

A time came when the kingdom suffered a great famine because of a wizard's spell. The spell could only be broken by the feather of the great bird known as the phoenix. The king called his three sons together and asked them to seek this feather.

Brave immediately went to the stable, saddled his horse, and went out into the world to seek the phoenix. But he knew nothing about this bird, so he didn't know where to search or what to do. He wandered through the world for seven years and never found the magic bird.

Smart realized he needed to know something about the home and habits of the phoenix. He went to the castle library and researched the habits of this bird. Every day he thought he would stay just a little longer in the library and learn a little more to help him find the phoenix. For seven years Smart never left the library.

Hugh sat and thought for a day because he felt so sorry for his people. Finally he also went to the library and read about the phoenix. After a month and a day, he went to the stable, saddled his horse, and journeyed into the world to search for the place where the bird was hiding. Courageously, he overcame the dangers that stood in his way. He came upon a wizard of ice and a dragon of fire, but he threw them down and found the great phoenix. He carried a feather home to his father, and the spell was broken. The people had food to eat, and everyone was happy again.

The king grew old and had to decide which of his sons should rule in his place. His youngest son was brave and adventurous, but he never thought before he acted. The middle son was very intelligent, but he never actually did anything. His eldest son was brave and adventurous, but he was also smart enough to think about what he was doing, so the king declared that his eldest son, Hugh, would rule the kingdom.[22]

A Skill Before Everything

This tale was adapted from a Serbian story teaching the value of skills and self-reliance over mere money.

A king set out with his wife and daughter to travel and see the world, but their ship was hit by a great storm and they were shipwrecked in a foreign land. Now, the king had no money and he had no skills to offer to an employer, so he was forced to work as a shepherd for a rich landowner. This man gave them a hut and a flock of sheep to watch. The family lived there peacefully for several years and without too much regret for their former magnificence.

One day, a prince passed through that area and fell deeply in love with the daughter of the shepherd. Returning his feelings, she agreed to marry him so long as he learned a trade. "Darling," he exclaimed, "I am a prince. People learn trades to earn their daily bread, but I have lands and cities, so I don't have to work." But she insisted she would never marry him until he had some skill he could use for hire or for business.

The prince apprenticed himself to a rug maker. His hands being unaccustomed to labor, it took time to learn the art. When he finally graduated he brought his certificate of proficiency and samples of his work to his beloved and her parents.

"How much," inquired the shepherd, "could you get for such a rug?"

"For a grass mat of this size," replied the prince, "I could get three pence."

"Imagine that! Now if you sold such a rug for two days you'd have a sixpence, and for two days more you would have earned a shilling! If I had only known this trade a few years ago, I would not be a shepherd." The father told the prince he was a shipwrecked king and how, without a trade, he could only herd sheep.

Thus the prince realized the wisdom of his beloved, and they held the wedding with great joy. After the celebration, the shepherd was given a ship and a strong escort so that he might return home and reclaim his throne.[23]

Why the Sky Removed Itself from the Earth

The response of creation to inappropriate use is
the subject of this story from the Kassena people of Africa.

In the beginning, the sky was close to the ground. An old woman was about to cook, but the sky was in the way, so, in her temper, she cut off a piece and made it into soup. The sky became angry and went away to its present place.[24]

How Thorstein Lost His Kingdom

This story is adapted from a far longer narrative from Iceland.

A long, long time ago there reigned a king and queen, who had an only child, a son named Thorstein. The boy was brave, strong, and handsome and was loved by everyone because of his kindhearted generosity. But as the years passed and he became a man, his kindness was without wisdom or good judgment. He gave whatever was asked to everyone who came to him. His mother and father tried to tell him that unwise generosity sometimes did more harm than good, but Thorstein would not believe them. He continued to give to everyone who asked him as long as he had anything to give. Before they died, the king and queen tried again to teach their son that a good and wise king must reign with kindness, and also with justice. Thorstein promised to do his best, but when he was crowned king, all his good resolutions to be wise were scattered to the winds. He kept an open house for all who chose to come and gave gifts to everyone who asked, so that all the riches and treasure his wise father had collected began to disappear.

Yet, no one was the better or happier.

Before many months had passed, the new king had nothing left but the kingdom itself. He decided to sell his throne. In exchange for a horse and a sack filled with gold and silver, Thorstein let go of his inheritance.

Once he had sold his kingdom, his so-called friends now began to disappear, and as the sack of gold emptied they became fewer and fewer. "We can't get anything more out of him," they said. Finally they all deserted Thorstein.

Realizing the sad situation he had brought upon himself and his kingdom, Thorstein decided to travel and leave his false friends far behind. Once a prince, he was reduced to poverty—and with nothing to show for it, as no one was made better off than they had been before, and some were worse off, for they had used Thorstein's gifts unwisely.

Now, it is said that Thorstein learned from his mistakes and became a king once again. He was always generous, but wisely so, giving his gifts not simply because they were wanted, but where they were most needed.[25]

The King's Son

While dated in its ideas about social birth, this story from Soviet Georgia points to the character of those who are truly children of the earth.

A certain king had a son and sent him out to be nursed by a blacksmith's wife. This woman put the king's child in an ordinary cradle and her own son in the bed of gold provided for the prince.

Several years later, the king brought the fake prince back to the palace and brought the foster brother as well. One day the king set out to ride in his favorite forest and took his false son with him. When they arrived, the king asked: "How do you like this forest, my son? Isn't this a wonderful place?"

"O Father," the boy replied, "if we could only burn all this wood, what a lot of charcoal we would have!"

The king was puzzled by this answer, which seemed more like that of a blacksmith than a prince. So, he called the other boy over and asked him the same question.

"There could not be a better forest, Your Majesty!" the boy exclaimed.

"But what would you do with it if it were yours?" inquired the king.

"I would double the guards, so it would be protected for the use of all."

The king saw how the blacksmith's wife had tried to cheat him. She was put in prison, and the true prince took his proper place.[26]

The Two Builders

Appropriate action to place and circumstances is essential to stewardship and is illustrated in this tale from Angola.

One man called himself Ndala, the slow and careful builder. The other man called himself Ndala, the builder of haste.

Ndala, the builder of haste, said, "I will go to trade my goods for what I need." Ndala, the slow and careful builder, also decided to travel and trade. Each man started out, and in the middle of their journeys a terrible storm began.

Ndala, the builder of haste, built a hut quickly and went inside it for shelter. Ndala, the slow and careful builder, started making his hut very slowly and carefully. The storm came and killed the slow and careful builder outside. Ndala, the builder of haste, escaped. Because his hut was finished, it sheltered him when the storm came on.

It is often better to build slowly and carefully, but sometimes speed is also important.[27]

The Farmer and the Magic Ring

This story is derived from a poem by John Godfrey Saxe.

A wandering fairy wished to reward an honest young farmer for a deed of kindness. She gave him a ring that was set with a magical stone. "Take it and wear it as long as you live," said the fairy. "It is a wonderful ring and will give you whatever you wish. But it is good for one wish only. Give the ring a twist just so and your desire will be granted."

The man wondered, what should he wish? He went home and consulted his wife. She asked, "How about a couple of cows?"

"No," he answered, "I can earn the price of the cows in a year." They considered land, a meadow next to their farm. But that they could also buy within a few years. Husband and wife decided to wait. After all, only one wish was allowed, and they should use it to some good purpose. And so they went, from day to day and year to year. By talent and hard work the farmer grew wealthy, and he never tried a wish with the magical stone.

Some said the young farmer was foolish to throw such an advantage away. But others nodded and considered the fact that wishes can easily run awry, and sometimes the wisest wish is not to wish at all.[28]

False Economy

Whereas extravagance may lead to an empty pocketbook,
in this story from China, being a miser leads to the same place.

There were two women who lived next door to each other. Both of their husbands were in foreign lands doing business. One woman cooked good meals for herself. She kept her home comfortable and well lit. In her spare time, she worked and earned additional income to improve her home.

Now, the neighbor thought the woman was terribly extravagant in heating her home, in her meals, and in spending money for oil to light her home. She was extremely careful of her own money. She ate only the tiniest bit of food, rarely heated her home, and, to save money on wicks for her lamp, pulled bits of cotton out of her blanket to use.

When the two husbands returned together from abroad, the first woman was healthy and cheerful. She welcomed her husband in a well-furnished home and showed him all the money she had saved. The other woman, having eaten little and having lived in the cold, was rather sickly. She'd been unable to do much work and had saved no money. When her husband went to bed that night, he asked why the blanket gave so little warmth. His wife told him that wishing to economize, she had pulled out all the cotton to make lampwicks.[29]

The Ants Who Pushed on the Sky

This story was adapted from a Native American tale
of the Pueblo people in the southwestern United States.

A handsome man lived in the pueblo. His name was Kah-too-oo-yoo, which means the Cornstalk Young Man. Kah-too-oo-yoo often went hunting with his friend, but this man was a poor hunter and became jealous when Kah-too-oo-yoo made a good catch. The Cornstalk Young Man offered to share everything he caught, but the friend always refused.

One day the friend challenged him to a game of climbing a tree. When Kah-too-oo-yoo began to climb, his false friend bewitched the tree to make it grow very tall, until Kah-too-oo-yoo was pushed against the sky. Days, weeks, and months passed, and he nearly died of hunger.

In the meantime, the people of his pueblo almost died as well, because Kah-too-oo-yoo was rainmaker for his people.

It wasn't until four years later that his friends, the ants, found him. Kah-too-oo-yoo doubted that creatures so small could be of any use. But the captain of the Little Black Ants knew his thoughts and said, "A person should not think so. This little is enough." They fed him through a magic acorn, and then the captain told him, "We will do our best."

The Little Black Ants pushed against the sky, and the Little Red Ants pulled on the trunk as hard as they could. After a mighty heave, the tree was pushed one-fourth of the way into the earth. Then they pushed and pulled again until the tree went one-half of the way into the ground. Then it was three-fourths of the way, then all of the way back into the dirt.

Kah-too-oo-yoo returned home and magically restored the food storehouses of his people. It began to rain, and the crops began to grow again. As for the false friend, he died of shame in his house, not daring to come out, and no one wept for him.[30]

The Elephant and the Ants

The strength of numbers, and not despising the weak,
are illustrated in this tale from the Santal Parganas of India.

In the days of old there was a great deal more jungle than there is now, and wild elephants were very numerous. One day a red ant and a black ant were burrowing in the ground when a wild elephant appeared and said, "Why are you burrowing here? I will trample all your work to pieces."

"Why do you talk like this?" asked the ants. "Do not despise us because we are small; perhaps we are better than you in some ways."

The elephant answered, "Don't talk nonsense. There is nothing at which you could beat me; I am in all ways the largest and most powerful animal on the face of the earth."

"Well, let us run a race and see who will win," challenged the ants. "Unless you win, we will not admit that you are supreme."

At this the elephant went into a rage. "We will start at once!" It set off to run with all its might. When it got tired it looked down at the ground, and there were two ants. So it started off again, and when it stopped and looked down, there on the ground were two ants; so it ran on again, but wherever it stopped it saw the ants. At last it ran so much that it dropped upon the ground from exhaustion.

Now, it is a saying that ants are more numerous in this world than any other kind of living creature, and what happened was that the two ants never ran at all but stayed where they were. But wherever the elephant looked at the ground, it saw some ants running about and thought they were the first two, and so it ran itself to exhaustion.[31]

The Hare and the Tortoise

This story has been attributed to Aesop, although variants are found in many cultures.

One day the hare laughed at the tortoise because he was so slow and clumsy. Thinking to make the tortoise look ridiculous, he challenged him to a race. The hare thought the whole thing was a lovely joke, and when the tortoise agreed to the race, they selected the fox to act as umpire.

The race started, and the hare soon left the tortoise far behind. When she got about halfway to the finish line, she began to play about, nibbling the plants and amusing herself in many ways. It was a warm day, so she thought she would take a nap in a shady spot, because even if the tortoise passed her while she slept, she could easily pass him before he reached the end.

The tortoise plodded on, without pausing and without resting, straight toward the goal. The hare, having overslept, started up from her nap and was surprised to find the tortoise nowhere in sight. Off she went at full speed, but when she reached the finish line, she found the tortoise was already there, waiting for her to arrive.[32]

The Traveler

This story has been attributed to Aesop.

A man was walking along a dirt road when he saw several rattlesnakes basking in the sun. Having almost stepped on them, he jumped back, and with much respect and compassion he walked out of the road to avoid hurting them.

Continuing his journey, it was not long before the man came across some earthworms that had come out of the ground after a rain shower. Unfortunately for them, they were in the middle of the road. The man paid no attention and carelessly crushed them to death under his feet.[33]

The Boy and the Young Hawks

This story comes from the Native Americans of the Arikara culture.
For an act of kindness, a boy is rewarded with great strength. Yet he is corrupted by his power and abuses his abilities by doing evil.

Outside the village a small boy wandered with his bow and arrows, shooting at birds and gophers. Day by day he went out looking for game. Once, he discovered a hawk's nest with four eggs in it. The mother hawk was nowhere to be found, and the boy realized she must have been killed; otherwise, she would never have deserted her nest.

The boy visited the nest every morning. Finally the eggs hatched, and the boy was pleased to see the young hawks. He brought insects to the young ones for them to eat. He did this every day, and the birds grew and finally began to try to fly. He wanted to take them home, but he thought he would wait two or three days longer.

When he went out to bring the birds home, he saw a man in front of him, so he ran, for fear the man would take the birds. The man reached the nest first, and the boy cried, "Those are my birds. Do not touch them, for they are mine."

The man told the boy to come in a hurry, yet the boy was frightened, for the man was a stranger.

"You have pleased me," said the man, "by taking such good care of my sons, and these birds are now your brothers. "You have won much favor, and I will reward you with great strength."

Before the young hawks flew away, they gave the boy some feathers to put on his arrows.

The boy became a good hunter and was known to be very brave. In the beginning, he served his people well and became known far and wide for his strength and courage. But then the boy began to change because he was strong enough to do anything he wanted. He did such wrong that his own people feared him and tried to stop him. But every time someone tried to stop the boy, he lost his courage and decided to forget the whole thing. As a result, the boy was called "Make-to-Forget."

Make-to-Forget grew into a very bad man.

One day a man fought and killed Make-to-Forget. The people thought it very sad, because Make-to-Forget started out brave and strong but then hurt his people by doing wrong deeds.[34]

The Eagle as King of the Birds

European versions vary about the contest between the birds to determine the kingship, wherein the wren wins by cheating. This tale, from the Ojibwa people native to North America, gives a different conclusion, whereby the eagle wins even greater honor for having carried the small bird.

The birds met together one day to see which one could fly the highest. Some flew up very swiftly but soon got tired and were passed by others of stronger wing. The eagle flew up above them all and was ready to claim the victory when the grey linnet, a very small bird, flew from the eagle's back, where it had been hidden. Being fresh and untired, the linnet succeeded in going even higher than the eagle.

The birds flew down and met in council to award the prize. They decided it should be given to the eagle because that bird had not only gone up nearer to the sun than any of the larger birds but also had carried the linnet on its back. For this reason the eagle's feathers became the most honorable marks of distinction a person could bear.[35]

The Bear and the Mouse

This story is from Finland. A variation by Aesop substitutes a lion for the bear.

Osmo, the bear, was caught one day in a net and thrashed back and forth until he was exhausted. Then he fell asleep. While he slept, a herd of mice began playing all over his great body. Their tiny feet tickled, and he woke with a start. The mice scampered away, except for one that Osmo caught under his paw.

"Squeeeeak, squeeeeeeeak!" the terrified mouse cried. "Let me go! Let me go! Please let me go! If you do I'll reward you someday! I promise I will!"

Osmo roared with laughter.

"What, little one? You will reward *me*? Ha! Ha! That's a good one! The mouse will reward the bear! That's a fine joke. But I will let you go anyway. You're too small and insignificant for me to kill, and too small to eat. So run along!"

With those words the bear lifted his paw, and the mouse scampered out.

"She will reward me for my kindness!" Osmo repeated, and in spite of the fact that he was fast caught in a net, he shook again with laughter.

He was still laughing when the mouse returned with a great army of her fellow mice. At once the tiny creatures began gnawing at the ropes of the net. They quickly freed Osmo.

"You see," the mouse said, "although we are small and insignificant, we can reward a kindness!"

Osmo was so ashamed for having laughed at the mice on account of their size that all he could say as he lumbered into the forest was "Thanks!"[36]

Small Hornbill Proves He Is Stronger

Though it is not always possible to choose where our struggles take place, this Bulu story from Africa illustrates that using one's head is useful regardless.

All the different tribes of the forest birds came together to debate about which tribe was the strongest. They finally decided that the bird that could shake the most leaves from a certain tree would be declared the winner.

One after another the birds took hold of the tree's trunk and tried to shake it, but they could not move it at all.

At last Small Hornbill, who had just arrived, was asked to try. He flew up into the top branches and was able to shake them hard until the leaves flew. Small Hornbill won because he was smarter than the other birds.[37]

The Shirt of a Happy Man

This story was adapted from a poem
by John Hay of the United States.

The king was sick. Of course, he looked healthy, but he said he was sick, and everyone believed him; he was, after all, the king. Dozens of doctors came to see him but could not cure him. He sent for more. At last a poor doctor was called to his side. He looked at the royal tongue and thumped on the regal chest but could find no trace of illness. Still, he wisely rubbed his nose and gave his prescription: "The king will be well if he sleeps for one night in the shirt of a happy man."

The messengers rode all over the kingdom. They found poor folks who wanted to be rich, and rich people who thought they were poor. They found people who complained of their taxes and poor roads, people who were sad because they had lost someone they loved, and others who argued all the time in their homes. But nobody said they were happy.

At last they came to a village gate where a poor man sat whistling. He laughed and sang as he lounged upon the grass.

The tired messengers looked at him and said, "Heaven save you, friend! You seem to be happy today."

"O yes," the man laughed. "I have no time to be sad."

"This is our man," the king's messengers agreed. "We will give you one hundred gold pieces, sir, for the loan of your shirt tonight."

The man lay back on the grass and laughed until his face turned red. "I would be glad to give it to you," he answered, "but I haven't a shirt to my back."

Each day the reports were given to the king. He heard the news of his country, the good people and bad, the sorrowing, the poor, and the discontented. He heard of suffering and poverty and hunger, and he grew ashamed of his useless life and his imaginary illnesses. So he opened the windows to let the fresh air into the room, then settled down to do the work of being a good king. Then the people blessed him and were glad.[38]

The Ten Fairy Servants

This tale of how a spoiled and lazy individual learns there are servants in her fingers comes from the part of Sweden known as Gotland.

Many years ago there lived a poor family who had one daughter. Her name was Elsa, and her parents spoiled her dreadfully. When she was an adult she won the love of a hardworking and honorable young farmer named Gunner, and before long they were married. In the beginning she enjoyed her work in keeping the home and helping on the farm.

But the labor grew tiresome, for she had never enjoyed working hard and would have preferred to have others do her work. One day she cried with frustration and threw herself upon the sofa to weep. "No!" she stated, "I won't put up with this anymore. Isn't there anyone who can help me?"

"I can," came a quiet voice, and before her stood a white-haired man with a broad-brimmed hat upon his head. "Don't be afraid," he continued. "I came to give you the help for which you have wished. I am called Old Man Hoberg. I knew your family ten generations ago. Your first ancestor asked me to be godfather to his first child. I could not attend the baptism, but I gave a proper gift, a wealth in silver. Unfortunately, the money I gave blessed no one as it only encouraged pride and laziness. Your family has long since lost the riches, but the pride and laziness have remained. Even so, I will help you, because at heart you are good and honest."

There was a long silence while Elsa considered his words.

"I will give you ten obedient servants," said Old Man Hoberg. He shook his cloak, and ten comical little creatures hopped out and began to clean the room.

"Reach out your fingers," said the old man.

Elsa reached out her hands, and the old man sang:

"Hop o' My Thumb,
Lick the Pot,
Long Pole,
Heart in Hand,
Little Peter Funny Man—
Away, all of you, to your places."

Instantly the little servants disappeared into Elsa's fingers, and the old man vanished.

Elsa sat staring at her hands, but she soon felt a strong desire to work. "Here I sit and dream," she said with cheerfulness and courage. "It's already seven o'clock, and there is much to do." She hurried out and started the day's work.

From that time forward, Elsa enjoyed her work, and everyone marveled at the change in her. No one was more pleased or satisfied than the young wife herself. Under her hands everything flourished, bringing wealth and happiness to the young couple.[39]

Why the Magpie's Nest Is Unfinished

This story is told in Great Britain to explain the untidy appearance of the magpie's nest.

Once upon a time, when the world was very young, the magpie for some reason did not know how to build her nest. She called upon the other birds to teach her, but as each came and showed how to lay the sticks and feathers, she proclaimed, "I already knew that." The birds continued with their suggestions, but the magpie said again and again, "I already knew that."

When the nest was half finished, the birds got tired of the magpie's conceit. "Well, Mistress Mag, as you seem to know all about it, you may finish the nest yourself," they told her. They left and refused to return, and ever since then the magpie's nest is sloppy and not quite finished.[40]

Why Is the Bee Busy and the Spider Sulky?

In the Romanian story "The Bee and Her Sting," the bee has a mean spirit. By contrast, this tale, which is also Romanian, attributes a sweeter nature to the maker of honey.

Once upon a time there lived a poor widow. She had two children, a son and a daughter, who, when they were grown, left home to find work. The girl went to a place where workers were building houses, and there she toiled day and night carrying bricks and mortar to the builders. The son met a weaver and learned how to make cloth.

One day the mother grew very sick and knew she wouldn't live long, so she sent a message to her children. When the message reached the daughter, she left her work at once and hurried home to her mother. When the message reached the son, he was sitting at his weaving and said he was too busy to come until his work was finished. So he stayed, quite alone, weaving away, grumbling all the while.

It is said that the sweet-natured daughter was later changed into a bee, busy and active, whose honey sweetens everything. The brother, who wove constantly without any joy in it, changed into the spider, who sits alone and sulky in the corner and weaves his webs, never finishing.[41]

Hercules and the Lazy Man

Variations of this fable have been attributed to Aesop. The idea that "God helps those who help themselves" is also often attributed to Benjamin Franklin of the United States.

As a man was driving his wagon through a muddy road, the wheels stuck in the mucky stuff and the horses could not pull it out. The man immediately dropped to his knees and cried out for Hercules to come and help him. Hercules appeared and said, "Lazy fellow! Get up and put your shoulder to the wheel. If you need help after that, then you shall have it, but I won't do what you are too lazy to attempt."

Moral: "The gods help those who help themselves."[42]

The Boy and the Nuts

This story has been attributed to Aesop.

A boy thrust his hand into a pitcher full of nuts and grabbed as many as his fist could possibly hold, but when he tried to draw it out, the narrowness of the neck prevented him. He burst into tears and bewailed his hard luck.

A fellow who stood nearby gave him this advice: "Take only half as many and you will easily get them."[43]

The Hunter Who Could Not Run

This telling of "practice makes perfect" comes from the Tahltan people native to North America.

A young man lived with his uncle, who gave him a bow and made many arrows for it, but the young man always shot them and came back from hunting without arrows or game. One day his uncle watched him. Some caribou ran by, and the young man ran after them for only a little while. The uncle ran ahead and killed a caribou to take home for food. He waited for his nephew to arrive.

When the young man came, his uncle asked, "Why aren't you running? You'll never catch any game in that way. Caribou run fast."

The nephew answered, "I am sorry, Uncle, but when I run a short time, my heart begins to beat so hard that I become afraid and have to walk."

They carried the meat to camp. But after that, the uncle took his nephew hunting every day. First he made him carry a sheep up a steep mountain. Then he made him run. At first the young man ran and then walked a while. His uncle followed, and when the young man went too slow, his uncle urged him to go faster until they reached the top of the mountain. "Don't be afraid," the uncle said. "You will not die, and you'll have more breath if you practice."

Every day they practiced. The uncle made his nephew run and climb steep slopes, every day a little bit more. Little by little, the nephew could go faster and faster until he could do things like other people did. In the end, the young man became a great hunter.[44]

The Two Brothers

This story comes from the Bulu people of Cameroon, West Africa,
and is told to advise prudence. Kindness also is important.

There were two brothers. The older brother was a foolish man, but the younger one was wise.

One day the father said, "My sons, I have begotten you, but I have no riches for you. If you seek riches, go to the crest of the hill you can see in the distance. You will see something there."

So the younger son started out for the hill. He came upon an old man on the path, and seeing that he was old and ill and had only a tiny load of firewood, the younger brother went out to cut firewood for him. The old man thanked him and asked, "Where are you going?" The younger brother replied, "I am going to seek my fortune." So the old man told him, "As you go, you will see a large man on the hill. Do not stand in front of him, but behind, and when you do, say to him, 'I wish to get riches.'"

The younger brother went along and did as the old man had instructed him. The large man gave him a small ivory tusk and said, "If you want anything, strike upon the ground with this tusk once; do not strike twice, but only once."

The boy did as he was told, and he became very rich.

The older son also set out to climb the hill. But he ill-treated the old man and showed him no mercy. Therefore, he didn't know what to do when he got to the hill and failed to obtain any riches.[45]

The Python and the Vine

In this story from the Umbundu people of Angola, Africa, the inattention or laziness of the vine results in three deaths.

The vine was in the tree where it had climbed. One day a large snake, the python, came and rested in the shade of the tree. A dove came as well and perched in the same tree upon the vine. Then a man came who had been following the bird with his gun.

The snake cried to the vine, "Scare away the bird and save its life!" The vine ignored him. Again the snake cried, "Scare away the bird! Think about it! Perhaps the man will shoot it, and in the death of one there may be the death of many." But the vine would not consent to scare away the dove.

Before the snake could say anything more or move away himself, the man came close and shot the dove, which fell upon the head of the snake. When the man saw the python, he grabbed his axe and killed it. Then he folded it up to carry it, but he couldn't handle it very well. He saw the vine climbing up the tree, so he pulled it down and used it to fasten the snake in a tight bundle.

Now it was too late for the vine, who sadly remembered the warning of the python: that in the death of one, there might be the death of many![46]

Why the Elephant Lacks a Tail

That there are some jobs you just need to do for yourself is a lesson the elephant learns in this story from the Vandau of South Africa, resulting in the proverb "The elephant lacks a tail because he sent for it."

The chief of the animals wanted to give tails to all the beasts. He sent a messenger to tell them that they should come to his house to receive their tails. All the animals went except the elephant; he sent the jackal to fetch his tail.

When the jackal arrived at the chief's house, he chose a large tail for himself. When he had what he desired, he remembered that the elephant had asked him to bring a tail. He seized a tiny tail and took it back home to give to the elephant. The elephant wasn't happy with the jackal's choice, but there was nothing he could do about it.[47]

Aesop and His Fellow Servants

This story is sometimes said to be by Aesop, whereas others say it is about Aesop. It explores the greatest resource of all—the mind.

A merchant ordered that everything be made ready for a journey. When the packs were divided among the servants, Aesop chose the basket of bread. The other servants laughed, because that was the largest and heaviest of all.

When lunchtime came, Aesop had barely managed to struggle along. But then he was told to give an equal share of bread all around. He did so, and this reduced his burden by one-half. When suppertime arrived, he got rid of the rest. For the remainder of the trip he only had the empty basket to carry, and the other servants could only applaud the way he had thought ahead.[48]

The Cock and the Jewel

This fable has been attributed to Aesop.

A young cock scratched in the dirt to entertain himself and turned up a priceless jewel. From that time he was proud to be the only cock to own such a valuable gem. But another cock said one day, "I'm sure jewels are very fine items to own. Yet for myself, I would rather have one grain of corn than all the jewels in the world."[49]

Plant Medicine

Modern medicine has learned much of the healing power of plants, and the importance of this points to the need for preserving species. This Cherokee myth explores the same subject.

In the old days, we are told, the animals could speak, and they lived in friendship with the human race. But humans multiplied so quickly that the animals were crowded into forest and desert. So the friendship between animals and people was soon forgotten. The peace was further shattered because humans developed powerful weapons to kill the animals for their flesh and skin.

The animals met in council and thought of ways to protect and avenge themselves. The deer decided that if a hunter did not ask pardon from the animal spirit, he would be stricken with rheumatism. The fish and reptiles decided to inflict nightmares upon the humans. The birds and insects decided upon further ills to torment the people.

But when the plants heard the plans of the animals, they decided to help the people. Each tree, shrub, and herb, down to the grasses and mosses, agreed to furnish a remedy for one of the diseases named by the animals. In this way medicine came into being.[50]

Hiring a Coachman

The cultural source for this story is unknown.

A man advertised for a coachman, and three men answered the advertisement. They all seemed like they would be good workers, and the man didn't know which one to choose.

Finally he hit upon a scheme. There was a road near his house that ran along the edge of a great ravine. The man asked each one of these coachmen how close he could drive to the cliff without going over. The first said he could drive within six inches of it; the second said he could drive within two inches of the edge. When the third man was asked, he said, "I'd keep as far away from it as possible!"

He said to the third man, "You are the coachman I want!"[51]

The Three Sons

This tale comes from the Bulu people of Cameroon, West Africa.

Once upon a time there lived a man who had three sons. When their father died, these sons were left as poor as beggars. But one night the spirit of their father appeared to them and said, "I want you to go tomorrow and sit under the butternut tree that stands at the north end of the path that leads to the marsh."

When day dawned, the three brothers rose from their beds and traveled to the butternut tree; they camped for one night. Then the spirit of their father came to them once more. "Of the fruits that will fall from this tree, the one that falls first belongs to the oldest, the second to the next son, and the last one will belong to the one who was born last. Take them and do not open the fruits until you have reached your home."

The brothers waited for the fruits to fall, and when each had one, they started for home.

As the oldest brother was going along, he said, "My fruit is too heavy; I will open it and see what is inside." He took a knife and split the fruit open. There were all sorts of riches in the fruit, but they spilled out and ran into the bush. The brother gave a great howl of disappointment.

Then the middle brother also grew tired because the fruit seemed too heavy. He took his knife and split open his fruit, and all the riches it held were completely lost to the bush.

The youngest brother, however, carried his fruit home and fastened the door shut before he took his knife and cut open the fruit. Riches of all kinds spilled from the fruit and entirely filled the house.

Thus did the older brothers fail to become rich, because they were too easily tired of a heavy load. Luckily for them, their younger brother shared some of his wealth.[52]

The Maid and the Pail of Milk

This story is often attributed to Aesop. There are variants in several cultures, including India and Mexico. In India, a Brahman sits with his rice pot, thinking that if there should be a famine he could sell his rice for a hundred rupees, with which he would buy some goats, which would grow to be a herd. Then he would buy cows, then buffaloes, then horses, which he would sell for gold. With that he would marry well and have a son named Somasarman. When the son was old enough, he would spend time at the stable, and the son would run too close to the horses' hooves, to be saved by his father. In trying to return the son to his mother, she would be distracted by domestic work, and thereupon he would kick her with his foot.... With that thought the Brahman gave a kick with his foot and broke the pot of rice all over himself, leading to the saying that "he who makes foolish plans for the future will be white all over, like the father of Somasarman."

Dolly, the milkmaid, had been a good and careful worker for many years, so her employer gave her a pail of new milk. With the pail on her head, Dolly headed to town to sell her milk. On the way, she thought about what she would do with the money.

"For this milk I will get a shilling," said Dolly, "and with the shilling I will buy twenty eggs. I'll put them under the old hen, and if only half of the chicks grow up and do well, I shall be able to sell them for several shillings. With that money, I will buy that jacket I saw in the village and a hat with ribbons. Then, when I go to the fair, I shall look quite splendid."

She tossed her head just thinking about it. Down came the pail, and the milk all spilled on the ground.

Moral: Don't count your chickens before they are hatched.[53]

The Mountain and the Squirrel

This fable is from the writings of Ralph Waldo Emerson, an American essayist and poet of the nineteenth century.

One day the mountain and the squirrel had a terrible quarrel. The mountain called the squirrel foolish.

The squirrel answered and said, "You are doubtless very big, but all things must be taken into consideration, and I think it is fitting to occupy my own place. If I'm not as large as you, you are not as small as I, and not half as nimble. I admit, as a mountain, you make a pretty place to lay my feet. Everyone has a different talent. If I cannot carry forests on my back, neither can *you* crack a nut."[54]

The Horse and the Dog

This fable comes from Russian author Ivan Kryloff.

A dog and a horse who served the same family began one day to discuss each other's merits and abilities.

"How grand and big you are, to be sure," said the dog. "But how noble can your service be, to plow a field or draw a cart? I've certainly never heard of any other proof of your merit. How can you possibly compare yourself with me? I work day and night. In the daytime I watch the cattle in the meadows; by night I guard the house."

"Quite true," replied the horse. "What you say is perfectly correct. Only remember that if it weren't for my plowing, you wouldn't have as much to guard."[55]

Ben-Ammi and the Fairies

This tale was adapted from a poem by John Godfrey Saxe, who derived it from a Judaic story of the Rabbinic tradition.

Once upon a time there was a rabbi named Ben-Ammi, and it must be admitted that he was both wealthy and a miser. At midnight one evening, a stranger came to Ben-Ammi asking him to perform a circumcision for his child. Despite his miserly ways, Ben-Ammi held his office in great regard and always served the poor without thought of how they could reward him. So, he followed the stranger to a great stone, where the father spoke some words and a doorway was opened to fairyland.

Ben-Ammi met the mother and learned her husband was the king of that magical land. She warned him to accept no gift from the king or he would be trapped in fairyland forever. The man performed the rite, and then the king asked, "How shall I reward your task?" Ben-Ammi wisely replied, "I only ask to return to earth." "No," answered the king, and led him to a treasure room, but Ben-Ammi said he only wished to go home.

They entered another room, where along the walls were thousands of rusty keys hung in rows. To his surprise Ben-Ammi thought he recognized his own set of keys. When he asked, the king replied: "They are indeed your own. In this place I hold the keys of all people who hoard and do not use their gathered gold. Here, take the keys. From now on, let your heart melt in pity for the poor. Everything you give away will impart a blessing upon you."

After this, the king sent him home, but Ben-Ammi never forgot. From that day, he understood the proper use of wealth, which is the art of doing good![56]

The Hunter

In this tragic story from the Wasco people native to North America, a son brings himself to disaster because he tries to cater to his father's unreasonable demands and does something wrong.

A boy grew old enough to shoot and began to kill birds and squirrels. He was a good shot. But one day his father said, "You don't do as I used to. I am ashamed to say you are mine. When I was your age, I used to catch young elk."

This made the boy feel bad. But one day he had a visit from an elk, and the elk said, "If you will listen to what I say, I will help you whenever you need me. You must not be proud. You must not kill too many of any kind of animal—only what you actually need. If you obey these rules I will be your guardian spirit."

From that time, the young man became a great hunter. He knew where every animal was—bear, elk, deer. He killed what he needed for his food, and no more. The old man, his father, said, "You are not doing enough. At your age I used to do much more." The young man was sad because of his father's scolding. The spirit elk was very angry at the old man.

Wanting to gain his father's approval, the young man went out and killed five entire herds of elk. He killed them all, and he even tried to kill his guardian spirit. This elk ran to a lake and pretended to be dead. The young man went into the water to pull the elk out, but as soon as he touched the elk, they both sank.

After touching the bottom of the lake, the young man woke suddenly and saw many, many bears, deer, and elk. They were all persons. The ones he had killed were there too, and they were groaning. A voice called, "Draw him in!"

Each time the voice was heard, the young man was pulled nearer his guardian spirit elk. When he was close beside her, the great elk asked, "Why did you go beyond what I told you to do? Your father asked more of you than he ever had before. Do you see our people on both sides? These are the ones you have killed, and you hurt them with many needless wounds. Your father lied to you, and you believed him instead of doing what was right. Now I shall leave you and never be your guardian spirit again."

When the elk had finished, a voice said five times, "Cast him out."

The young man went home and lay on his bed for five days and nights. Then he called the people together and told them, "My father was never satisfied with me, because he said I had not done as well as he had done. He always said I had disgraced him, but he was lying about what he had done in the past. My father wanted me to kill more than was needed, so my guardian spirit has left me. Now I die."[57]

A Man Turns into Stone

This story about a bad employer comes from the Lamut people of Siberia.

Once there was a man who owned many reindeer and employed other people to work for him. He had a very bad temper and often struck his assistants for the least little thing.

One day the reindeer herd wandered away from their usual pasture. One assistant searched, but the hoofprints disappeared after a short distance. He walked for many miles and grew tired before he returned home and said, "I could not find the herd."

The man gave him a severe beating and then said, "Why couldn't you find it? Where can it be? I will go and look for it myself." The man went to the pasture and walked all around it, but he was also unable to find any tracks. When he was tired, he climbed onto a large boulder in the pasture, resting his head on his hands and thinking about the problem.

"Byra!" a voice said.

The man sprang to his feet and looked up. High on the rock there stood an old man, as high as the sky. "O man, do you see me?" the old one asked.

"I see you."

"Do you hear my voice?"

"Yes, I hear your voice."

"What are you doing?"

"I am resting myself."

"And where are your reindeer?" asked the old man.

The man grunted, "I do not know."

"Ah … why do you strike your assistants? Isn't each one of them a man like yourself? Look upward! There are your reindeer."

The man looked up and saw his reindeer mounting up to the sky—all of the herd, bucks and does and fawns. He stared and could think of nothing to do.

"So you will stand here forever," said the old one before he vanished.

It felt almost like he was waking from a dream. The man tried to climb down from the stone, but his feet stuck to it. He pulled and pulled but could do nothing. After a while his feet and legs began to sink into the stone.

The next morning, his people came looking for him. The man's feet had sunk into the stone up to his ankles. They tried to pull him out, but he cried in pain, "Leave me alone! I cannot stand it. It looks like I am done for, so you'd better go away and tell the other people."

In a couple of days the man had sunk into the stone up to his knees. His people talked to him, but he did not answer—only the look in his eyes was still lifelike. By springtime he was all stone, and he still stands there to this day.[58]

Too Much Care

In this story adapted from India, a raja learns that too much pampering can be a problem.

A young raja once asked his wuzeer, "How is it that I am so often ill? I take care of myself, I never go out in the rain, I do not work enough to get tired, I wear warm clothes, I eat the very best and richest food and take every care for my health. If I feel bad I take every possible medicine. Yet I am always catching cold or getting a fever."

"Ah," said his wuzeer, "too much care can be as bad as none at all."

The wuzeer invited the raja to join him for a walk in the fields. Before they had gone far, they met a poor shepherd. The shepherd spent all his days tending his flock. He had only a coarse cloak that did not seem thick enough to protect him from the rain or cold. He ate mostly parched corn and water and lived in the field in a small hut made of woven palm branches.

The wuzeer said to the raja, "You must know how hard these poor shepherds work. Ask this one if he suffers much illness."

The raja did as the wuzeer told him and asked the shepherd about the state of his health.

The shepherd answered, "Perhaps it will surprise you, sire, to hear that I almost never am ill. From childhood I have lived like this, so I suppose the weather does not affect me."

The raja was astonished and said to the wuzeer, "Doubtless this man must be extraordinarily strong and healthy and nothing would affect him."

"We shall see," said the wuzeer, and he invited the shepherd to the palace. There for a long time, the shepherd received the same care as the king. But one day his feet grew chilled on a damp marble floor, and he grew very sick.

"How can this be?" asked the raja.

"Too much care," said the wuzeer, as he had done once before. "Too much can be as bad as none at all."[59]

The Woman Pounds the Sky

Creation responds poorly to abuse in this tale
from the Ashanti people of Africa.

In the beginning, the sky was close to the ground. One day a woman was pounding yams, and the sky got in the way so that her wooden pestle hit it continually. It grew so angry that it withdrew from her reach.[60]

4

Room for Improvement

Why the Crab Has No Head

This tale is from the African Fjort in present-day Congo.

Nzambi the creator had already given the crab a body and legs, and she promised the next day to give him a head. The crab sent invitations to everyone to come see Nzambi place his head on his body. When they had all arrived, he was so proud he could hardly walk straight. But Nzambi scolded him for his pride and vanity. She told those who were present that, as a warning to them not to be self-centered and vain, she would not give the crab a head after all. And thus it happens that when the crab wants to see where he is going, he has to lift his eyes out of his body.[1]

The Wren's Presumption

In this very short story from Scotland,
the wren suffers from an inflated view of himself.

The wren dipped his beak into the sea and boasted, "You're less because of me!"[2]

The Young Man and the Stream

In folktales, punishment or justice is often extreme for defects of character such as pride, boasting, and ingratitude. In this tale from Russia, the punishment is for all three.

A young man was riding to Smorodina, and its stream lay in his path. Politely he asked the water to show him a place to cross; the stream obligingly provided a shallow place where he could safely ford. But after he was on the other side, he began to boast. "People talk about the Smorodina waters, saying that no one can cross it whether on foot or on horseback—yet it is no stronger than a pool of rainwater!"

The young man went merrily on his way. However, when it came time for his journey home, the river took its revenge and swept him away, saying, "It isn't I but your own boasting that has done this."[3]

Coyote Father and His False Colors

This tale comes from the Pueblo people native to the southwestern United States.

The coyote father became jealous of the woodpecker's fine colors. He felt the woodpeckers put on airs because of their bright plumage.

One day the woodpecker invited the coyote family for dinner. The coyote father told his wife and children to bring a great pile of wood and make a fire. He then lashed a burning stick under each of their arms with the burning end pointed upward. "When we get to the woodpecker's home," he told them, "lift your arms often to show your bright colors. We will prove we are as good as the woodpeckers."

His wife and children did as the coyote father had said. But when they sat down to dinner, one coyote girl shrieked, saying that her fire was scorching her arms.

"Be patient, my daughter," said the coyote father, "and do not fret about little things."

Then another daughter cried that her fire had gone out.

The woodpecker inquired how it was that their bright colors were so bright at first but soon became black. "Oh, that is the beauty of our colors," said the coyote father. "They are not always the same—like other people's—but turn all shades."

The uncomfortable coyotes made an excuse to hurry home as soon as they could, and the coyote father scolded his family for exposing him to be laughed at.

The woodpecker gathered his own children. "Now, my sons and daughters, you see what the coyotes have done. Never in your life try to appear to be what you are not. Be just what you really are, and put on no false colors."[4]

The Fox and the Raven

This story comes from China.

The fox is an old expert at the art of flattery and is a master trickster. Once he spied a raven who had landed on a tree with a piece of meat in his beak. The fox seated himself beneath the tree, looked up at him, and began saying words of praise.

"Your color," he said graciously, "is the purest black, like blackened diamonds. And it is my belief this shows your wisdom, which shines like a gem in the richest collection. I have also noted that the courage of ravens is greater than normal. In truth, you are the king of birds!"

The raven was filled with joy and pride. "I thank you! I thank you!" he exclaimed. As soon as he opened his beak, the meat fell to the earth.

The fox snapped up the meat and devoured it. He laughed. "Remember this, my dear sir: If someone praises you without cause, he is sure to have a reason for doing so."[5]

The Boastful Geese

This fable from Russia explores the folly of expecting honor because of the accomplishments of one's ancestors.

A farmer was driving some geese to town for sale. Hoping to make a good bargain, he hurried them with a long rod. As a consequence, the geese complained loudly to every passerby.

"Were there ever any geese more unfortunate than we are?" they asked. "This farmer drives us along as though we were common, ordinary geese. He is such an ignorant peasant and he does not know that he should pay us great honor. After all, we are the noble descendants of those famous geese who once saved Rome from destruction."

"And is that your reason for expecting people to honor you?" one of the passersby asked them.

"Of course! Our ancestors, the geese of Rome—"

"I know, I know. I have read all about that. But what I am asking you is what use have you yourselves ever been? What have *you* done?"

"Us? Why, nothing, but our ancestors—"

"Then why should you expect any honor? Let your ancestors rest in peace; they received their reward. But you, my friends, are only fit to be roasted."[6]

The Magic Jar

Several cultures tell stories that teach that elderly relatives should be respected. In this story from China, a farmer is repaid for his unkindness to his grandfather.

A poor farmer once found a large pottery jar in his field. He took it home, and his wife began to brush out the dirt on the inside. But the jar suddenly filled with brushes. No matter how many were taken out, others kept taking their place. The wife carried brushes every day to the village and sold them, and the family lived in comfort.

Then one day a coin fell into the jar by mistake. The brushes disappeared, and the jar filled with money!

Such riches! Such luxuries! Such wonders were theirs because there were always coins in the jar!

Now, the farmer had an elderly grandfather who lived in his home, and he thought it was terribly unfair for the old man to enjoy this wealth without doing any work. So the farmer handed his grandfather a spade and told him it was his job to shovel the money out of the jar. The old man was weak and shaky, and sometimes he could not shovel as fast as his grandson wanted.

"Worthless old man!" the farmer would shout. "What a lazy and good-for-nothing wretch! You don't want to work, that's all. Dig harder! Faster!"

Grandfather tried, but it was so hard when his hands shook and his old bones ached. One day his strength gave out and in the middle of a shovelful, he fell forward into the large jar and died.

Instantly the coins disappeared. The whole jar filled itself with dead grandfathers. The farmer had to pull them all out and have them buried. Every day, more dead grandfathers. It used up all the money the farmer had received. Finally the jar broke, and he was just as poor as ever.[7]

The Boasting Traveler

Aesop may have told this fable about a man who wanted others to think well of him.

A man entertained a group of fellows with stories of the wonders he had done when on his travels. "I was at Rhodes," he said, "and you know the people of Rhodes are famous for jumping. Well, I took a jump that no other person could come close to. That's a fact, and if we were there I could bring you ten people who would tell you about it."

"Why do we need to go to Rhodes?" asked one of those who were listening. "Just imagine you are there now, and show us your jump."[8]

The Fly and the Chariot

This fable is attributed to Abstemius.

A fly seated himself on a chariot that raced along the ground. As they ran at full speed, the feet of the horses and the rims of the whirling wheels flung up great clouds of dust. The fly took all the credit for himself and proudly cried, "See what a dust I am raising!"[9]

The Ass and the Lion

This story from the Shans of China carries the moral that "anyone who forgets his poor brothers when he is rich is just the same as an ass."

A lion once asked an ass to go walking with him. The ass swelled with pride; it was such an honor to go about with such exalted company. He thought to himself that he must be a very special creature indeed, and he decided that if he met any of his friends or family along the way, he would pretend not to see them.

Before long, they met some donkeys who said hello to the ass.

The ass asked, "Who are you? I do not know you."

Then the donkeys said, "Even if you go about with a lion, you are still an ass."[10]

The Spider and the Silkworm

This is an English fable.

A spider busied himself and spread his web from one side of the room to the other. An industrious silkworm was watching and asked to what purpose he spent so much time and labor in making such a number of lines and circles.

The spider snorted and replied, "Do not disturb me, you stupid thing. I pass my genius on to posterity. I shall be famous!"

Just as he had spoken, a woman came into the room to feed her silkworms. She saw the spider at his work, fetched a broom, and swept it all away.[11]

The Coyote and the Fox

The Native Americans of the Thompson River area of British Columbia, Canada, tell this story of how the trickster Coyote was in turn tricked because of his own vanity.

Coyote found some meat and bones. After eating all the meat, he gathered the bones together, lit a fire, and put part of the bones into the kettle to boil. He wanted to get the fat out of the marrow. Fox came along and acted surprised that such an important personage as Coyote should be doing such work.

"You are a chief," he said. "Let me do your work for you."

Flattered, Coyote agreed, and going a distance from the fire, he lay down on his back. He put on the air of one who was much too dignified to notice what was going on around him.

Fox boiled the bones. Then he skimmed off the fat, put it in a dish, and set it aside to cool. "I have nearly finished my work," he said to Coyote, "and as soon as the fat stiffens, we shall eat."

The vain Coyote barely paid attention.

As soon as the grease was stiff, Fox took it up and ran away with it. Coyote chased him, but he couldn't catch Fox. His vanity caused him to be Fox's dupe.[12]

Good Deeds Should Be Repaid with Good

Variations upon the motifs of this tale can be found in numerous cultures, but this version from Brazil puts the issue in terms of the proper response to good deeds.

One day a fox was taking a walk when he discovered a jaguar in a hole. He had gone into the hole long before and grown too large to get out. Now he asked if the fox would help him roll the stone away.

The fox helped the jaguar out. "Now I am going to eat you!" said the jaguar. He caught the fox and asked, "How is a good deed paid for?"

"Good is repaid with good," the fox answered. "Nearby there is a man who knows all things; let us ask him."

They crossed to an island, and the fox told the man how he had rescued the jaguar out of the hole, and how the jaguar, in payment, wanted to eat him.

The jaguar said, "I wanted to eat him because good is repaid with evil."

"All right!" said the man. "Let us go see the hole." So they all went and arrived at the hole. "Go in," the man said to the jaguar. "I want to see how you were lying."

The jaguar went in, the man and the fox rolled back the stone, and the jaguar was a prisoner again. "Now," said the man, "perhaps you will learn that good deeds should be repaid with good!" So the jaguar was left, and the others went away.[13]

The Hyena and the Crane

This version of the fable is from the Vandau people of South Africa. There is another African variant with a fox and a crow, and another attributed to Aesop with the wolf and the crane.

One day a hyena ate his meal so quickly that a bone stuck in his throat. It was very painful, and he ran howling through the bushes, calling out that he would richly reward anyone who would remove the bone.

Finally he met a crane.

"Crane," he said, "I will give you a great reward if you can put your head into my throat and remove the bone that is choking me."

The crane thought the reward would be nice, so she put her head into the throat of the hyena and pulled out the bone. Afterward she said, "Now give me the reward you promised."

"Reward!" exclaimed the hyena. "How much of a reward do you want? Haven't I done enough for *you*? You should thank *me*, because I was the one who did you a great kindness when I allowed your head to enter my mouth and then leave. Under any other circumstances, anything that entered a mouth of a hyena would never come out again. Get away with you, and don't come near me again."[14]

Dog and the Kingship

This tale comes from Angola.

The people decided to give Dog the kingship. They looked for all the things of royalty—the crown, the scepter, the rings, and the robe. "Everything is ready," they said. "The day has come to install the king."

The headmen all came. They sent for the players of the drum and marimba. They spread coarse mats and fine mats. In the place where the king was to sit, they first laid a coarse mat, then a fine mat, then last of all a chair. They said to Dog, "My Lord, sit down." The people began to divide the food.

Dog, on seeing the breast of a fowl, became greedy. He stood up quickly, grabbed the breast of the fowl, and ran into the bush.

"Look!" said the people. "We were going to install Dog as king, but he has run away with the meat into the bush!"

So the people did not give Dog the kingship. No one who is greedy or a thief could make a good king.[15]

Why Spiders Are Always Found in the Corners of Ceilings

Most cultures tell trickster tales. Anansi is the trickster figure of Africa, comparable to Coyote in southwestern Native American groups and to Raven in the Northwest. Anansi sometimes appears as a man, other times as a spider.

Once upon a time, Egya Anansi worked with his wife and son to prepare a much larger farm. They planted yams, maize, and beans and eventually harvested ten times as much food as they ever had before. Egya Anansi was quite happy.

He was, however, a very selfish and greedy man who never liked to share anything—not even with his own wife and son. When he saw that the crops were ripe, he thought of a plan in which he could get everything. He called his wife and said, "We have all worked hard to prepare these fields. We will gather the harvest and pack it into our barns. When that is done, we shall be in need of a rest. You and our son should go back to our home in the village and take a vacation for two or three weeks. I have to go to the coast on business. When I return we will all come to the farm and enjoy our well-earned feast."

Anansi's wife and son thought this a very good, sensible plan. They went back to their village, leaving Egya Anansi to start on his journey. But he didn't plan on going anywhere. Instead, he built himself a comfortable hut near the farm, took a large store of the corn and vegetables from the barn, and prepared all of it for himself. This went on for two weeks.

As the third week began, Anansi's son began to think it was time for him to return to the farm to weed the fields. He journeyed home and worked for several hours. While passing the barn, he happened to look inside. Great was his surprise to see that more than half of their magnificent harvest was missing! Thinking that robbers had been at work, he wondered how he could prevent further mischief. He returned to the village and told the people what had happened, and they helped him construct a rubber man. When evening came, they carried the sticky figure to the farm and placed it in the midst of the fields to frighten away thieves. Some of the men stayed with Anansi's son to watch from one of the barns.

When all was dark, Egya Anansi came out of his hiding place to fetch more food. On his way to the barn he saw in front of him the figure of a man, and at first he felt very frightened. Finding that the man did not move, however, he gained confidence and went up to him.

"What do you want here?" he asked. There was no answer. He repeated his question with the same result.

Anansi then became very angry and dealt the figure a blow on the cheek with his right hand. Of course, his hand stuck fast to the rubber. "How dare you hold my hand?" he exclaimed. "Let me go at once, or I shall hit you again." He then hit the figure with his left hand, which also stuck. He tried to get loose by pushing against it with his knees and body until, finally, knees, body, hands, and head were all stuck fast to the rubber man.

There Egya Anansi had to stay till morning, when his son came out with the other villagers to catch the thief. They were astonished to find the evildoer was Anansi himself.

Anansi was so ashamed to be caught in the act of greediness that he changed into a spider and hid in a dark corner of the ceiling.

Since then spiders have always been found in dark, dusty corners, where people are not likely to notice them.[16]

Why the Blackbird Isn't White

In some folklore, the blackbird and raven were both once white and became black for a number of reasons. In France, the cause was the bird's greed.

Once upon a time, the blackbird was as white as snow. One day, while lurking in a thicket, he saw the magpie, who was very busy. In the hole of a tree, she was hiding diamonds, jewels, and pieces of gold coin. He inquired the means by which he might acquire a similar treasure.

The magpie replied, "You must seek, in the bowels of the earth, the palace of the Prince of Riches. Offer him your services, and he will allow you to carry off as much treasure as your beak will hold. To reach him you will have to pass through many caverns, each one more abundant in riches than the last, but you must not touch a single thing until you have actually seen the prince himself."

The blackbird, on hearing this, went to the spot indicated by the magpie, where he found the entrance to an underground passage. He reached a cavern, the walls of which were bright with silver. But mindful of the magpie's advice, he continued to pursue his way till he entered a second cavern, all ablaze with gold.

The bird forgot everything in his desire for the gold, and he plunged his beak greedily into the glittering dust strewn upon the floor. Immediately there appeared a terrible ogre, vomiting fire and smoke, who rushed upon the wretched bird with such lightning speed that he only escaped with the greatest difficulty. But, alas, the thick smoke had forever dirtied his white feathers, and he became quite black, with the exception of his beak, which still preserves the color of the gold he was so anxious to carry away with him.[17]

The Greedy Crow

This tale about the greedy and foolish crow comes from the Philippines.

One day the crow was eating a piece of meat. He had found it on the ground, picked it up, and flown to the top of a tree. While he was sitting there eating, a kasaykasay (a small bird) passed by. She was carrying a dead rat and was flying very fast. "Kasaykasay," called the crow, "where did you get the dead rat?"

But the small bird said nothing and flew on her way. The crow became angry because she had ignored him. "Kasaykasay, kasaykasay, stop and give me a piece of that rat, or I will follow you and take the whole thing for myself!"

Still the small bird paid no attention to him. The crow was furious and decided to do as he had threatened. He left the meat he was eating and flew after the other bird.

Now, although she was small, the kasaykasay could fly faster than the crow, so he could not catch her.

While the crow chased the kasaykasay, a hawk happened to pass by the tree where the crow had left his meat. The hawk seized the meat and flew away.

The crow pursued the kasaykasay a long time but could not catch her. At last he gave up and flew back to the tree where he had left his meat. But the meat was gone and he was almost ready to die of disappointment and hunger.

After a while, the hawk passed by the tree again. He called to the crow and said, "Mr. Crow, do you know I am the one who took your meat? If not, I will tell you now, and I am very sorry for you."

The crow said nothing, because he was so tired and weak he could hardly breathe.

The moral of the story is this: Do not be greedy. Be content with what you have, and do not wish for what you do not own.[18]

The Spirit of Wealth

This story has been attributed to Aesop.

A good man became poor and elderly. Because he had no one to care for him and because he had always been good, the fairies invited the man to live with them. During his first few days there, he went to visit all the fairies and spirits who dwelled in Fairyland. There was only one, the Spirit of Wealth, whom he never visited or greeted.

The fairy queen finally came and asked him for an explanation. "Well," he answered, "I have seen that spirit in the company of such rascals when in the world that I did not know whether it would be considered respectable to be seen talking to him here!"[19]

The Discontented Water-Carrier

This story is adapted from a poem by John Godfrey Saxe.
The tale came originally from Turkey.

Once upon a time, a water-carrier by the name of Hassan watched the wealthy people pass him by and grumbled at the unfairness of life. He thought it a terrible thing that one man should wear rags and another a cloth of gold.

Suddenly a little fairy elf appeared before him. "Choose any gift you desire," said the elf.

With great joy, Hassan considered the many possibilities. "I should like," he finally replied, "to have a hidden well, filled to the brim with jewels and with gold."

She led him to a secret place and removed a great slab of stone to reveal a treasure to his sparkling eyes. "Take what you will," she told him. "There is no end to the riches here. But remember, once you stop to eat, your work is finished and you can have no more. The stone will move back into its place."

Delighted, Hassan bent to his task. He filled three water skins with gold but was not satisfied. He took his shovel and dug into the hoard and piled it beside the well. "Another hour of digging will do it," he said. But when that hour had passed, he determined that one more hour was necessary. The sun set and the sun rose, but Hassan kept saying to himself, "Just an hour more."

He built a mound of treasure greater than that of any king on earth. Then, as he threw a last shovelful on the mountain of gold and jewels, it began to slide. The whole shining heap tumbled upon his head and buried him forever.[20]

The Hoopoe from Rugen

This story, telling the origin of the hoopoe bird, comes from the Isle of Rugen in the Baltic Sea.

The hoopoe bird was once a human, a maker of clothing. He lived in a large rich city and carried himself like a smart fellow. He wore a colored silken coat and went from one grand house to another and from one palace to the next. From these he carried home expensive materials from which he made clothing. Because he was handsome and polite, all the great people took him for their tailor, so he had plenty of work. He even made the dress for the queen to wear when she was crowned.

Mr. Hoopoe became very rich, but he was never satisfied. He always looked for more work, and when he carried home his load of fabric it was so heavy it made him groan like a mule. As he climbed the stairs, he sighed, "Hoop, whoop!"

Now, wanting more and more work can be excused, if it is necessary, but in this case, in the end, it turned to greed. The tailor began to steal some of the pieces of fabric he had been given to make clothing. This couldn't be tolerated. As he climbed upstairs with his heavy load, sighing "Hoop, whoop!" he was suddenly changed into a colored bird. Ever since then he has kept sighing, "Hoop, whoop!" and is known as the hoopoe bird.[21]

The Punishment of Greed

In this ghost story from China,
it is a teacher who learns a lesson.

A teacher once took a job in a small village. When he arrived, he found that the schoolhouse was not yet completed. But a two-story building in the country had been rented where he could live and teach until the schoolhouse was finished.

The house was near the river and had a fine view of the countryside. One evening as the teacher stood on his front steps and enjoyed the sunset, he noticed a fiery glow near the river. What a strange thing! He had never seen anything quite like it. As the sun disappeared, the light shone with an eerie brilliance.

The teacher decided to investigate the strange sight, so he set off for the river.

A coffin lay there, and the strange light came from underneath its wooden cover!

The teacher then realized what must have happened. The dead person had been buried with his or her jewels, and it was the gems that gave off the light. To think of the riches that must be contained within that coffin!

Greed made him forget everything. He forgot that it was a terrible thing to steal from the dead. He forgot that the dead should be treated with respect. He thought only of the riches that lay before him.

Seizing a stone from the riverbank, he smashed it upon the coffin cover again and again, until he had shattered the wood and made a large hole. Dropping the stone, he looked inside.

A young man's corpse lay there. His face was more pale than the mists rising over the river, and a dark shadow lay over his eyes. He was wrapped in large cloths and wore straw sandals upon his feet.

The hand of the dead man lifted. With a gasp, the teacher stumbled backward. The corpse lifted itself and sat.

The courage of the teacher shattered into smaller pieces than the wooden coffin cover. Lifting his heels, he flew back to his home, but he sneaked a glance over his shoulder and could see the corpse stumbling after him! Lurching through the door, he slammed it shut behind him and thrust down the lock.

He leaned against the door, panting for breath. Not a sound could be heard beyond his beating heart. Perhaps the corpse had not followed him all the way to the house. Barely breathing, he tiptoed upstairs to a window. He opened it and peered down. The corpse was leaning against the wall of the house!

Suddenly the corpse saw that the window was open and leapt up and through it. The teacher wailed and thundered toward the stairs. But his legs felt like strips of wet paper, and they deserted him on the way down. Thump, thump, thump—it felt like he fell endlessly, until the final crash upon the bottom floor. There was not a sound after that save for a dull thud on the floor overhead.

All night the teacher lay on the floor below.

All night the corpse lay above.

The next morning the students came as usual to their classes. But the door was closed, and when they called, no one answered. Finally they forced the door open and found the teacher lying on the floor like a dead man. They sprinkled him with ginger, but it took a long time for him to open his eyes and tell them what had happened.

The corpse was taken away, and it never walked again. But the teacher gave up his job in the village and returned home. He often said, "Because of a moment's greed, I nearly lost my life!" For the rest of the days of his life, he never again spoke of trying to gain wealth.[22]

The Dog and the Loaf of Bread

This story comes from Hindu sources.

A dog, thinking only of his empty stomach, stood at the gate of a village and saw a loaf of bread roll out of the gate and start a journey toward the desert. The dog ran in pursuit of the loaf and cried, "Oh staff of life, strength of the traveler, object of my desire! Where are you going?"

"To the desert," replied the loaf of bread, "to see my friends, the wolves and leopards."

"Your boasting speech doesn't frighten me," replied the dog. "I would follow you down the throat of a crocodile, or between the teeth of a lion. I would chase you through a dung heap. If you rolled around the world I would still pursue you."

"I see," answered the loaf of bread. "Those who live by bread alone will put up with anything for the sake of it."[23]

The Man and the Foxes

This fable has been attributed to Aesop.

A man had some vines and orchards that had suffered a great deal because of the foxes. One day he caught one of these animals in a trap. In a terrible rage he tied the fox's tail with a rag soaked with turpentine and set fire to it.

In awful pain and fright, the fox ran toward the river to douse his tail. But on the way he went through a large cornfield ready to harvest. The corn caught fire, and the flames spread and destroyed the man's entire field. The man was very sorry he had not chosen something less cruel to solve his problems.

Moral: There is a difference between justice and revenge.[24]

The Monkey's Rebuke

This tale about dishonesty and the milkman's just reward for it comes from India.

In a certain village there lived a dishonest milkman who filled his cans only half full of milk. The other half was water. The people of that village were all very honest, so they never dreamed their milkman was cheating them. If the milk seemed thin, they simply thought the cows must have been drinking a great deal.

By watering the milk, the milkman got together a great sum of money—four hundred silver pieces. He decided he would go try his tricks in another place, where there were a greater number of people to be cheated. He put his four hundred silver pieces in a bag and set out on his journey.

After traveling an hour, he came to a pond. He sat down by the water to eat his breakfast and laid his bag of money by his side. Now, it happened this was the very same pond where the milkman had come to water his milk. He came this far out of the village because he did not want to be seen by anyone.

But there was one who had seen him: a monkey that lived in a tree overhanging the pond. Many times this monkey had seen the milkman pouring water into the milk cans and chuckling over the profit he was making. This monkey knew as well as anyone that when you sell milk, you should put no water in it.

The monkey sneaked up behind the man, snatched his bag of money, and scampered back into the tree. He opened the bag and started throwing coins into the pond. At first, the man didn't realize what was making little splashes in the water, and then—oh, horror!

"Wait, you monkey," shouted the milkman, "that's my bag! What are you doing? Bring me back my money!"

"Not yet," said the monkey, and he went on dropping the silver pieces, splash, splash, splash!

The milkman wept and tore handfuls of hair out of his head, but the monkey kept dropping money into the pond just the same.

At last the monkey had dropped two hundred pieces of silver into the pond. Then he tied up the bag and threw it down to the milkman. "There, take your money," said the monkey.

"And where's the rest of my silver?" demanded the milkman.

"You have all the money that is yours," said the monkey. "Half of the money was the price of water from this pond, so to the pond I gave it."

The milkman felt ashamed of himself, and he went away a wiser man. Never again did he put water into his milk.[25]

The Magic Pot

This story comes from Newfoundland.

A woman came to the judge complaining that someone had stolen a pair of blankets that she had washed and put on the clothesline to dry. The judge suspected a certain man, but he had no proof. He asked the woman if she had a good crowing rooster. She said no, but her neighbor did. He told her to ask the men of the neighborhood to come to the house at dark.

That evening, when the men had arrived, the judge placed the rooster under a large iron pot inside a small room of the house. He extinguished the lamp. "Go into the room," he said to the men. "I want you to go one at a time and touch the pot. When the guilty one touches it, the cock will crow."

Each man did as he was instructed, but the rooster never made a sound.

The judge then called everyone into the house and lit the lamp again. He told them to hold up their hands, and then he pointed to one. He said, "You are the guilty man."

"Nonsense!" the man blustered. "You heard, the rooster never made a sound."

"That's true," answered the judge, "but you never touched the pot because you were afraid it *would* crow."

Everyone's hands were black from the soot on the pot except this man's, whose hands were clean. At first he kept saying he was innocent, but he finally confessed and returned the blankets.[26]

The Judgment of the Chief

This tale was adapted from a story by Samuel Taylor Coleridge.

In his march to conquer the world, Alexander the Great came to a people in Africa who lived in a remote area and knew neither war nor conqueror. Alexander wished to know their manners and customs. While he visited with the chief, two citizens entered to seek a decision of justice.

"I bought from my neighbor a piece of land," said the first man. "While I was digging a trench, I found a treasure. This is not mine, because I only bought the land and not any treasure that might be hidden beneath it. Yet, the former owner of the land will not receive it from me."

The defendant answered, "I hope I have a conscience as well as my fellow citizen. I sold him the land with all it holds, and thus the treasure is his."

The chief repeated their words so they might see whether or not he had understood them correctly. Then after some thought he said to one, "Friend, you have a son, don't you?"

"Yes."

"And you," he said to the other. "You have a daughter?"

"Yes."

"Well, then," said the chief, "why doesn't your daughter marry his son? Give the treasure to them both for their beginning in life."

Alexander seemed surprised and puzzled.

"Do you think my decision is unfair?" the chief asked him.

"Oh, no!" replied Alexander. "But it astonishes me."

"What decision would be made in your country?"

"To confess the truth," said Alexander, "we would have seized the treasure for the use of the king."

"For the king!" exclaimed the chief. "Tell me, does the sun shine on your country?"

"Oh, yes!"

"Does it rain there?"

"Of course it does."

"Wonderful! But are there animals in the country, ones that live on the grass and other plants?"

"Very many."

"That is the answer," said the chief. "It is for the sake of these innocent animals that the sun continues to shine, and the rain comes upon your country, since its people are clearly unworthy of such blessings."[27]

The Cloud

This tale describes how a man's fear, and perhaps his belated conscience, brought him to justice. The story comes from Asia.

Many years ago two men lived in the same village, and they agreed to take their money and go together to trade in a distant country. They told their wives that they might be gone for two or three years, and then they started to go through the jungle.

When they reached a far country, one of the men said to himself, "If I kill this man, take his money, and go home, it will be good for me."

He was stronger than his friend and in fighting him hurt him so badly that he fell to the ground. The dying man said, "Because we are so far from people in the jungle, you think no one will know what you have done, so I will tell that cloud floating in the air above us that you have killed me. Oh cloud! My friend has killed me; go to my home and tell my wife."

Then he died.

The murderer laughed and thought nothing of it. He took the dead man's money and returned to his own country. His wife was very glad to see him, and the wife of the dead man came and asked for news of her husband.

"Your husband and I separated when we reached a distant country; he went one way, and I went another."

So the wife of the dead man went away to her home.

Soon after this the murderer was lying on his patio and looking up at the clouds and laughed, then shivered a little and went back inside. As weeks passed, he began to avoid going outside when there was bad weather. A while later he stopped going outside at all. During rainy nights he dreamed and called out with terror. His wife kept asking what was wrong.

"Nothing," he exclaimed, "nothing at all!" But his nightmares grew worse until he finally told her what had happened.

The man's wife kept the secret for some time, but it troubled her also. She became so unhappy in her mind that she told her sister. After a while her sister told a friend, and so the story traveled throughout the village until it reached the chief, who sent his men to arrest the murderer. When he was questioned, the man confessed his crime, and although he knew he would suffer the punishment, he felt almost relieved the truth was known.[28]

The Owl Embarrassed

This European version of the wren's attempt to become king of the birds concludes with the owl's faithlessness to his responsibility.

The birds decided that whichever of them could fly the highest would become king. The eagle succeeded in the task, but when he was tired, the wren, who had perched on his tail, rose up and flew yet higher. For this deceit the birds confined the wren in a mouse hole and appointed the owl to guard the entrance. But while the other birds were taking counsel as to the wren's punishment, the owl went to sleep and the prisoner escaped. Never since has the owl dared to appear in the daytime.[29]

How Beasts and Serpents First Came into the World

This Anansi tale comes from West Africa. Anansi comes to grief because of greed, ill temper, discourtesy, and his unwillingness to follow instructions.

Once upon a time, there was a famine that had lasted nearly three years. Kweku Tsin daily searched the forest hoping to find some food. One day he discovered three palm kernels lying on the ground. He picked up two stones with which to crack them. The first nut slipped when he hit it and fell into a hole behind him. The same thing happened to the other nuts, so Kweku decided to go down the hole to see if he could find them.

The hole was an entrance to a hidden and deserted town. He called out, "Is there nobody in this town?" A voice came in answer. He went in that direction and found an old woman sitting in one of the houses. She asked why he was there.

After he told her what had happened, the woman was very kind and promised to help. "You must do exactly as I tell you. Go into the garden and listen carefully. You will hear the yams speak. Pass by any yam that says, 'Dig me out, dig me out!' But take the one that says, 'Do not dig me out!' Bring it to me."

When he brought it, she told him to take the peel from the yam and throw the yam away. He was then to boil the rind, and, while boiling, it would become a yam. This is what happened, and they sat down to eat it. Before beginning their meal the old woman asked Kweku not to look at her while she ate. Being very polite, he did exactly as he was told.

In the evening the old woman sent him into the garden to choose one of the drums that stood there. She told him to take the drum that says "ding-dong" on being touched, but not the one that sounds "dong-dong." He obeyed her directions. When he showed her the drum, she looked pleased and told him that he had only to beat it when he became hungry. That would bring him food. He thanked the old woman and went home.

As soon as he reached his hut, he gathered his family together and beat the drum. Food of every kind appeared before them, and they all ate as much as they wished. The next day Kweku gathered the villagers and fed them with the drum. Every family got enough food and all thanked Kweku sincerely.

Kweku's father, Anansi, was not at all pleased to see his son feed the whole village. He was jealous and thought he would also like to have a drum. Then the people would be grateful to him instead of to Kweku. So he asked his son where the drum had come from. Kweku wasn't very happy about telling him, but Anansi gave him no peace until he'd heard the entire story.

Anansi set off. He had taken with him an old nut that he pretended to crack, then he threw it down the hole. He jumped in after it and hurried through the silent village. He shouted for someone in the town; the old woman answered, and Anansi entered her house. He was very rude to her and asked her to hurry and get him something to eat. But every time the woman told him to do something he did the opposite. When he insisted he would look at her while eating, she left her meal untouched, so he ate his food and hers as well. After he had finished, she told him to go to the garden and take the drum that said "ding-dong." Yet Anansi insisted on taking the drum that said "dong-dong." He left without saying so much as "thank you" to the old woman.

When he got home, he gathered the villagers together and told them he was going to provide them with food. Anansi began to beat his drum. Instead of the multitude of food that Kweku had summoned, Anansi's drum brought forth beasts and serpents of all kinds. Such creatures had never been seen on the earth before.

All the people ran away except Anansi, who was too scared to move. The animals presently scattered in every direction, and ever since they have roamed wild in the great forests.[30]

The Wren as King of the Birds

This version of the wren as king of the birds comes from Ireland.
A similar story is told in Germany, Scotland, and other parts of Europe.

During a grand assembly of all the birds of the air, it was determined that the kingship of the feathered tribe should be conferred upon the one who could fly highest. The favorite in the betting was of course the eagle, who at once, and in full confidence of victory, commenced his flight toward the sun. When he had far outdistanced all competitors, he proclaimed with a mighty voice his monarchy over all things that had wings.

Suddenly, however, the wren, who had hidden himself under the feathers of the eagle's crest, popped from his hiding place, flew a few inches upward, and chirped out as loudly as he could, "Birds, look up and behold your king!"

The wren didn't win much by cheating. He was called king but has never been honored or obeyed, because he was dishonest.[31]

Squirrel and the Kingship

Impatience lost Squirrel the opportunity to become king in this story from Angola.

The people of the forest met to choose a king. "Let us give Squirrel the kingship," they decided.

"It shall be today," Squirrel announced.

"Not today," said the people. "First we are looking for the symbol of the kingship."

"It shall be today, at once!" Squirrel insisted.

"Oh, dear," the people exclaimed. "We said we had to look for the symbol first, but Squirrel says it has to be today. We can't give him the kingship; Squirrel is too impatient. If we gave it to him, he could not govern the people."[32]

I Have a Crow to Pluck with You

The cultural source for the crow-plucking story may be British.

The crow was about to be elected king of the birds because he seemed so beautiful and unusual. But the truth was that the crow had decorated itself in the feathers that had fallen from the other birds. The owl came up, recognized one of its own feathers, and plucked it out, setting an example for the other birds. Soon, they had left the crow with only his own plumage.[33]

The Tortoise and the Fox

This Persian tale gives a lesson about greed but also speaks of the difference between saying words and actually doing something.

Once upon a time there was a tortoise who was sowing seed when a fox chanced to pass by and said to him, "May God give you strength." Then he continued on his way. The wheat sprang up, the summer passed, and the time came for reaping it. The fox turned up again and said, "May God give you strength." Again he went on his way.

He did not reappear until harvesttime, when the tortoise had threshed and winnowed the wheat. Then the fox threw several big bags over his shoulder and came to the threshing floor. "I have come for my share," said he.

"You crazy rascal!" said the tortoise. "Your share of what?"

"Didn't I say to you, 'May God give you strength'?"

"Yes, no doubt you did," replied the tortoise, "but what makes you think that gives you a right to share with me as though you did some of the work?" And so they fell to quarreling.

Finally, the fox said the only way he would agree to settle it was a race. "We will go off a long way and then race back to the threshing floor, and whoever gets there first will be the owner of all the grain."

The poor tortoise didn't know what to do but agree, as it looked like the fox might do anything to him in order to get the wheat. But he did have a plan in mind. He went and told his brother the story privately.

"Now, you go to the threshing floor and hide there," said the tortoise. "I can't possibly race the fox. When he comes running up, say: 'Eight and twenty, you've lost!' Then you'll have scored off him, because he won't see any difference between us."

After that the brothers went off, and the one hid himself by the threshing floor, and the first tortoise went away with the fox and started their race.

But the tortoise hid himself under a small bush while the fox went on running as hard as he could till he came to the threshing floor. Just as he got there, the tortoise brother cried out, "Eight and twenty, you've lost."

The fox screamed with anger, but the tortoise brother only shrugged. "You're not allowed to stand about here. Be off!"

Then the fox hung his head in embarrassment and went off about his own business. And so everyone who is greedy is put to shame.[34]

The Fox and the Hypocrite

Inconsistency of word and action is a hallmark of hypocrisy in this tale attributed to Aesop.

A fox was being hunted and chased when he saw a man working in the woods. He begged the man to help him find a hiding place, so the man said he could go into his cottage.

The fox was no sooner hidden than the hunters arrived. "Have you seen a fox pass this way?" they asked.

The man said, no, but he pointed toward the cottage where the fox was hidden. The hunters didn't understand and rode off again at full speed.

The fox, however, had seen everything through a hole in the wall. He walked out of the cottage and started away without a word. "What's this?" exclaimed the man. "Don't you have the manners to thank me before you go?"

"Well, of course," said the fox. "If you had been as honest with your fingers as you were with your tongue, I would never have left without saying good-bye."[35]

The Camel's Neck

The danger of laziness and of having foolish wishes granted is illustrated in this tale from India. Compare this story with "The Farmer and the Magic Ring (Part 3)."

Once upon a time there was a camel who happened to catch the favor of a magical being. "I have come to reward you," said the enchanted one. "Choose what you like, and it shall be yours."

"O mighty one," answered the camel, "more than anything, I would like to have a neck eight miles long."

The magical being answered, "Be it so!"

Immediately the camel felt his neck shooting out like a telescope, until it was eight miles long. It grew so fast the camel found it hard to avoid running his head against the trees. However, he steered it successfully, barring a bump or two. By the time his neck stopped growing, he was so far out of sight of the magical being, he could not even say thank you.

Why did he want a neck eight miles long? The reason was that he was a lazy camel, and he wanted to graze without the trouble of walking. Now he could easily graze for a distance of eight miles all round in a circle without moving from the spot where he lay. Of course, he never considered that it might be rather dangerous; for when his head was grazing a few miles away, hunters could stick a spear into his body, or tie his legs together, without his seeing them.

All summer the camel enjoyed himself while he lay still and comfortable and sent his head foraging around. But then the rainy season began. There were storms every day, and the camel wanted to keep dry, but he had problems finding a shelter eight miles long. At last he discovered a long winding cave that would hold most of his neck. He ran his neck into the cave and lay still, with the rain pouring upon his body.

It happened that a pair of jackals lived in this cave. When they saw this strange neck winding along their cave, they were frightened and hid themselves.

"What is this snake?" said the he-jackal to his wife.

"Oh, dear, I don't know!" whispered his wife. "I never saw a snake like this."

They kept quiet, and the head passed out of view into the inner part of the cave, then lay still.

"Let us smell him!" said the she-jackal.

They smelled him. "He smells nice," said the he-jackal. "Not a bit like a snake."

"Let us taste him!" said the she-jackal.

They took a bite; the camel stirred restlessly. They took another bite, and liked that better still. They went on biting.

The camel curled his head around to see what was going on, but before his head could get back more than a mile or two, he grew so weak from loss of blood he could move no more, and he breathed his last. So the camel died because he was lazy and was granted his foolish wish.[36]

The Frog Who Wished to Be as Big as an Ox

This fable has been attributed to Babrius and Aesop.

An ox grazing in a meadow scared a brother and sister frog, who ran to tell their mother what had happened. "The monster was huge!" they said.

The mother was a vain old thing and thought she could make herself as large. "Was it as big as this?" she asked, blowing and puffing herself out.

"Oh, much bigger than that," replied the young frogs.

"As this, then?" she cried, puffing and blowing again with all her might.

"No, Mother. If you were to try till you burst yourself, you would never be so big."

The silly old frog tried to puff herself out still more and burst herself on the spot.[37]

The Boy Who Cried Wolf

Although it is likely the best known of Aesop's fables, this story bears repeating. Most good stories do.

A boy was sent to take care of the sheep. It was his job to watch over the animals and keep them together—and most of all, to keep an eye out for wolves.

The boy thought it was terribly boring out there in the meadow with nothing to do, so he decided to play a joke on the rest of the town. He knew his job was to run and call for them if there was a wolf, but what if he ran and yelled without having seen a wolf? Wouldn't that be great fun?

"Wolf! Wolf!" he screamed, and everybody in town dropped whatever they were doing and ran to the meadow. They found the boy lying on the grass and howling with laughter. "You should have seen yourselves," he cried. "You were all white and scared and running and huffing and puffing. You were sooooo funny."

The next day he got to thinking about how much fun it had been to scare the villagers, so he screeched "Wolf! Wolf!" The people dropped everything they were doing, grabbed clubs, and ran to the meadow. Once again they found the boy laughing himself sick over their pale faces and raised clubs, and they went back to the village angry over his lies.

A week later, the boy was really bored and yelled, "Wolf! Wolf!" Once more, everybody in town dropped whatever they were doing and ran to the meadow ready to fight the wolf. But the boy laughed again and pointed his finger at their fright and puffing lungs.

The next day as the boy was watching the sheep, he saw a suspicious gray animal slinking toward the flock. It was a wolf! "Help, help," he cried for the villagers to come. "It's the wolf! Come and help!"

Everybody in town looked at each other, rolled their eyes, and went on with their chores. "It really is a wolf!" the boy shrieked. "You've got to come!"

But the people ignored the boy, because they had learned better than to pay attention to the words of a liar. And so the wolf ate the sheep because the boy didn't know how to tell the truth.[38]

The Cat and the Bat

This story has been attributed to Aesop.

A cat had devoured the canary beloved by the people with whom she lived, and she overheard them threatening to put her to death the moment they could find her. In her fright, she lifted up a prayer, vowing that if she were delivered from her danger, she would never again eat another bird.

Not long afterward a bat flew into the room where puss was purring at the window. The question that troubled her was this: On the one hand, she was very hungry, and on the other, she had made certain promises in her prayer.

Finally, she thought up a convenient excuse. As a bird, the bat was certainly not a lawful prize, but it was also a sort of mouse and as such she could properly eat it. Within minutes, she was licking her whiskers over her meal.

It is very easy to rationalize the breaking of a promise.[39]

The Owl and the Raven

In Greek mythology, the raven became black because he carried gossip; in this Eskimo story it was the consequence of impatience.

The owl and the raven were fast friends. One day the raven made a new dress, dappled white and black, for the owl. In turn, the owl made a pair of boots of whalebone for the raven. Then he began to make a white dress for his friend. But when he was about to have the raven try it on, the raven kept hopping about and would not sit still.

The owl became frustrated. "Now, sit still, or I shall pour out the lamp over you." The raven continued hopping around, and so the angry owl poured the oil upon it. The raven cried, "Qaq! Qaq!" and since that day he has been black all over.[40]

The Mean-Spirited Tortoise

If the tortoise could have kept his mouth shut at the appropriate time, he would not have lost his life in this story from India. This story is also told in China; and a version with the frog in place of the tortoise is told in North Carolina, United States.

A tortoise and two geese lived together in great friendship at a small pond. When the water got very low, the geese knew they would have to leave, but first they went to say good-bye to their friend, the tortoise. The tortoise remarked that the evaporating water was dangerous to himself also, but he had a problem—he was almost as helpless on dry land as a ship would be. He begged the geese to find a way to take him with them.

After much thought, the geese brought a piece of wood. They proposed to each take an end while the tortoise bit down in the middle and suspended himself beneath the wood. This way they could carry him to a new stretch of water. For his own safety, they strictly ordered him not to utter a word during their flight.

They had not flown far when some persons below saw what was passing over their heads and cried out in surprise. The tortoise was annoyed by this. "May their eyes be plucked out!" he yelled. Of course, when he opened his mouth, he lost his grip on the wood, fell to the ground, and was killed.[41]

The Man and the Partridge

Aesop may have first told this fable.

A partridge was taken in the net of a man and begged to be set free, promising he would lure other partridges into the net.

"No," replied the man, "even if I had been tempted to let you go, I wouldn't now. There is nothing worse than a scoundrel who tries to save himself by betraying his friends."[42]

Wickedness and Fortune

This story has been attributed to Aesop.

Fortune and Wickedness had an argument about which of them could make humankind the most unhappy. Fortune boasted that she could take from people every visible good and bring upon them every endless misfortune.

"Perhaps," replied Wickedness, "but this is not enough to make them miserable without my assistance. However, without your help, I can make any individual completely wretched. I can do that, even if you try your best to make them happy at the same time."[43]

The Blind Sheep

This story has been attributed to Aesop.

A certain sheep became blind in his later years, and an owl offered to cure him. On the morning when the operation was to be performed, the sheep seated himself and asked the owl if everything was ready for the cure. The owl assured him everything was prepared.

"By the way," said the sheep, "without my eyes I'm a little behind on the news. Tell me, how is the world these days?"

"Very much like always," answered the owl.

"Really?" asked the sheep. "In that case, leave me blind. I wouldn't give a blade of grass to recover my sight if I must be punished by watching the terrible deeds of the world and its people again."[44]

The Prince and the Flea

This is a Turkish fable.

A prince of royal blood was once badly tormented by a flea. At last he caught the troublesome pest and was about to kill it when the flea said, "I beg of you, do not kill me. After all, I did not harm you very much." "Yes," replied the prince, "but you did me all the harm that you could!"[45]

The Debt

This tale from Kashmir illustrates the truth that those who are willing to hurt their fellow human beings are not to be trusted in other matters as well.

A Musalman owed some rupees to a Pandit but refused to pay him. Eventually they brought the case before the governor, who heard everything they had to say. He put the men in separate rooms and eventually ordered the Pandit to come back. He asked him whether his claim was true. The Pandit said it was.

"Then take this knife and go and cut off the man's nose for his dishonesty," said the governor.

But the Pandit begged to be excused, saying he didn't care so much for the money that he would cut off a man's nose for it. The governor ordered him to return to a separate room to wait, and as soon as he was out of hearing he sent for the Musalman and asked him if he owed the Pandit anything. The man said he didn't.

"Then take this knife," said the governor, "and go and cut off the Pandit's ear for his false accusation."

The wicked Musalman took the knife and left with the intention of cutting off the Pandit's ear.

The governor called him back. "I see," he announced. "You must pay the amount demanded by the Pandit, and also a fine. Tell me no more lies. The man who would not hesitate to take the ear of a fellow creature is not a man to be trusted."[46]

Why Dogs Can't Talk

In contrast to popular images of the dog as faithful and true, the Tahltan people native to North America tell how dogs lost the power of speaking like people because they were once liars.

In early times dogs used to talk, but they told lies. When a hunter went home, his dog would run ahead and tell the people he had killed game. Then, when the hunter arrived, the people learned he had killed nothing. When hunters killed game, the dogs always said they had killed nothing. They always lied.

Once, the people were starving. A man went out hunting with his dog and searched all day but could find nothing. On his way home the dog ran ahead and told the people his master was bringing in some nice fat game. The people were delighted and got the wood together to cook it. When the hunter arrived, they learned he had brought nothing and were very disappointed.

The man said to the dog, "From now on, you won't be able to lie because you will be unable to talk." This is how dogs lost the power of speaking like people.[47]

The Crane Who Quarreled with His Mate

This English story is from the Odo of Sherington.

A crane once quarreled with his mate and pecked out one of her eyes. Afterward, he felt quite ashamed for having done her such a terrible injury. So he prepared to leave home and travel to a distant country. A crow met him as he was setting out and asked the reason for his journey.

"I have pecked out my mate's eye with my beak," replied the crane. "I am so ashamed, I feel I must leave the country."

The crow said, "Don't you have the same beak?"

"Certainly," answered the crane in surprise.

"Then," the crow returned, "where will you run to? Wherever you go, you must carry your beak with you."[48]

Quetzalcoatl and Tezcatlipoca

In this tale from Mexico the peace and plenty of the land were destroyed by the lord's alcohol abuse. Tezcatlipoca might be cast in the role of "drug pusher."

In the days of Quetzalcoatl there was enough of everything needed for life. There was plenty of corn to harvest, the calabashes grew thick as one's arm, and cotton came in all colors without having to be dyed. Beautiful birds with lovely feathers filled the air with their songs, and gold, silver, and precious stones were abundant. In the reign of Quetzalcoatl, all people enjoyed peace and plenty.

But there were those who were envious of this happy land, especially Tezcatlipoca, an evil wizard. He disguised himself as an old man with white hair and presented himself at the palace of Quetzalcoatl. "Please present me to your king. I wish to speak with him."

The servants advised him to return another time, because the king wasn't feeling well and could see no one. He kept pressing them, however, and they finally allowed him to see the king.

When he entered the king's room, Tezcatlipoca pretended to feel very sorry for the suffering king. "How are you, my son?" he asked. "I have brought you a drug that you should drink, and it will heal your illness."

"You are welcome, old man," replied Quetzalcoatl. "I am feeling quite ill. The sickness affects my entire body, and I can't use my hands or my feet."

Tezcatlipoca promised if he took the medicine the king would immediately feel better. Quetzalcoatl drank the potion, and he did feel much better. The cunning Tezcatlipoca urged him to take another and still another cup of the potion. Because it was nothing but wine, the king soon became drunk, and Tezcatlipoca was able to do whatever he wanted with both the king and the country.[49]

The Lion and the Council of Beasts

This story has been attributed to Aesop.

One day in council, the need for a tax was discussed, but what kind of tax should it be? The lion gave his opinion that the fairest way would be to lay a tax on sin, and that each beast should decide upon the quantity of sin for his neighbor. That way, it would prevent any selfish partiality.

"No, no," said the elephant, "that will never be fair, because it gives power to ill will and oppression. The best way, in my judgment, would be to make a tax on virtues. Each one will give a list of his or her own, and I have little doubt that this will provide an adequate income for our forest."[50]

The Mosquitoes and Thunder

Apart from the irony of a mosquito being the hero, this story from the Native American Lillooet people of British Columbia, Canada could open a discussion of if and when lying might be the "moral" thing to do.

There were many mosquitoes who lived in the upper world, where they were ruled by a chief. Thunder lived there also, but not with the mosquitoes. The mosquitoes began to visit earth to get something to eat, and they found they liked human blood very much. They drank it more and more, until that was almost all the nourishment they ever desired.

Thunder heard that his neighbors, the mosquitoes, were living on blood, so he went and asked one where they got the blood. The mosquito told him that he sucked it from treetops. Then Thunder went down and sucked treetops, but he could not get any blood from them. He went back to the mosquito and asked him again. "I suck it from the rocks," the mosquito answered.

If the mosquito had told the truth, Thunder would have shot the people and sucked their blood instead of shooting the trees and rocks, as he does now. In this way the mosquitoes saved people from being shot by Thunder.[51]

How the Raven Became Black

This tale comes from Greek mythology.

Once upon a time the raven's feathers shone white as snow, and he was proud to be known as the messenger of Apollo. Yet despite his important position, the raven's nature was petty, for he enjoyed spying upon people and spreading gossip.

Apollo loved a young woman named Coronis. One day the raven saw Coronis talking with another man and carried the news to Apollo, who believed Coronis had lied about loving him. Apollo became angry. He took up his bow and shot his arrows at Coronis.

When Apollo realized what he had done, his heart filled with sorrow and he tried desperately to save the life of Coronis. Nothing helped, and she died in his arms.

Nothing could excuse Apollo's actions, but the gossiping raven was also at fault, so Apollo dismissed him as his messenger. "From now on," he told the raven, "to match your character, your feathers will be blacker than night."[52]

The Extortionate Sentry

Variations upon this story can be found in many cultures.
This version comes from the Santal Parganas of India.

There was once a sentry outside a raja's palace who would let no one go in to sell anything to the raja until they first promised to give him half the price they received from the raja. The poor traders had to promise, for their livelihood depended on selling their goods.

One day a fisherman caught an enormous fish, and he hoped the raja would give him a big price for it. He went off to the palace, but when he came to the gate the sentry stopped him and would not let him go in until he agreed to give him half of what he was paid. After some argument he had to promise. So he was admitted to the raja's presence, and when the raja asked what was the price of the fish, the fisherman said, "A hundred blows with a stick."

The raja was astonished and asked the meaning of such a request. Then the fisherman said that the sentry had extorted a pledge that he should get half the price, and he wanted the sentry to get fifty blows. At this the raja was very angry and had the sentry receive the full price of the fish, one hundred blows, and then dismissed him from his job.[53]

The Wolf and the Lamb

Power corrupts in this fable from Aesop.

A hungry wolf saw a lamb drinking at a stream and wished to find a plausible excuse for making him his victim. "What do you mean by muddying the water I am going to drink?" he demanded.

"Pray forgive me," answered the lamb meekly. "I would be sorry to displease you, but as the stream runs from you toward me, you will see I cannot spoil your water."

"That's all very well," said the wolf, "but you know you spoke badly of me behind my back a year ago."

"No, believe me," answered the lamb, "I am only six months old, so it could not have been me."

"It must have been your brother, then," growled the wolf.

"But I never had any brothers!"

"Well," responded the wolf, "I know it was a sheep of some kind, so make no more excuses." He seized the poor lamb and carried him off to the woods to eat.

Before he died, the lamb gasped out, "Any excuse will serve a tyrant!"[54]

The Lion's Share

This story about the abuse of power and resulting tyranny has been attributed to Aesop.

A lion, a wolf, a jackal, and a fox agreed to share whatever each caught in hunting. A fat stag fell into a snare set by the fox, who called the rest of the group together.

The lion divided the stag into four parts and took the best piece for himself. "This is mine, of course, because I am the king of beasts."

Taking another portion, he added, "This too is mine because I am making the division." He put aside the third piece. "That is for me as the strongest, and as for the remaining part, I'd like to see any of you so much as lay a paw on it."[55]

The Elephant and the Assembly of Animals

This story can be found in various sources, including a poem by John Godfrey Saxe.

The wise elephant always tried to help his society and saw among the beasts many abuses that called loudly for reform. Therefore, one day he gathered them together and with respect and humility made a speech. He spoke about vices such as laziness, selfishness, cruelty, dissension, and envy.

Many of the animals listened with approval and humbly thought about how they could improve their own habits. Among these were the innocent dove, the faithful dog, the obedient camel, and the industrious ant.

Another part of the audience was terribly offended. This included the cruel tiger and the savage wolf; the serpent, which hissed with all his might; the hornet; and the fly. The lazy grasshopper left, and the sloth was indignant.

The elephant ended his speech saying, "My advice is given equally to all, but remember that those who feel angry about any remarks of mine may be feeling the sting of their own guilt."[56]

Play Fair by the Moon

The importance of fair play is illustrated
by this tale from the Cherokee people native to North America.

Two towns once played a ball game against each other. One of them had the best runners and had almost won the game when the leader of the other team picked up the ball with his hand. This was not allowed in the game, but he did it anyway and tried to throw it to the goal. Then it struck against the solid sky and fastened itself there to remind players never to cheat. That is where the moon came from.[57]

The Ass and the Driver

This story is from the Yoruba people of Africa.

An idol was to be moved from one temple to another through a town. To move it, the people placed the idol on the back of an ass. While the ass and its burden passed through a small town, the people bowed before the idol.

The ass thought, "My, the people are worshiping me. I must be very important, so why should I move along like a common animal?"

The driver of the ass grew angry because the animal wouldn't move anymore, so he struck him across his hindquarters; the ass then began to kick and pitch, and the idol fell and broke into pieces. The driver took a splinter of the idol and carried it by hand into the temple.

It was at this time that the ass found that the people stopped bowing before him and realized that it is unwise to take the credit that is due to someone else.[58]

The Wily Tortoise

This fable comes from India.

A man was bird-catching in the jungle, and he snared a wild goose. On his way home, he sat by a pond where a tortoise lived. The tortoise started waddling out of the pond.

"Take care, friend!" warned the goose. "This fowler has caught me, and he will catch you!"

The tortoise waddled into the water again. "Many thanks, friend goose," he answered. "One good turn deserves another." He dived into the pond and brought up a ruby. "Here, Mr. Fowler, take this ruby, and release my friend the goose."

The fowler took the ruby, but he was very greedy, so he said, "If you bring me a pair to this, I will let the goose go."

The tortoise dived and brought up another ruby. Then the fowler released the goose. "Now, hand over that ruby!"

"Forgive me," said the tortoise, "I have made a mistake and brought up the wrong jewel. Let me see the first, and if it does not match, I will try again."

The fowler gave back the first ruby. "As I thought," the tortoise commented. He disappeared into the pond.

The fowler waited a long time but never again saw the tortoise, who had ventured to safety at the bottom of the pond and stayed there. The fowler tore his hair and went home, wishing he had not been so greedy.[59]

The Boy Who Lied About His Scar

This story comes from the Wishram people native to North America.

A boy was gathering kindling in the forest when he slipped and was scraped on the head by a stick. The wound healed but left a scar. His father was looking at his head one day and saw the scar.

"How did you get that scar?" the father asked.

The boy was embarrassed to say how it happened, so he said, "A deer once struck me with his horns."

The boy became older and went hunting deer for food. But the deer never appeared to him because he had lied about their having made the scar on him.[60]

The Magic Boat

In this story from the native people of Guyana, South America, a man learns the danger of not following instructions.

A group of men were traveling together, and in the afternoon they came to a landing by the river. A beautiful canoe was there with a paddle beside it. An old man in the group warned them, "Don't get into that boat! It is magic, and if you get into it, even without touching the paddle, you will be carried off and we shall never see you again."

All of the men listened and followed the old man's instructions. They lay down and went to sleep—except one man. This one man could not sleep; the more he thought of the boat, the more he wanted to go have another look at it. He tossed and turned, but finally he couldn't resist the temptation. He quickly slipped out of his hammock and went to the canoe. He admired its graceful lines and began wishing that he had a beautiful canoe like this for himself. He stepped nearer and nearer, admiring it more and more, until he finally jumped inside. As soon as he was inside, the boat slid into the river and went off with him; he was never seen again.[61]

The Lucky Pot

This story comes from the Warraua people of Guyana.

On his way home from the bush, one day a man came across a campsite with a pot simmering on the fire. The pot spoke to him, asking if he was hungry, and when the man said he was, the pot said, "All right, I will cook a bird for you." The pot began to boil, and after a time the man ate what was inside and went home. His wife gave him some fish, but he wasn't hungry.

After a while, the man made an excuse to leave his home and visit the campsite in the bush again. He said to the pot, "I am hungry. You must cook meat now."

So the pot boiled away and served him good meat. Once again he returned home and refused the cassava his wife offered him. After a couple of days, he paid another visit to the lucky pot and gorged himself with meat. When he returned home, he still wanted none of the food his wife brought him.

Now the man's two sons looked at him and at each other and then whispered to each other: "What does this mean? Our father stays at home two whole days and isn't hungry. He goes into the bush and even when he returns he will not eat. Where does he get his food?" So they watched him carefully and the next day followed him at a distance. They heard him talk to the pot and help himself, and then when he returned home he again refused to eat the food his wife offered him.

The man's household was growing short of food, so the man went away to fish. The sons visited the campsite and asked the pot to cook food for them. After eating, they washed the pot carefully, so there wouldn't be even a trace of smell in it.

The man came home and gave his wife the fish he had caught, but he refused to eat any himself. "I do not want it; I am satisfied," was all he said. He then sneaked away to his lucky pot and told it to cook for him, but it would not boil anymore for him or for anyone else because it had been cleaned out so carefully.

The man began to cry, but the pot spoke up and said, "You were greedy. You wouldn't give the bird or the meat to your wife or to your children. You ate it all yourself, and this is what has happened."[62]

After a Flood

Most cultures tell flood stories. This one from the Navajo people of the southwestern United States tells of greed and impatience among the "unruly" ones after the flood.

A great flood came, and the people climbed and climbed until they reached the upper world. Now, one group of people heard that another tribe, the Kisani, were in a camp a little distance away. They also heard that the Kisani had brought with them from the lower world an ear of corn for seed.

Some of the unruly ones said, "Let us go to the camp of the Kisani and take the corn away from them!"

But there were others who were wiser and more kind, and they insisted this would be wrong. "The Kisani have had as much trouble as the rest of us. If they had more foresight, they have a right to profit by it."

But some of the unruly young men still went and demanded the corn from the Kisani. There was an argument, but the Kisani finally offered to break the ear in two and let them choose whichever half they wanted. The young men agreed to this bargain, and the woman who owned the ear broke it in the middle, laying the pieces down for the others to choose.

The young men couldn't decide which piece they should take, and Coyote, who was among the unruly ones, became impatient with them. He grabbed the tip end of the ear and ran off with it. The Kisani kept the butt and always after that had better corn than their neighbors.[63]

5

Beauty & Virtue

The Thief and the Honored Gentleman of Cathay

In this story from China, the kindness of a man shown to a thief brings happiness to them both.

In the region of Cathay, there lived a gentleman whose worth was plain to his neighbors, for he was always just and kind. It was the birthday of this honored man. The friends and neighbors sent many gifts and congratulations to show their respect, and the honored gentleman's sons and servants were kept busy receiving the messengers bearing gifts.

A thief lived in the district, and he knew there would be articles of value among the presents. He sneaked into the room and hid himself by lying facedown on a large roof beam that crossed the great hall where a banquet was to be served that evening. From this spot he could see the opening of the gifts, the parcels of silk, jade, and jewels. He made sure he remembered where the most valuable items were deposited. This way he could carry them away after the guests had departed and the family had gone to sleep.

Late at night, when the guests had all taken their leave, the honored gentleman lingered to look upon the gifts and consider the kindness of his friends. The thief considered this a good opportunity to study once more the layout of the room, before the lights were extinguished, so he might move through it without stumbling and alerting anyone. What he did not realize was that the lights shone behind him and cast his shadow on the floor.

The honored gentleman showed no sign of having seen the moving shadow. But he soon called a servant and told him to bring the best of foods and to lay the table for a single guest. When this was done, the honored gentleman sent the servant to bed and remained in the great hall by himself. Turning toward the beam on which the thief lay, and bowing as though to an important guest, he said: "Will the gentleman who is on the roof beam now come down and join me for supper?"

Not knowing what else he could do, the thief descended. He was led to the table by his host, who served him while he ate and treated him with great respect. When the thief had finished eating, the honored gentleman handed him a bag of silver coins. "Please make good use of these, with honor," he told the thief. Then he led him to the door and gave a courteous farewell.

Tens of years passed and brought the eightieth birthday of the honored gentleman. The years had only increased the love and respect of his neighbors and his many descendants. Once more his friends and family determined to show their respect and sent many costly gifts. They were all invited to dine with the gentleman that evening. His grandson received the presents at his door and brought them to show his grandfather.

Toward evening, his grandson came to him with a priceless gem. It had been brought by a stranger who would not tell his name, and who insisted upon seeing the master of the house.

The stranger was brought to the old man's room, where he expressed great joy in seeing the honored gentleman alive and in good health. His host did not recognize his guest. "I beg your pardon, sir," he said, "my sight is failing and perhaps my memory also. Could you tell me your name?"

The guest replied that he was a sincere friend, an honest man, and rich enough to bring many such gifts. The host answered that he could not accept gifts without knowing the donor. Also, he wished to invite the stranger to the banquet that evening but could not do so without knowing his name.

"Why don't you invite me in this way," the stranger told him. "'Will the gentleman who was on the roof beam now come down and join me for supper?'" The thief went on to tell the honored gentleman that under the influence of his host's kindness he had repented of evil. With the coins he had been given, he had gone into foreign trade and had greatly prospered. Always he had sought to practice truth and mercy.

The stranger stayed to banquet with the other guests. Among them all, none were happier than he and his kindly host.[1]

The Wren and the Camel

This story comes from Moorish literature.

A pair of wrens once built their nest in a hedge beside a highway. Once, while the father wren was in the fields, a camel happened to pass that way. The little wrens saw him, and when their father returned they said, "Oh, Papa, a monstrous big animal came by here!"

The wren stretched out one leg. "As big as that, my children?"

"Oh, Papa, much bigger than that!"

The wren stretched out a leg and a wing. "As big as that?"

"Oh, Papa, much bigger."

Finally the wren spread both wings and legs. "As big as that then?"

"Oh, yes, much bigger!"

"That is impossible, my children, for there is no animal bigger than I!"

"Just wait and see for yourself," said the little wrens.

Presently the camel came back, browsing along the hedge. The wren was perched beside his nest; and the camel bit off a bunch of leaves, taking the father wren with them. The wren managed to fly out safely from between the camel's big teeth and hurried back to his children.

"You are quite right," he said. "The camel is a monstrous big animal. But I am not ashamed of myself, just the same."[2]

The Bird That Brought the Yellow Flower

This tale of friendship and gratitude comes from China.

One day a man saw a bird, wounded by an arrow, fall to the ground. Filled with sympathy, the man carried the bird home. He drew out the arrow and nursed the creature back to health. When it was well, the man carried the bird into the open air, opened his hands, and let it fly to freedom.

Many months later, the man fell ill until it was feared he would be unable to live. Growing weaker daily, he lay in his bed by the window, watching the blue sky and wondering how much longer he would look upon the clouds drifting across the heavens. A faint scratching came, and the man roused himself enough to open the glass. The bird flew inside the house and laid a yellow flower beside the man. Then it explained that if the man would make a tea from the flower petals, his life would be saved.

The wife of the man quickly brewed the tea, and his health soon returned. The man and the bird remained friends for the rest of their lives.[3]

The Eagle and the Man

A fable attributed to Aesop, this story is similar to one in China where a man rescues an eagle who finds ways to repay him.

A man caught an eagle in a snare. He cut the bird's wing feathers and kept him chained to a stump in his yard. While he was there, a kindhearted fowler saw the sad-looking bird and took pity on it. He bought the eagle and treated him well until his wings were grown again, then let him go free.

The first thing the bird caught was a fine fat hare, which he gratefully laid at the feet of the generous fowler.

A fox saw this and said the eagle would have done better to make friends with the first man. After all, he was the one who had caught him and might do so again.

"Your advice may be all right for a fox," replied the eagle, "but I prefer showing my gratitude instead of living through fear of what the other man might do."[4]

A Poor Man's Gratitude

This story, origin unknown, has similarities to a Tolstoy tale and stories from the Middle East.

A very poor man, rich only in the vast number of years he had lived, busied himself in planting and grafting an apple tree. A stranger happened by and interrupted him, demanding: "Why do you plant trees? You cannot hope to eat the fruit of them."

The old man raised himself up, leaned on his shovel, and answered, "Someone planted trees for me before I was born, and I have eaten the fruit; I now plant for others, so that the memorial of my gratitude may continue when I am dead and gone."[5]

Lekambai and the Sky King

From Fiji and Samoa, this story of delayed gratitude also relates to obedience or faith.

In the old days Lekambai went out in his canoe, and once while he was fishing, a terrible storm arose that drove him far out to sea and nearly swamped his canoe in the waves. A great wave came and threw the canoe against a rock. Lekambai clung to the rock while his canoe floated away, dashed to pieces. Lekambai climbed and climbed up this rock, but he could find no place to dwell, or food or water, except what there was in the hollows of the rock. So, after climbing many days, he became weak and ready to die. The earth was hidden from his sight because he had climbed so high. He could see nothing but the sun by day and the moon and stars by night; even the clouds lay far beneath his feet. He went on climbing, higher and ever higher, until in the middle of the night his strength failed, and he fainted.

When he awoke, the man looked around and saw he was in a pleasant land, full of trees and sweet-smelling flowers upon which the sun was shining brightly. But there were no coconut trees, and he could see no other people. He became very sad when he thought of his home and his friends, and how he might never see them again.

Now, this land to which he had climbed was the sky; and the Sky King heard his sorrow. He called to Lekambai, "You wretched man there! Why are you weeping?"

"I am weeping, sir," Lekambai answered, "because I am a stranger in a strange land. My country is Samoa, and I know I shall see it no more forever."

The Sky King pitied him and said, "Weep not, for you shall see your land again, and your wife and your children and your friends. See this turtle? It will carry you safely to Samoa. When it begins to move, hide your face in your hands and don't look up until the turtle crawls ashore. If you do not follow my words, a terrible evil will happen. When you reach your land, please remember to give the turtle a coconut and a coconut-leaf mat, so we may plant the nut and learn how to make mats out of its leaves. As you can see, we have none in this country."

So Lekambai thanked the Sky King and promised faithfully to remember all his words. Then he hid his face in his hands, climbed upon the turtle's back, and felt it leap with him down into the sea. They sank down deep in the midst of the waters until Lekambai was nearly choked, but he remembered the words of the Sky King and kept his hands tight over his eyes. Then the turtle rose to the surface and swam swiftly over the waves with Lekambai on its back. Many voices sounded in the man's ears, trying to persuade him to uncover his eyes, but he refused. The sharks called after him and said: "We are coming! We, the sharks, are coming to eat you!" But still Lekambai covered his eyes.

The wind howled past him, screaming into his ears: "I am strong! I will blow you off into the sea." The waves roared at him: "We will swallow you up!" The dolphin leaped up: "See! Here comes a canoe from your own land, from Samoa. It is your friends looking for you." But Lekambai covered his eyes tightly with his hands, for he remembered the words of the Sky King.

All night they went on, and when morning came, a great bird flew past and called to him, "Lekambai! Lekambai! Look up; Samoa is in sight." But he would not. Soon his feet struck against the ground, and the turtle crawled upon the beach. Then Lekambai found he had landed close to his own town. He leaped to the ground and ran to his people, who welcomed him back, weeping for joy because he had returned when they had thought him dead.

In his joy Lekambai forgot about the turtle, thinking of nothing but his wife and his children and his friends who were kissing him, weeping over his return, and asking many questions. Several hours passed before he remembered the turtle. Then he recalled the mat and the coconut that he had promised to provide the Sky King. He ran to the beach and found the turtle gone. It had grown tired of waiting and had become hungry, so it had swum out to the reef to look for some seaweed to eat. There, some of the townsfolk speared and killed it.

Then Lekambai was sorry, and great was his grief. "What is this? You have killed my friend—he who brought me over the sea. What shall I do? Why did I delay? How can I send my gifts to the Sky King? A miserable man am I!" And they all wept.

Together, they dug for five days and made a grave. At the bottom, on the sixth day, they laid the turtle, and buried with it a mat and a coconut.[6]

The Eagle's Gratitude

This story has been attributed to Aesop.

A man was out walking one day when he discovered an eagle caught in a snare. Impressed by its beauty, and being a kindhearted fellow, he released the bird.

The day was hot, and the man soon found a cool spot in the shadow of an old wall and sat down upon a stone. A few moments later, the eagle made a swoop upon his head and carried off his hat. The bird flew quite some distance before letting it fall.

The man ran after his hat and wondered why a bird to whom he'd shown so much kindness should play such a mean trick in return. He turned around to go back to his seat by the wall. Great was his surprise and gratitude when he returned and found the wall had crashed into a heap upon the stone where he had been sitting.[7]

The Shepherd Judge

Stories of good and impartial judges appear in many cultures.
This one comes from the country of Georgia.

The king had four viziers who helped him judge the people. There was also in the land a shepherd whose wisdom and fairness became known throughout the countryside. One day, the shepherd even corrected the judgment of one of the viziers. After this the king decided to make him the chief judge for all the people.

But the shepherd refused to take this high position unless the king put out both of his eyes. He said he did not want to see those he must judge. The king wasn't happy about blinding the shepherd, but he insisted, so it was done.

Then the king and the people built the shepherd a fine house and gave him all the help he needed. He began to do justice in such an honest way that people came to him from everywhere: important people and poor, old and young, friend and enemy. Everyone who came praised his decisions.

Once there came a man and a woman. The man said to the judge, "I came to this woman's house on a mule, and its calf came with us. This woman ran out, seized the calf, and asked how it came to be with my mule. She tried to drag away the calf, but I wouldn't allow it. I won't give up my property to her. In God's name, judge between us!"

This is what he said to the judge, but he secretly sent the shepherd a large bribe and a message saying, "Take the money, and don't embarrass me in front of this woman."

But the judge wouldn't receive the bribe and asked the woman what had happened.

"Sir," she replied, "this man rode up to my house on a mule; I have nothing in the world but one calf and its mother, both of which I love. My calf went up to this man's mule and seemed to nurse as though it were its mother. The man must have thought this was a way to take my calf from me. He dragged it home, but it wasn't his, so I have come to you for justice."

When the judge had heard both sides, he announced his decision. "Because a mule has never borne any baby, it certainly cannot have borne a calf. Take the calf from the man and give it to the woman who owns the cow."

Everyone who heard the judge's decision was pleased.

It is said that God was merciful to this good shepherd and the woman's handkerchief made his eyes whole again. After this he saw with both eyes, but until the day of his death he judged as though he were blind and could not see the wealth of one or the importance of someone else.[8]

The Man Who Was Afraid to Die

This is adapted from a narrative in a book by Annie Slossen, who recorded it from a "mountain" child in the United States named Elizabeth York, known locally as Story-Tell Lib. The child was lame and in failing health. This was the last tale Elizabeth told before her death.

There was once a man named Reuben who was very ill, and it was whispered that he was going to die. This scared the man deeply.

A friend tried to comfort him and spoke of how the caterpillar makes its cocoon and goes to sleep, then comes out as a beautiful butterfly. "I wouldn't want to miss doing something like that, would you?" asked the friend.

But somehow nothing anybody said made any difference. There were many things around Reuben that talked and tried to help—trees, and flowers and grass, and crawling things that were always dying and living, and living and dying. The man thought it didn't help him any, but it might have, just a little, because he couldn't help thinking about it once in a while. But he was scared just the same.

One summer he grew even weaker and felt more ill than he had before. Reuben was scared always now.

Then, one afternoon Reuben awakened from a nap and realized he felt better. Gladly he arose from his bed to take a walk. Then he began to think about what the flowers and trees and creatures had said about dying and how they laughed at him for being scared about it. He said to himself, "Somehow, I don't feel quite so frightened today, but maybe that's just my imagination."

As he was walking, Reuben met a man who was so handsome, he was suddenly convinced the stranger was an angel. He had never seen one before, but he was sure just the same. And the angel said, "Aren't you happy?"

"I would be," Reuben replied, "except that I'm so terribly afraid of dying. It must be terrible to be dead."

Then the angel laughed, a bright, beautiful, joyful sound. "Didn't you know? You are dead."[9]

Why the Hare Has a Split Lip

There are several variations of this story, adapted from the Bushmen of Africa. A very similar story is told among the Native American Chitimacha people of present-day Louisiana, but it has a different conclusion.

One day the moon and the hare had an argument. The moon said people would be like the moon, who died and then lived again. The hare said no, people would die and always be dead. The moon said the hare wasn't telling the truth and people would live again after they died. The hare still insisted death would be forever.

Finally, the moon became angry because the hare wasn't speaking the truth. The moon struck the hare on the face, and the lip of the hare became split. Ever since then, people see the hare's split lip and remember the moon said death would not be forever.[10]

Not Lost, but Gone Before

The cultural source for this story is unknown.

Once upon a time, there lived a grub in the bottom of a nice muddy pond. Every day the grub watched the frog swim to the top of the water and disappear.

Now, the frog was a very important person in the pond, and the grub was a little afraid of him. Still, he was very curious about where the frog kept going. So, one day, the grub scraped up his courage. He went to the frog and bowed politely. "Mr. Frog, please, Mr. Frog," he began, "there is something I must ask you."

The frog turned his great goggle eyes to the grub.

"Indeed!" he stated. "Proceed!"

"Mr. Frog, what is there beyond the world?" stammered the grub, so afraid he could hardly speak.

"What world do you mean?" inquired the frog.

"This world, of course—our world," answered the grub.

"This *pond*, you mean." The frog laughed at him. "This isn't a world, this is just a place."

"Well, what is outside of this place?"

"It's dry land," said the frog in his most pompous manner.

"But what's dry land?"

The frog was puzzled. How could he explain dry land to a creature who had always lived in the water? "Why, you silly grub," said the frog, "dry land is like the mud on the bottom of the pond, only there isn't any water. It is a beautiful place out in the air."

"No water?" The grub simply couldn't understand a world where there wasn't water.

The grub was so confused that the frog felt sorry for him. "You are a silly fellow," said the frog, "but I admire your spirit, so I'll make you an offer. If you sit on my back, I will carry you up to dry land and let you see for yourself. Hold tight!"

The frog swam to the top of the pond, climbed up on the bank, and turned to the grub. "Here we are," he said. "What do you think of it?"

But the grub was nowhere to be seen.

What happened to the grub? The moment he reached the surface of the water, a terrible feeling had come over him and he jumped off the frog's back, panting and struggling for life.

"Horrible, just horrible!" he said when he got back to the bottom of the pond. "Mr. Frog was lying to me. Outside of this world is nothing but death."

He went and told all his friends about how he had gone on an adventure and barely escaped with his life.

In the evening, the frog came back and started a quarrel with the grub, because the grub hadn't held on tight. The grub was angry also and forgot to be polite when he accused the frog of lying about the world outside the pond and trying to kill him.

They might have had a serious fight because of it, but the frog suggested the grub tell his side of the story. Then the frog insisted on telling about what had happened to him.

"I waited for you," said the frog, "and though I didn't see you, I saw something that will interest you more than any creature that lives. I saw a grub just like you climb out of the water on a reed. I was surprised, because I know how you grubs like the shady bottom of the pond. So I stayed and watched and saw a wonderful thing happen. The body of the grub seemed to split open, and after much squirming and struggling, something came out of it—a glorious dragonfly. Oh, little grub, you cannot imagine what a beautiful creature the dragonfly is! It has wonderful silvery wings, and its body gives out rays of glittering blue and green. I watched it fly in great circles and then I plunged below to tell you the splendid news."

Now, the grub thought this was a very pretty story, but he doubted it could really happen to him. Weeks passed, and the grub often thought of it. Then, one day he felt sick and weak and had an overwhelming desire to climb upward. The other grubs gathered around him and made him promise that if the wonderful change should happen to him, he would return and tell them so. He promised and slowly climbed up the reed. His friends and relatives watched, but they couldn't see past the surface of the water.

And then the wonderful change did take place. The grub burst his shell and became a beautiful dragonfly.

He tried to keep his promise. But when he flew into the water he had the same feeling as before when he had tried to come into the air. But although he could not go back to them, he often flew close to the surface of the pond because he wished so much he could tell his friends of the great joy that was waiting for them.[11]

Good Deeds Are Counted Riches in the Spirit World

The people of China tell this tale of what constitutes wealth after death.

Just before a man died, he whispered, "I have been to the spirit world, and I met a good friend. After we greeted each other, I asked why he had not brought his riches with him. He scolded me, saying riches could be brought to the spirit world, but people are not willing to bring the right kind—virtue and merit; those are the things of wealth after death."[12]

Preparing the Way

This story can be found in the notes of Jacques De Vitry of France.

A stranger visiting a distant country was surprised to be crowned king upon his arrival. Suddenly, he had every comfort he had ever desired, and in gratitude he tried to reign with justice. Then he learned the fate of the previous kings of that country: It was the national custom that the king reign for a year, after which he was sent to an island exile.

This man was wiser than some of his predecessors. During his yearlong reign, he sent servants to build a palace upon the island and to prepare it for his coming. The island was supplied with food, clothing, and all the comforts he could enjoy. As time passed, instead of fear or dread, the island became a place he anticipated with joy.[13]

Seasons with an Attitude

As in "The Golden Purse and the Seeing Eyes," (Part 6) this story illustrates the truth that appreciation is in itself a blessing, for the eldest sister notices, values, and enjoys the world in a way the younger cannot. In a symbolic fashion, the gifts of the four seasons grant no more than she already has. There are similar stories from all over Europe.

Two sisters once lived together in a cottage deep in the forest. The oldest sister thought nothing but good thoughts and sang while doing her daily work. The other sister hardly seemed related to her, for she was lazy and mean-tempered. She often sneered at her sister and made fun of the poor young man who wanted to marry her.

One day in the early spring, the older sister went into the forest to gather sticks for firewood. She met two women and two men. Now, she didn't know these people were actually the four seasons of the year. Winter was a tall blustery fellow dressed in black and gray. Spring was a beautiful young lady dressed in green, blue, and pink. A handsome hearty man was Summer. Fall was an older woman, in russet, orange, and brown.

"Good morning," Summer greeted the older sister.

"Hello," she said. "Isn't it a beautiful day?"

"Yes," answered the beautiful young lady dressed in green, blue, and pink. "Isn't this the most beautiful time of year?"

"I often think so," commented the sister.

"Such a relief, when spring ends the terrible winter," said the tall blustery fellow.

"Perhaps," answered the girl, "but winter is very nice as well. The plants need the sleep they receive in winter, and the rain makes a lovely sound on the roof. Besides, it's so cozy to curl up by the fire."

"Then you must dislike summer with its heat and hard work," stated the hearty man.

"Not at all," she replied. "Everything grows so quickly. There are fruits and vegetables, and the animals have time to raise their young. What would we do without summer?"

"Surely then," the older woman said, "fall must be disappointing."

"How could it possibly disappoint me?" cried the girl. "The last of the harvest comes in, and the leaves turn glorious colors. Such a sweet smell of change is in the air."

The older sister said good-bye and continued her search for firewood.

When she was gone, the seasons discussed how polite and generous she had been when speaking about each of them. They decided to reward her. Winter gave the gift that when she walked in the snow, strawberries would spring up and ripen. Spring declared that whenever she spoke, the rarest of flowers would fall from her lips. Summer said her garden should produce larger fruits and tastier vegetables than anyone else in the district. Fall said she might share her gifts with whomever she pleased.

When the older sister returned home, she was startled to find flowers dripping from her lips. Their fragrance was so sweet, she gathered them into bouquets and sold them in the village.

The younger sister ground her teeth with jealousy at her sister's good fortune. She determined to seek her own fortune in the woods. But when she met the four seasons, she had nothing except bad words to speak about them. She hated the cold sharp winter, sneezed at the flowers of spring, and disliked the heat and work of summer. Most of all she despised fall, because it was a season that couldn't make up its mind.

The gifts the seasons gave to this sister were of another sort. Winter declared her feet and hands would always be cold. Spring said she should sneeze all the more. Summer decided her garden would be poor. Fall promised she would be unable to share her gifts with anyone else. From that day, the younger sister lived alone, a sourpuss to the end.

Meanwhile, the fortunes of the older sister improved. In summer, she sold her extra pickings from the garden. Everyone wanted her strawberries during the winter. Soon, the sister and her poor young man married. Though they never became rich, they had enough, with some left over to share, and they were always happy.[14]

Robin as Fire Quencher

This brief and unusual tale is from the part of Wales known as Caermarthenshire.

Far, far away, there is a land of woe, darkness, and fire. Children suffer terribly in this land. The robin loves children, so every day he bears in his bill a drop of water to quench the flame. He flies so near to the burning stream that his feathers are scorched. This is why some people call him Bronrhuddyn, which means "breast burned" or "breast scorched." Because he spends so much time in this land of fire, when the robin returns, he feels the winter far more than his brother and sister birds. It is to serve children that the robin dares approach the flames.[15]

The Flower That Lives Above the Clouds

The cultural source for this story is unknown.

Long ago the plants of the world were given the choice of where they would live.

"I will cover the ground and make the bare soil bright with green blades," cried the grass.

"I will live in the sunny fields and by roadsides," laughed the daisy.

One by one the plants and flowers chose where they would be happiest and most comfortable. The roses and pansies wanted to be cared for in gardens. The violets and forget-me-nots chose the cool shady places. The cactus loved the warm dry sun, so it chose to go to the sandy desert. The water lily decided it would be happiest in ponds and lakes.

Finally all the places in the world had been chosen, except for the high ridges of the mountains. To this place, no one wanted to go. They complained of its cold and height and the fact that little food could be found there.

"Let the gray moss go," they all decided. The gray moss didn't want to go, but all the flowers insisted. They believed the mountains would just have to do without pretty flowers and make do with moss.

So the gray moss went up to the high mountains because it was told to go. It climbed over the bare rocks beyond the places where forest stopped growing. All was cold and barren.

When it reached the top, the gray moss stopped in amazement. What did it see but a quiet star-shaped flower clinging to the crags and blooming! It was white like the snow around it, and its heart was of soft yellow. Because of the cold, the flower had encased its leaves in soft wool to keep warm and alive.

"Oh!" cried the gray moss, stopping short. "How can you be here, where it's so awful? It is high above the forests, high above the clouds! I came because I was sent. Who are you?"

Then the little starry flower nodded in the cold wind. "I am the edelweiss," it said. "I came because there are no other flowers here. The mountains need flowers also."

"And they didn't tell you to come?"

"No," said the edelweiss. "I came because I was needed."[16]

Robin as Fire Bringer

Many cultures tell stories of how humanity received fire. This one comes from the Island of Guernsey in Great Britain. A similar story is told by the Swampy Cree people of northern Manitoba.

It is said that the robin was the first who brought fire to the Island of Guernsey. He grasped the fire in his beak and set out across the water. But the fire burned hot upon him. His breast was singed and has remained red ever since. The people were grateful, for what would they have done without fire?[17]

The Inchworm and the Mountain

This legend of Yosemite's El Capitan is told by the Miwok people native to North America.

One day some boys went fishing in a beautiful lake in the Yosemite valley, and after they had grown tired they lay down in the sun upon a rock beside the lake. They soon fell asleep. Upon awakening, the boys found that during their sleep the rock upon which they lay had been stood on end. They were now nearly a mile high in the air. They had no way to climb down and didn't know what to do.

The animals in the valley saw their misfortune and held a conference on how to help the boys. They decided the only thing to do was to climb up the face of the cliff. But the rock was too steep, so they tried to jump. First, the raccoon leaped upward, then the bear, the squirrel, the fox, and finally the mountain goat. But none of them were able to reach the boys. They had nearly given up in despair when the inchworm came along. "I will try," she said.

The animals laughed. "What could you do with your snail's pace? We are stronger and faster and can do nothing."

But she would not be laughed out of her purpose, and she began climbing up the cliff. Slowly, inch by inch, she crawled, so slowly it seemed she would take a thousand years to get there. But as she passed crag after crag, the animals below stopped making fun of her and began to shout encouragement. At last she reached the top. Then the Great Spirit turned her into a huge butterfly so strong that she flew down, with the boys on her back, to safety.[18]

A Child Saves the Land Beneath the Sea

This is a famous tale from Holland.

This story takes place once upon a time in a marvelous land where the people lived beneath the sea. This is not to say that they were mermaids and mermen. No indeed, they were humans like everyone else. They lived beneath the sea, but not in it.

There are many areas of the world beneath the sea. Most of them are surrounded by higher land, even mountains, so the ocean never has the chance to rush in and swallow up the countryside. In this marvelous country, however, the sea was next door, and the only thing that stopped the water from covering the towns and people were long, thick walls of earth called dikes.

In this land was a boy whose name was Peter. Like every other boy of his country, Peter knew that he lived beneath the sea and that the wonderful dikes kept back the ocean. One day, Peter's mother called him. "I want you to take some cakes to the blind man."

Peter was always happy to visit the blind man, who told such wonderful stories. They visited for an hour, then Peter said good-bye and started home. Walking along the top of a dike, Peter stopped to watch the ocean. It had rained a great deal in recent days, and the waves looked dark and angry. Yet Peter knew he was safe, for hadn't the great dikes always protected him and his people?

As he watched, and as the sun began to sink, Peter heard an odd gurgling sound. He was always curious about strange things, so he set off to look for the source of the noise.

A tiny stream of water was leaking through the dike!

It was only a little water coming through a hole no bigger than Peter's finger. Yet Peter knew about water and dirt. Water always softened the soil and then moved it away. That tiny stream of water would soon turn into a giant spout, and very soon after that the entire dike would collapse! The water would rush in and swallow up the land, the animals, and the people!

He looked about for help, but there was no one. The water must be stopped!

Peter quickly stuck his finger into the hole, and the water stopped. "Soon," he thought, "someone will come and help me. They will fix the hole, and everyone will be safe again."

An hour passed. Two. Three. The sun set and the stars came out, and it grew cold. Peter did not know that his mother thought he had decided to stay with the blind man for the night.

It was so hard to stand still and make his finger keep back the ocean. Peter's knees trembled, and he shivered and wondered if he could possibly last the entire night. Every time he thought he surely must rest, at least for a few minutes, he remembered how the water would cover up his family and friends. All through the dark, cold night he stayed at his task.

In the early morning hours, a man was out for a walk.

"Say, lad," he asked. "What on earth are you doing?"

"I'm keeping the water from coming through the dike," said Peter. "Please hurry and get some help."

The man rushed quickly indeed. Many people came to fix the hole. They took Peter home and told his parents what a hero he was. It is said that all parents in Holland still tell their sons and daughters about the hero who stuck his finger in the dike and stayed there faithfully to save their country.[19]

The Brave Bobtails

Courage, friendship, self-sacrifice, and service are the character traits of the bobtailed animals in this Native American story from the southwestern United States.

Sun Arrow was a very good man, kind to his neighbors and to all the animals. He had only one enemy. One day his enemy used a giant magic toad to entrap him. The toad began swallowing Sun Arrow, starting with his feet.

The animals gathered to help their friend.

First the bluebird told Sun Arrow to grasp her tail. She pulled with all her might, caring nothing about the pain, but her tail came off and Sun Arrow was still being swallowed. Then the bear pulled until his tail came off, and still Sun Arrow wasn't released from his trap.

Then the coyote tried. But the coyote was a coward and proud of his tail, so he gave Sun Arrow his ears. When it started to hurt, the coyote stopped pulling. Even so, his ears were tugged forward upon his forehead.

Then the badger gave Sun Arrow his tail. Just as Sun Arrow was beginning to be pulled from the toad, the badger's tail came off, leaving only a stump. Now, the badger cared nothing for the pain; he only wanted to help his friend. He dug into the dirt around Sun Arrow and gave him the stump of his tail, but the short stump slipped out of Sun Arrow's hands. The badger dug around some more, then had the man grasp him around the body behind the forelegs. The badger pulled with all his might—and Sun Arrow was freed! Then all the other animals killed the toad so it could never hurt their friend again.

Sun Arrow wanted to reward the bluebird, bear, and badger, but they refused, saying that they had acted out of gratitude for Sun Arrow's many kindnesses. They even refused to go to the medicine men of their tribe to have their tails mended to grow again, for they were proud that they had suffered to help their friend.

Ever since that day, the cowardly coyote is laughed at, and his ears still flop forward. But the brave bobtails are honored by all animals, and by all true believers.[20]

The Kind Crow King

The Shans, who live along the border of India and China, tell this tale of gratitude and self-sacrifice.

Once a crow was so wise and good, all the other crows chose him to be their king. In a time of hunger, the good crow king went one day to seek some rice from the kitchens of the human king. Now, when the human king's dinner was prepared, the chief servant put it on a tray and walked along the path to the palace. The crow king dived toward the servant's head, hoping some food would spill so he could gather it. The servant set down the tray and managed to catch the bird, saying, "Oh, crow! Now you will die!"

Another crow watched. He had received much kindness from his king. "That servant has caught my lord," he said. "I must try to save him, even if I die for it."

The crow flew down and pecked at the servant. Furiously, the servant let the crow king go and caught the second bird. He ran with him to the king of humans.

The human king was puzzled and asked, "Little crow, why did you peck at the eyes of my servant?"

"Because he had caught my king, who has always been good to me, so I thought I could save him, even if I died doing so."

When the human king heard this, he nodded wisely. "This little crow is so grateful for the kindness of another, he is ready to die for him. Let us learn from him to be always grateful for kindness shown to us."

The kindly human king set the crow free and gave orders that food from his table should be placed each day in a bamboo basket and hung on a tree outside the palace for the birds.[21]

Ocotochtli's Unselfishness

In this story from ancient Mexico, an animal known as an ocotochtli shows self-denial, service, and consideration for the other animals.

Ocotochtli went out to hunt, for animals eat meat, and there was no other way to obtain it. He hid behind a tree and waited for his prey. When the creature came near, Ocotochtli sprang out and killed it instantly by passing its poisonous tongue over the creature's eyes. Ocotochtli climbed a tall tree and with a loud voice cried until he could be heard far away. When the mountain lions, tigers, and ocelots heard this signal, they understood it was an invitation to eat. They hurried to the spot and enjoyed a fine dinner.

All the while, Ocotochtli stayed apart from the animals, watching. He waited until everyone had finished and then contented himself with the leftovers. He did this out of kindness to the other animals, for his tongue was so poisonous it would poison the meat and cause the death of any animal that ate after him. Ocotochtli did this every day, to serve the other animals.[22]

Snake and Hunter

This Suriname, South America, story is similar to "The Story of the Peasant, the Snake, and King Solomon" (Part 6) but has a different ending. See also "Good Deeds Should Be Repaid with Good" (Part 4).

There was a big fire in the wood. All the trees were in flames. To escape the terrible heat, Snake lowered himself into a deep hole. The fire raged for a long time, but at last a heavy rain fell and put it out. When all danger was past, Snake was unable to climb the steep sides of the hole. He cried out and begged for someone to help him, but nobody would come close because of his deadly bite.

A hunter came along. He took pity on Snake and pulled him out of the hole. But as soon as Snake was free, he turned and tried to bite the hunter.

"I did you a kindness," the hunter exclaimed. "You must not bite me."

"Why shouldn't I bite you?" asked Snake.

"Because you should never harm anyone who has shown you an act of kindness."

"Everybody does," hissed Snake.

The hunter answered, "Let us find someone to judge between us."

They soon met a horse, then an ass, then a cow. To each of these the hunter and Snake told their story and asked, "Ought anyone to return evil for good?"

The horse neighed, saying he was often whipped for his good services to humans. The ass hee-hawed, saying he was beaten with a stick for his good services to humans. The cow bellowed that she expected to be butchered for her good services. *"Boen no habi tangi,"* they all said. "Good has no thanks."

With such poor witnesses to the importance of doing good, Snake announced that he had won the case. But the hunter said, "I don't agree yet. Let us put the case before Anansi, who is very wise!" Snake agreed, so they traveled to see Anansi.

They came to the city where Anansi lived and found him at home. Snake and the hunter explained what had happened and how the animals, having suffered evil from humans, believed that "good has no thanks."

Anansi looked thoughtful and shook his head before saying, "My friends, I cannot say who is right until I have seen with my own eyes how everything happened. Let us go back to the exact spot."

The three walked back to the hole in the wood where Snake had escaped from the fire.

"Show me how it happened," Anansi said.

Snake slid into the hole and began calling for assistance. The hunter pretended to be passing, and turning to the hole, he was about to help Snake out again. Anansi stopped him. "Wait," he said, "I will settle the dispute now. You must not help Snake this time. Snake must try to get out without any assistance so that he may learn to appreciate a kind act." So Snake stayed in the hole and suffered much from hunger. At last he managed to get out. But experience had taught him much.

One day Snake heard that the hunter had been thrown into prison. He decided to help the man and hurried to the king's palace. Secretly he bit the king and escaped. Then he went to the prison where the hunter was kept. "Don't be afraid," Snake told him. "A while ago you did me a favor, and now by experience I have learned to appreciate it. I come to help you."

Snake told the hunter what he had done and gave him three different kinds of leaves to cure the king. Following Snake's advice, the hunter cured the king and later married the king's daughter.[23]

The Theft of Fire

Coyote is usually a trickster in Native American stories, yet in a few tales from the Karoks of California he seeks to serve humankind. In this story he uses trickery to help people obtain fire.

There was no fire on earth, so the Karok people were cold and miserable. The only fire lay far away to the east, hidden in a treasure box that belonged to a couple of hags. Coyote decided to steal fire for the people. He called a great council of the animals and lined them up from the land of the Karoks to the distant region where the fire was kept.

Then Coyote took a Karok man with him and hid the man under the hill. Coyote went to the tepee of the hags. He said "good evening" and asked if he could sit by the fire. They let him sit beside the fire because he was only a coyote. Pretending to be asleep, he spent all night watching and thinking, but he had no chance to get a piece of the fire.

The next morning Coyote had a counsel with the man and told him that when he, Coyote, was inside the tepee, the man should attack. Then Coyote went back and stood close by the casket of fire. The man made a dash at the tepee, and the hags rushed out after him. Coyote seized a firebrand in his teeth and flew over the ground. The hags saw the sparks flying and chased after him, but Coyote reached Lion, who ran with it to Grizzly Bear. Grizzly Bear ran with it to Cinnamon Bear; he ran with it to Wolf, and at last the fire came to Ground Squirrel.

Squirrel ran so fast that his tail caught fire. He curled it up over his back and burned the black spot you still see on his shoulders. Squirrel came to Frog, but because Frog couldn't run, he opened his mouth and swallowed the fire. He jumped, but the hags caught his tail. Frog jumped again, and the hags kept his tail, which is why frogs have no tail to this day. Frog swam underwater and came up to a pile of driftwood. He spit the fire into the dry wood, and that is why there is fire in dry wood even today.[24]

The Triumph at Tara

This story of heroic actions, large and small, comes from Ireland.

A long, long time ago, when Conn was king in Ireland, all the lesser kings with their nobles and warriors were assembled together in his castle hall at Tara. They were holding a great feast, but there was no laughter or cheer. A deep gloom rested over all of them.

After the meal, the king arose and spoke to those gathered. "Kings and men of Ireland," he said, "there is no rest or peace for us tonight. On this evening, for many years, the enchanter Aillen has come from the mountains to destroy the castle of Tara, burning it to the ground. Tonight he will surely come again. Is there any among you who will take it upon himself to keep guard over Tara and kill this enchanter? If there is, I will give him lands and wealth."

The kings and nobles looked at each other in silence. None dared to offer his services. They remembered how, in past years, the enchanter had played a sweet, low music, putting them all asleep. They remained silent, angry and ashamed.

Suddenly a young voice called out, "I will guard Tara this night." It was the boy Fionn. "I will pledge my life that no hurt shall happen to it."

The kings and nobles thought it very funny that a boy should try to do what they feared to attempt. But Conn saw a special courage in the boy and agreed.

Out into the starlight and the snow went Fionn. He waited. In the darkness, an old man came to Fionn's side and handed him a spear and shield. He explained that Fionn's father had been very kind to him, and so he had brought these weapons to help Fionn in his encounter with the enchanter. They had been made by the great craftsman Culain.

"Thank you," said Fionn. "It was kind of you."

As the old man turned to go, he paused, then came back to look into the boy's face. "Neither in song nor story," he said, "will my name go down to my children's children as the doer of noble deeds or as one who has conquered evil. My days have been spent in performing the little things."

"One who faithfully does a day's work of little things," said the boy, "is often nobler than one who has performed great deeds."

"You speak wisely." With slow footsteps he went his way.

At midnight, the magic music reached the ears of Fionn, but he raised the spear, and the enchantment fell away from him. The enchanter came near, but Fionn raised his shield; it caught the magician's fire and scattered it in harmless sparks on every side. Then the enchanter Aillen knew that great magic was defending Tara, so he was afraid and ran away. Fionn pursued him and hurled the spear at the enchanter. Aillen fell and died.

Thus Fionn conquered the magician with the shield and spear that had been given him by the old man who spent his days doing the little things.[25]

The Robin and Mary

In Basque culture, from which this tale derives, the robin is known as "Chindorra."

Once upon a time a bit of straw blew into Mary's eye. A robin, sitting on a bush nearby, saw her tears. At once he flew off to tell the swallow; then, carrying some clear water from a neighboring stream, he returned with his friend and perched on Mary's face. While the redbreast tenderly let the liquid fall into her eye, the swallow gently passed his long tail feather under the lid, and so removed the straw.[26]

The Burning of the Rice Fields

This story comes from Japan.

Once there was a good man who lived on a flat mountaintop with his grandson, Yone. Rice fields grew all around their house, and at the foot of the mountain, next to the blue sea, there was the village.

One day, when the fields were dry and nearly ready for harvest, the grandfather stood alone in front of his house, looking far down upon the people and out at the sea. Suddenly he saw something very strange in the distance where the sea and sky met. Something like a great cloud was rising there, as if the sea had lifted itself into the sky. The old man looked again, as hard as his old sight could allow. Then he turned and ran into the house. "Quick, quick!" he cried to his grandson, "bring a brand from the hearth!"

Yone could not imagine why his grandfather wanted some fire, but he still ran quickly and brought the firebrand. The old man already had one and was running for the rice fields. Yone followed.

What was this! His grandfather thrust his burning brand into the ripe dry rice. The rice! The food for the people to eat; the crop with which they would trade!

"Oh, Grandfather! Grandfather!" screamed the boy. "What are you doing?"

"Hurry! Set the fire!"

Yone was afraid his grandfather had lost his mind. In an instant the fields were blazing, and thick smoke poured up the mountainside and rose like a cloud, black and fierce.

In the village below, the people saw that their precious rice fields were on fire. Oh, how they ran! Men, women, and children climbed the mountain, racing as fast as they could to save the rice; not one stayed behind in the village.

When they came to the mountaintop and saw the beautiful rice all in flames, beyond help, they cried bitterly, "Who has done this thing? How did it happen?"

"I set the fire," said the old man.

"Why? Why?"

"Look!" he said and pointed to the sea. "Look!"

They all turned and looked. And where the blue sea had lain calm and peaceful, a mighty wall of water, reaching from earth to sky, came rolling in. No one could scream; the sight was far too terrible. The wall of water rolled upon the land, passing far over where the village had been, and broke with a roar upon the mountainside.

But the people were safe.[27]

The Singer for the King

The beauty of the nightingale's song wins honor in this tale from Romania.

The king of the birds wanted to discover which of his subjects had the finest voice. So he asked the birds to select from among themselves those whom they thought to be the best singers.

The birds counseled together and chose the yellow thrush, the blackbird, and the nightingale. The thrush had lovely golden feathers that glowed in the light of the sun. He insisted on going first because he was the most beautiful. The blackbird had a yellow beak and black feathers shining like silk, so he insisted upon walking behind the thrush. The nightingale was a small bird with drab feathers. She followed modestly behind.

When they reached the palace, the king placed the beautiful thrush at the head of the table. The thrush swelled with pride and began his song. The king was pleased and praised the thrush. Then came the blackbird's turn. The king admired his lovely black feathers and ordered a chair to be brought to the table. He sang even more beautifully than the thrush, and the king was delighted.

The nightingale was last. When she entered the room, she bowed meekly before the king, touching the floor with her beak. When the king saw that plain little bird, he wondered why she had come and demanded, "What do you want?" He never thought to offer her a seat as he had done for his other guests.

"Please," said the nightingale, "do not be angry with me. I was selected by the other birds to sing before Your Majesty."

"Very well. Sing. I will see what you can do."

The nightingale cleared her throat and began singing in the way she alone knows how to sing. The king and his court were stunned by the beauty and sweetness of her voice and were filled with admiration, for she had thrown the other birds into the shade.

When the nightingale finished her song, the king called her to the head of the table and gave her the thrush's seat. When the meal was over and all the guests rose from the table, it was the nightingale who walked first, then the blackbird, and finally the thrush, who in spite of his grand feathers had failed to give the best song. From that day onward, the nightingale has always been recognized as the best singer, and all the birds bow their heads before her.[28]

The Spirit of the River and the Woodsman

This tale is attributed to Aesop.

A man was chopping down a tree by the bank of a deep river when his axe slipped from his hand and dropped into the water, sinking to the bottom. Because he was very poor, the loss of his axe was a terrible misfortune, and he wondered what would happen to him.

He was much surprised when the river spirit arose and asked what was the trouble. The man explained, and the spirit dived to the bottom of the water. He brought up a golden axe and offered it to him.

"I'm sorry," said the man. "I wish that were mine, but my axe is the ordinary kind." The spirit dived again and brought up a silver one. Again the man explained it wasn't his. The spirit dived a third time and brought up the axe that the man had lost. The poor man took this with great joy and gratitude. The spirit was so pleased with his honesty that he gave him the other two in the bargain.

When the man returned to town, he told his friends about his adventure, and one of them set off at once for the river and let his axe fall in on purpose. He lamented his loss with a loud voice. The river spirit appeared and asked the cause of his grief. After hearing the second man's story, he dived, then brought up a golden axe and asked if this was his.

Amazed at the sight of the precious metal, the fellow said that of course it belonged to him. The spirit was disgusted by his dishonesty and not only refused to give him the golden axe but refused to bring up his own.[29]

The Three Brothers and Their Pear Tree

This story comes from Serbian sources.

Once upon a time there lived three brothers who were very poor. Their only possession in the world was a pear tree. Each morning, one of them would stay and watch over the ripening pears while the other two hired themselves out for pay.

One night an angel came to see what kind of men these three men were. The angel first approached the eldest brother, whose turn it happened to be guarding the tree. Disguised as a beggar, the angel told the brother he was hungry and asked for a pear.

"I cannot give you any of the fruit belonging to my brothers," the eldest explained, "but here are some from my share of the tree." On the following day, the angel came again and asked the middle brother for the gift of some fruit. Gladly, this man also shared the pears, carefully taking them only from his portion of the branches. The third day the angel came to the youngest brother and begged for food, and the youngest said, "I cannot give you any that are the property of my brothers, but I will gladly give you some from my section of the tree."

Impressed by the generosity of the brothers in the midst of their poverty, the angel determined to give them their wishes. The oldest brother asked for a river of wine. Instantly, this was done, with barrels and servants and wagons to carry the wine to market, and a fine large home as well. The youngest brother saw a flock of doves and asked that they might become his own herd of sheep. Immediately, a large flock of sheep, grazing land, and a house were his, with shepherds to guard the flock, milkmaids to milk the sheep, and servants to clip and carry the wool to market.

Then the angel turned to the middle brother and asked what was his wish. The man replied that all he wanted was a sincere loving wife. Before long, the brother was married and living in a small cottage inside the forest.

A year passed, and the angel came to see how the brothers were faring. Again disguised as a beggar, the angel came to the eldest brother, who had grown immensely wealthy off his flowing river of wine. "May I have a small glass?" inquired the angel. "Be off with you," the brother replied. "If I gave everyone a glass of wine, where would I be?"

Disappointed, the angel continued to the youngest brother's home. "May I have a small slice of cheese made from your sheep's milk?" he inquired. "Go away," growled the man. "I can't give something to everybody."

Last of all, the angel arrived at the middle brother's home in the woods. The man and his faithful young wife welcomed him. Their only regret was the poor food they had to offer. The bread they made came from flour pounded from the bark of certain trees, and there was only water to drink. But when the loaf was taken from the oven it was somehow changed to good wheat bread, and when the water was poured from the pitcher it came out as rich new milk. They were grateful for the miracle, which meant they had something fine to offer their guest.

The angel transformed their small cottage into a grand manor house, with fields and herds and servants to care for them. The modest man and the loving woman lived happily ever after, sharing with all those who needed their help.

As for the two brothers upon whom wealth had such a poor effect? The angel sent them back to their pear tree.[30]

Rabbi Simon and the Jewels

This story comes from the Jewish Talmud.

Once upon a time there was a rabbi named Simon. He bought a camel from an Ishmaelite. His disciples took it home and removed the saddle. Underneath they found a fortune in diamonds. "Rabbi! Rabbi!" they exclaimed. "God has blessed you with this new wealth."

"Take the diamonds back to the man from whom I bought the animal," answered the rabbi. "He sold me a camel, not precious stones."

The diamonds were returned, to the surprise of the proper owner, and the rabbi was glad he had kept the jewels he valued most: honesty and integrity.[31]

The Raja Who Went to Heaven

A ruler is affirmed in his good deeds in this tale from the Santal Parganas of India.

Once upon a time there was a raja who had many water reservoirs and tanks, and around their edges he planted trees, mangoes, pipals, palms, and banyans.

One of these banyans was a magic tree. On a bright summer day, the raja climbed into the magic banyan and was carried up to the kingdom of heaven. He climbed out of the tree, and it disappeared, so he had to stay for a while.

The raja wandered about and came to a place where he saw some men laboring to build a palace. He asked them for whom the palace was being built. To his surprise, they gave his own name. He asked why it was being built for him, and they said that it was because he had always been a good ruler who did not oppress his people, who gave to the poor, and who took care of widows and orphans.

When the raja returned to where the banyan tree had been, he found it had reappeared, so he climbed into the tree and was carried back to earth.

When some years had passed, the raja knew he would not live very much longer. He divided all his money among his friends and the poor. A few days later he died and was taken to the palace that he had seen being built.[32]

A Lesson for Kings

This story is part of the Jataka or birth tales of Buddhism in India.

The king of Benares wished to discover whether he was really a good person, so he asked the people around him. When these voices gave only praise, he realized it was because people were afraid of him. He left his country to travel in disguise. In the meantime Mallika, the king of Kosala, was making the same quest. It happened that the two kings came face to face in a narrow road where there was room for only one chariot.

Then the charioteer of Mallika said to the charioteer of the king of Benares, "Take your chariot out of the way!" But the other said: "Take your chariot out of the way! In this chariot sits the lord over the kingdom of Benares."

Yet the other replied: "In this chariot sits the lord of the kingdom of Kosala. Take your carriage out of the way and make room for the chariot of our king!"

Then the charioteers didn't know what to do, as both passengers were kings. Finally the driver for the king of Benares suggested they decide by whoever was the eldest. But it turned out both kings were the same age. Then the charioteers inquired about the size of each lord's kingdom, his army, his wealth and fame, and many other subjects. Both lords were equal in all of these. They finally decided that the one who was most righteous should go first.

The charioteer of the king of Kosala proclaimed:
"The strong he overthrows by strength,
The mild by mildness, does Mallika;
The good he conquers by goodness,
And the wicked by wickedness too.
Such is the nature of this king!
Move out of the way, O charioteer!"
But the charioteer of the king of Benares said:
"Anger he conquers by calmness,
And by goodness the wicked;
The stingy he conquers by gifts,
And by truth the speaker of lies.
Such is the nature of this king!
Move out of the way, O charioteer!"

And when the charioteer of Benares had spoken, both Mallika of Kosala and his driver left their chariot. They unharnessed the horses, removed their carriage, and made way for the king of Benares![33]

The Magic Mirror

The virtue of a clear conscience wins the heart of a king in this story from Spain.

It was proclaimed throughout the kingdom of Granada that the king had decided on marrying. After the news had become somewhat stale, everyone asked, "Who is the king going to marry?"

The question of the king finding a worthy woman for his queen was much discussed. A test must be made. The king's personal barber owned a magic mirror. If a person looking into this mirror was not thoroughly good, the blemishes on his or her character would show as spots on the mirror's surface.

"Is looking into the mirror one of the conditions?" everyone asked.

"This is the only condition," replied the barber. "Any woman from eighteen years upward is eligible."

"Then you will have every woman in Granada claiming the right to be queen!" all exclaimed.

"But first they will have to justify their claim, for I will not take any woman at her word. No. She will have to gaze into the mirror with me by her side," continued the barber.

The sole condition imposed on those who wished to become queen of Granada was made known, and many people laughed. Yet, strangely, no woman applied to the barber to look into the mirror.

Days and weeks went by, and the king was no closer to marriage. It must be understood, the king was a very handsome man and was loved by all his subjects for his many virtues; thus it was surprising that none of the lovely ladies who were members of the court should seek to become his wife.

Every morning the king asked the barber if any lady had tried to look into the mirror; but the answer was always no. The fact was, no one wanted to face the magic examination.

Finally, the barber suggested that the shepherdess on the mountainside might brave the magic, if the king did not object to marrying a woman of such low rank.

The king was quite agreeable, and so the shepherdess was brought to court. All the fine ladies and gentlemen had gathered to watch the trial, and the shepherdess felt very shy at being surrounded by so much grandeur. The magic gifts of the mirror were explained to her.

"Sir," replied the maiden, "we are all sinners in the sight of God; but I have known what it is to be loved, because the sheep come to me for protection. I have desired to be good, and although I am not ambitious to become queen, I will look into the mirror."

Saying this, she walked up to the mirror and gazed into it, and it reflected her loveliness without a single spot.

The court ladies and gentlemen surrounded her; and when they saw the magic mirror showed no stains on its surface, they snatched it from her and exclaimed, "There is no magic in it—a trick has been played on us!"

"No," said the king. "You have only yourselves to thank. If you had been as innocent as this shepherdess, who is going to be my queen, you would not have feared looking into the mirror."

So, the shepherdess and the king were married and lived happily ever after.[34]

The Story of the Squirrel

This tale is told by the Shans who live along the border between India and China.

Prince Gautama became discouraged in his quest for truth and considered returning to his life in the palace. He came to a lake and saw a squirrel that was dipping its tail in the water and shaking the water off onto the land.

"Little squirrel," the prince asked, "what are you doing?"

The squirrel answered, "I am trying to drain the lake."

The prince said, "How can you drain the water by dipping your tail into it and shaking it on the shore? The lake is so large, and your tail is so small."

"I am not like Prince Gautama," replied the squirrel, "who is easily discouraged. He wishes to return to his palace because he thinks he cannot find the truth. Yet, he has searched for only a short while."

The prince, feeling ashamed, returned to his search and never stopped until he became Buddha, the Enlightened One.[35]

The Poor Man and His Wealthy Neighbors

This story was adapted from Jacques De Vitry of France.

There was a poor man who earned a modest living. When he returned home to his wife, they sang together and slept happy and secure. His wealthy neighbors, in comparison, were always troubled, and they certainly never sang. One of them, a very rich man, said, "I will make my poor neighbor lose his desire to rejoice and sing." Secretly he threw a bag of gold pieces in front of the poor man's door while he was away from home.

The poor man returned and found the bag. At first he was very happy to find the treasure, and he rushed inside to hide it in some secret place. But that night he began to worry, because he was afraid either the bag would be stolen from him or he would be accused of stealing it. He and his wife could not rejoice or sing as they had always done.

Eventually, the poor man's neighbors began to ask him what had made him so thin and sad. At first he did not dare confess the truth, but then the rich man told him he knew his secret. "I was the one who left the bag of coins at your door," he said.

The poor man exclaimed, "Take back your money! Only then may I be happy and sing again!"[36]

Honesty Is the Only Policy

This story about an honest man comes from Judaism.

The queen had lost her crown! The servants searched everywhere, but it could not be found. As a last resort, the situation was proclaimed in the streets, and a grand reward was offered to whoever returned the crown within thirty days. However, if someone delayed in bringing the crown until after the thirty days, then his head would be lost.

Among the people was a good man who went strolling one evening beside the river. In the moonlight he saw the crown, glimmering with gold and jewels. He seized it quickly and brought it to his home, where he guarded it carefully. Thirty days passed. After the time when the reward was promised, he wrapped the crown in a cloth and carried it to the palace, where he requested an interview with the queen.

When the man stood before the queen, he bowed and unwrapped the crown.

"What do you mean by this?" asked the queen. "Why did you wait until now? Don't you know the punishment?"

"Yes, I knew the punishment," the man answered calmly. "I waited until this time so you would know that I did not return the crown for the sake of a reward, or for fear of the punishment. I returned it simply because my beliefs forbid me to withhold anyone's property from her."

And the queen told the man to go home in safety, for he had done what was honest, simply because it was the right thing to do.[37]

Choosing a King

This story comes from the Ibo people of Nigeria.

Once upon a time the birds came together to elect a king. Their choice fell upon Okili, who was richly dressed in green plumage. The birds told Okili that after three days of probation, he would be formally installed as king of the birds. From that moment, Okili began strutting about, his head high, proud and looking down upon the other birds. He boasted of his power and what he intended to do after he was crowned. He acted so lordly and superior that the birds became frightened and felt they really could not trust such a king. They reconsidered their decision and immediately canceled the arrangement.

Their choice then fell upon a tiny, white, swallow-tailed bird named Ebwe-Awba, and he was put on a probation similar to Okili's.

The bird's mother was worried about her son. She thought of ways she could help strengthen him so he could resist the temptations found in being a king. Most of all she wished he could be endowed with wisdom and honor, so that he might not be spoiled by power or have his judgments perverted by bribery. The mother went into the countryside and gathered certain leaves to make a medicine to help her son. She pounded them and placed them in a pan and left them to steep in water.

The tiny swallow-tailed bird came along and thought the water was for bathing. He dipped himself in the liquid with disastrous results. From pure white he was changed to jet black! He rushed to the river and washed himself over and over, but the stain would not wash away. He hid himself for two days until, weak with hunger, he whistled a sad little song: "Cha, cha, chigo, chigo," which means "I have washed over and over again."

The mother recognized the voice of her son and hurried to help him. She bemoaned the change in his appearance, but there was nothing to be done except explain the situation to the rest of the birds.

"I hope," she told the birds, "that his change of color will not influence you against my son."

The birds were united in their decision. Ebwe-Awba had been chosen because of his amiable and generous qualities. The birds declared that color should make no difference in the king's election.

From that time forward, Ebwe-Awba has been king of the birds.[38]

The Vain Cereals

This story is Armenian and/or Turkish.

The different cereal grains argued among themselves about which of them was best and should rule over the others.

"I am the best," declared Barley, "for I have sixty grains."

"No! I am the most worthy," said Millet, "for I have a hundred grains."

Wheat was the only one who remained silent.

The king noticed Wheat's humility and appointed him above all the others, second only to the king himself![39]

Smiling at Trouble

This story comes from Liberia.

The chief was known in the country surrounding his town as a rich man, but misfortune came upon him. Sickness carried off his cattle and sheep, the rice crop failed, and a famine began. Then a neighbor raided the chief's town and destroyed everything. But the chief set about mending his fortune so cheerfully that he was a wonder to all his people.

"This is the way," said the wise man of the village, "that every true man should meet trouble."[40]

Pandora's Box

Without curiosity, nothing new would be invented or discovered, yet curiosity can also lead to trouble, as Pandora and Epimetheus find in this ancient story from Greece.

Once upon a time Epimetheus and Pandora lived in a small cottage in a beautiful meadow. Every day they played with the animals and sniffed the flowers and lay for hours looking for cloud pictures in the sky. They never had to work and had no troubles of any kind.

There was only one thing that bothered Pandora. A stranger had left a box with them and said he would return someday for it. He'd had a mischievous look in his eye when he put the box down, tied only with a small golden cord. Pandora wanted to know what was inside. Whenever she looked at it, she felt almost as though there was a voice inside the box calling to her.

"Perhaps we should find out what is in that box," Pandora told Epimetheus.

"No, indeed," he protested. "It wouldn't be right, for it isn't ours."

"But don't you want to know what's inside?"

"Not at all!"

Of course, Epimetheus wasn't really telling the truth; he did want to know what the box contained, but he didn't want to admit that to Pandora.

One day Pandora found herself alone in the cottage with the box. She could hardly bear it, wondering what might be hidden beneath the lid tied down with the golden cord. Finally she couldn't withstand her curiosity any longer—she tiptoed over to the box. For a while, she pretended that she was just looking at the pretty knot the cord made, but all the while she was loosening the threads, until the knot was undone.

Meanwhile, Epimetheus returned to the outside of the cottage and watched Pandora's activity from the window. Carefully he stayed out of sight, for he wanted to be able to see, but he didn't want to be blamed for raising the lid himself.

Up popped the top of the box.

Alas! There were no treasures or interesting things inside, but mean, ugly creatures that flew from the box and laughed a hideous laugh. They whispered words Pandora and Epimetheus didn't yet understand, words like Pain, Hate, Prejudice, Disease, War, Slavery, and Selfishness. Pandora could tell that the words were something terrible. She slammed down the lid of the box, but it was too late; all those awful things were loose in the world.

Pandora sat and wept while Pain stung her forehead and Sulking whipped around to catch Epimetheus on the way out the window. Epimetheus came to sit beside Pandora, and they both wept together.

"Let me out! Please let me out!"

The tiny voice was so soft that Pandora and Epimetheus hardly heard it at first; there was only the sound of their weeping in their ears.

"Please let me out."

When Pandora finally understood the soft whisper, she exclaimed, "I certainly will not! There are enough of your friends already free." Her voice was very firm now. Epimetheus paid no attention; he was still grumpy from the sting Sulking had given him on the cheek.

"I want to help you," the voice answered. Pandora noticed that it wasn't hideous like the other voices, but pretty like a bell ringing in a spring breeze. "I am not like the others, really I'm not. All those others are troubles, and you will need me around, now that you have let them out."

Now, even Epimetheus was listening.

"Shall I open it?" Pandora asked. "She sounds nice."

"Yes," he replied. "And this time, I will help you, and take the blame if there is any, as I should have done before."

Together, Pandora and Epimetheus raised the lid of the box, and out sprang a lovely silvery creature with a joyful smile on her face. As soon as they saw her they could not help feeling better.

"Do not worry," she said. "My name is Hope, and although you have let loose all the troubles, I will always be here to comfort you."[41]

The Burning of the Dwarf Trees

This story of hospitality and self-sacrifice comes from Japan.

In the reign of the Emperor Go-Fukakusa, his regent, Tokiyori, cared very much about the people. Most of all he hated to hear stories of how the poor folk suffered at the hands of power-hungry officials. He decided to disguise himself and travel from place to place to find out firsthand what was happening.

Tokiyori set out and eventually came to a distant region of the land. It was winter, and he became lost in a heavy snowstorm. After tramping about for several hours, he was about to make the best of things by sleeping under a tree when, to his joy, he noticed a nearby cottage. The husband and wife welcomed him and apologized that the hospitality they could offer was very humble.

Tokiyori cared nothing for the lack of grand surroundings for the night and happily ate the simple meal he was offered. The fact that millet, and not rice, was provided clearly showed that the husband and wife were indeed poor, but they had a generosity that went straight to his heart. When the meal was over, they gathered around the fire that was dying out for lack of wood.

The husband turned to the fuel box. Alas! It was empty. Without a moment's pause, he went out into the garden, heavily covered with snow, and brought back three pots of dwarf trees—pine, plum, and cherry. Now, in Japan dwarf trees are held in high honor, and much time and effort are given to their care.

Tokiyori urged his host not to sacrifice his dwarf trees, but the husband broke up the little trees and thus made a cheerful blaze in the fireplace.

All these signs of a kind and gentle heart made Tokiyori curious about his host. The fact that he had owned these valuable little trees indicated that this generous man had probably not been born a farmer. This proved to be true. His host reluctantly explained that he was a samurai by the name of Sano Tsuneyo. He had been forced to take up farming because of the dishonesty of one of his relatives.

At this, Tokiyori remembered the man's story and suggested he apply to the emperor to obtain justice. Sano explained that the previous regent had been a good and just man, but as he had died (so he thought) and as his successor was very young, he had felt it was useless to present a petition. But he said that if there should ever come a call to arms, he would be the first to serve his emperor. It was this thought of someday being of use to his country that had sweetened the days of his poverty.

The following morning, Tokiyori warmly thanked his host and hostess for their hospitality.

Now it happened that in the following spring a call to arms was made by the emperor. No sooner had Sano heard the news than he set out to obey the summons. His armor was shabby, his shield rusted, and his horse old and tired. He certainly presented a poor figure among the well-clad knights who had also gathered. Many of these knights made rude remarks about Sano, but he bore their rudeness without a word. There he stood, a lonely and ragged figure among the sparkling ranks of samurai around him.

A messenger approached, riding on a magnificent horse and carrying a banner that held the regent's crest. With a loud, clear voice he ordered the knight wearing the shabbiest armor to appear before the regent. Sano obeyed the command with a heavy heart. He thought that the regent was about to rebuke him for coming into the grand company so poorly clad.

Sano was surprised by the cordial welcome he received, and still more surprised when his last winter's guest, Tokiyori, came forward to greet him. Tokiyori had not forgotten the unselfish burning of the dwarf pine, plum, and cherry trees. Now it was time for Sano to receive justice for all he had lost. The property that had been stolen from him was returned, and the regent bestowed an additional gift: the lordship of three villages, whose names in the Japanese language were the same as pine, plum, and cherry.[42]

Why the Stork Has No Tail

In this story from Romania, only the disabled stork has the courage to attempt the heroic task for his king.

The king of the storks had a good friend, Floria, who happened to be a human. Floria had once saved his life, and in gratitude the king had given him a feather. This was no ordinary feather, for if Floria were ever in danger, he was to take up the feather and the king would come to him.

Floria never expected to be in great danger, yet through no fault of his own, it happened that his human king became very angry with him.

"You will be put to death," proclaimed the king, "unless you bring me the Water of Death and the Water of Life."

In despair, Floria wondered what he could do. The Water of Death was a magic fluid that, if poured over a body that has been cut into pieces, will bring those pieces together and heal them. The Water of Life would then bring the person back to the living. Floria knew this much, but not where such waters were to be found. Indeed, even if he did know their location, it would be nearly impossible to get to it. Waters that could do such wonders were sure to be guarded by very powerful magic.

There was nothing to do. He would have to tell the king it was hopeless. Perhaps the king would be kind, although he would more likely be angry. Then Floria remembered the feather. Was it possible the stork king could help him? Well, he could lose nothing by trying. Floria took up the feather. At once the stork appeared and asked how he could help.

"Ah, my friend," Floria replied. "Is it possible you could bring me the Water of Life and the Water of Death? Without them, my own king may have me killed."

"I don't know where they are myself," the stork king told him, "but I have a large kingdom, and surely one of my subjects will know the answer. If it is at all possible to get the water, we will."

The king returned to his palace and called the stork kingdom before him.

"Have you seen or heard of the Water of Life and the Water of Death? Where are they to be found?"

The strong young storks looked at one another, and not even the oldest one said a word. The king asked again.

"We know nothing," they all replied.

At last there came from the far end of the crowd a sad old stork. He was lame in one foot and blind in one eye, with a shriveled-up body and half of his feathers missing.

Laughter skittered through the room behind the old bird.

"May it please Your Majesty," said the ragged creature, "I have been to the place where these waters may be found. It is where the mountains knock one against the other. It was there that my eye was blinded and my leg was crushed."

The king looked kindly upon the old bird and then turned to the other storks. "Is there any one among you who will run the risk and go to these mountains to find the water?"

Not one of the storks answered. They kept silent and avoided looking anyone else in the eye.

Only the lame stork stepped forward. "For your sake, O King, I am willing to go."

But the stork king felt it was impossible for the poor lame bird to attempt such a quest, so he asked the others again if any would go. When he saw they were all unwilling to take the risk, he turned to the ragged stork.

"Do you think, disabled as you are, that you can do this thing?"

"I will certainly try," replied the stork. "Tie two bottles for the water onto my legs."

The other storks laughed. "What a conceit," they sneered. "He thinks he shall succeed at what no one else dares try."

But the old stork paid no attention to their laughter, and the king was pleased with the stork's courage and dignity. He himself tied the bottles onto the old stork's legs and tied about his wings some pieces of fresh meat so he would have food for the journey.

"Farewell," said the king.

The old stork spread his wings and rose into the sky. He flew straight to the place where the mountains were knocking against each other, which kept anyone from approaching the fountains of life and death. He watched and waited to find a time when the mountains had drawn furthest away from each other. He planned to then plunge into their depths and seize the water. Yet, suddenly there came to him a swallow from the heart of the mountain.

"Fly no further, for you are surely lost if you try this."

"Who are you, and why do you try to stop me?" demanded the stork.

"I am the guardian of the mountains. My task is to save the creatures who have the ill fortune to come near this place."

"What can I do to be safe?"

"Have you come for the waters of life and death?"

"Yes, and I must succeed, for I have promised my king."

"If you must do this, wait until noon, because that is when the mountains rest for half an hour. When they are quiet, rise into the air as high as possible, then drop straight down to the bottom of the mountain. You will find a ledge on the stone between the two waters. Fill your bottles, then rise straight up. Beware! Do not touch the walls of the mountains; don't even brush the tiniest pebble, or you will be crushed."

Grateful, the stork waited and watched as the swallow had told him. Midday arrived, and the mountains trembled, then settled back with a sigh. They were completely still. The old stork rejoiced and flew straight up. He could see the sparkling waters below, resting between the mountains. Like an arrow, he winged his way downward, so swiftly the air whistled between his ragged feathers. It wasn't easy to get the stoppers out of the bottles, for they were tied to his legs, but he managed somehow to get his beak around the edge of the stopper and pull. First he hopped forward and filled the bottle on his left with the Water of Death and struggled to stop it up again. He didn't want to lose a drop. Then, the Water of Life. The bottle filled very slowly. When would the mountains start knocking together again?

Finally his bottles were full. They were so heavy he could not fly quickly. He beat his wings with all his strength. At last—the top of the mountain! He was growing tired but kept stroking. Then, disaster! Almost at the top of the mountain, his crippled leg swung out and barely touched a tiny stone.

The mountains roared and crashed upon him!

Yet he was high enough that only his tail was caught and became locked between the two peaks of the mountains.

Well, a tail was not so important, he thought. After all, he had the water and had escaped with his life. He pulled and twisted until his tail separated from his body.

Swiftly he flew away with the waters of life and death. Although he was very tired, he never stopped until he reached the palace of the stork king.

The news spread quickly that the lame stork was returning. All the storks in the kingdom gathered at the palace. They wondered what had happened to this lame, half-blind bird who had tried to put them to shame. "Look," they exclaimed. "He has lost his tail!"

"Hah, hah," they laughed. "Look at the absurd creature. He already looked funny enough, and now he is the most ridiculous bird alive."

The stork king squinted in anger, and his wings trembled. "Why are you laughing and making jokes? Just look behind you and see what you think now!"

The storks each looked behind himself. They were dismayed to find that their own tails had disappeared.

"It is your own fault," declared the king. "You laugh at this faithful messenger who lost his tail with courage and honor. Well, you haven't lost your tails for any reason except your cowardice and ill humor."

And this is the reason storks have remained without tails until this very day.[43]

The Three Sons

This is adapted from a story from Mexico.

A man had three sons. One day the eldest said to his father, "I am going to seek my fortune," and off he went. He walked and walked until he came to a hut where an old man lived.

The boy said, "Good day, sir!"

"Good day, son!" replied the old man.

"Have you any work, sir?"

"Certainly," the old man said. "Come in and be seated. Let us take lunch and then you shall go and deliver a letter for me."

After the boy had eaten, the man said, "Sweep the house, saddle this donkey, and go and take this letter to the town of Monjas."

The boy went, but when he came upon a red river he was frightened. He threw the letter into the water and returned to the hut. The old man said, "Have you come back already, son?"

"Already, sir."

"Did you deliver the letter?"

"Oh, yes."

Of course, the old man knew the letter had not been delivered, because the river had brought it back to him. But he asked, "Now, what do you want for your wages? Money or virtue?"

"Money!" the boy replied promptly.

"Then take this napkin," the man told him, "and you will have in it whatever you wish for."

The boy went home well satisfied. "Father," he said, "here I bring this napkin, and we must lunch with it. Napkin, I ask you to give me a lunch."

Suddenly a table appeared with plenty of good food to eat upon it.

After this the second brother said, "Father, I am going to seek my fortune." He went the same way his brother had gone and found the old hut and the same old man.

"Good day, sir!"

"Good day, my son!"

"Have you any work, sir?"

"Certainly," the old man said. "Come in and be seated. Let us take lunch and then you shall go and deliver a letter for me."

After the boy had eaten, the man said, "Sweep the house, saddle this donkey, and go and take this letter to the town of Monjas."

The boy did as he was told until he came to the red river, where he also was afraid, and threw the letter into the water and came back.

Back at the hut the old man said, "Have you come already, son?"

"Already, sir."

"Did you deliver the letter?"

"Oh, yes."

As before, the river had returned the letter to the man. But he still asked, "Now, what do you want for your wages? Money or virtue?"

"Money!" the boy replied promptly.

The man gave the boy an empty trunk, took a small pole, touched the top of the trunk with it, and said, "Pole, pole, put this trunk in his house," and the trunk was transported to the house of the boy. The boy told the old man good-bye; and when he came to his home, he found the trunk full of money.

Then the younger brother said, "Father, I will also go to seek my fortune." Like his brothers he came to the hut and found the old man.

"Good day, sir!"

"Good day, my son!"

"Have you any work, sir?"

"Certainly," the old man said. "Come in and be seated and let us first take lunch."

The man served the boy some very stale cakes, and the boy said to himself, "Poor old man! How can he keep himself on these stale things?"

The old man had heard the boy and said, "Sweep the house, saddle this donkey, and go to Monjas to deliver this letter for me."

The boy went. First he came to the red river. He called upon his courage and forded the river, and the water only wet the hooves of his donkey. He went on. He walked and walked until he came to a white river. He crossed it. Then he came to a green river, then a grassy hill with lean cattle roaming upon it. He came to a barren hill with fat cattle upon it. He walked on and on and came to rocks that were striking one another.

Finally he arrived at Monjas and delivered the letter.

On the boy's return, the rivers and hills were gone, and he had only to follow the road. He reached the hut of the old man, who asked him, "Have you come already, son?"

"Already," replied the boy.

"Well, tell me about what you have seen on the road."

So the boy told him about the red and the white and the green rivers, the grassy hill with lean cattle, the barren hill with fat cattle, and the strange place where the rocks were striking one another.

"Well, son," said the man, "and now what do you want for your wages? Money or virtue?"

"Virtue," the boy told him.

"All right!" replied the man. "Take this piece of wood, and on it you will find a present every day."

The boy left well satisfied. When he arrived at his house, he carefully kept the piece of wood, and every day when he awoke, he found two dollars on it.

One day, when the brothers were eating, they saw in the distance an old man wrapped in a sheet. His skin was full of ulcers and he was disgusting to see. The man came to the door and said, "Good day!"

"Good day, sir!" replied the youngest boy. But his brothers began to cover the food, because the old man was so disgusting to look upon. Only the youngest brother gave the old man food to eat.

The old man left, and the youngest brother prospered. But the brothers found their magic food full of grubs.[44]

6

Wisdom & Foolishness

Don't yell "Fried Fish!" until you catch them — Eleuthera proverb • A bald-headed person does not care for a razor — Yoruba • In at one ear and out at the other — English, Italian • He who has not tasted the bitter does not understand the sweet — German • "You should never curse the crocodile, until you have crossed the river — Africa • One who rides a tiger must continue to go fast — Japanese / Chinese • There is nothing so eloquent as a rattlesnake's tail — Native American • By night all cats are gray — English/French.

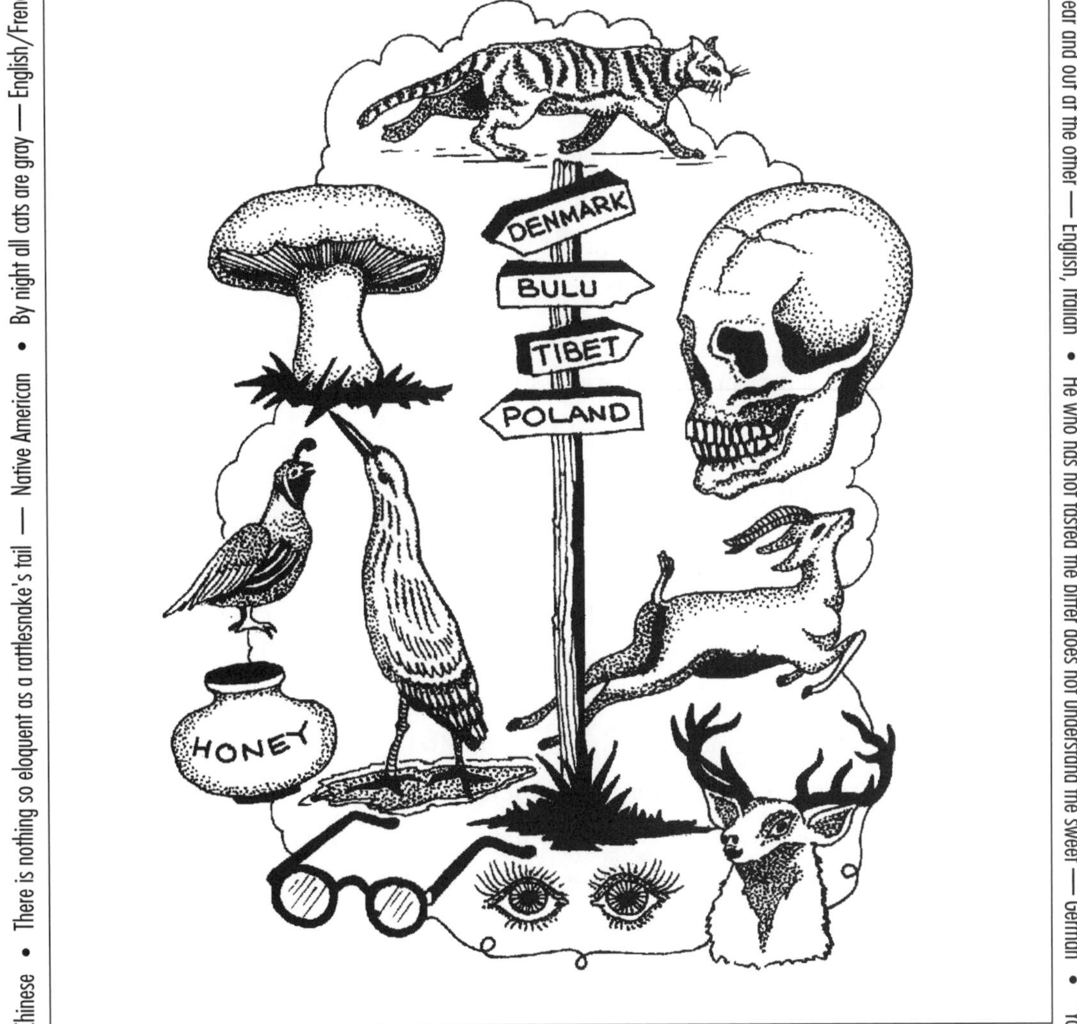

The Paharias Away from Their Place

This story is about wise people who know from where their importance comes.
It is adapted from a tale of the Santal Parganas in India.

Once upon a time there was a paharia, a man who leads the village. Almost every day, he sat in the sunshine and made decisions for his town.

Sometimes, when people argued and could not come to an agreement, they came to the paharia. On a warm afternoon, two men came before him.

"This man promised to give me one-half the fruit from his tree," one proclaimed. "It was in payment for the money I gave him at the time he planted his fields. Now the fruit is ripe, and he refuses to give me my fair share."

"That is not true," the other protested. "I said if I could not sell my fruit, I would give him half. But I have been offered much money for my crop. The fruit is worth far more than the coins he lent me."

The paharia listened carefully to the story of each man. He must decide who was telling the truth and who was lying.

Neighbors came, and he questioned what they knew and finally decided what he thought would be fair.

"Each man misunderstood the other. Sell the fruit," he said to the one who owned the tree. "But save that which grows upon one branch. Repay the man his coins and give him the fruit that remains."

The men were happy with the judgment of the paharia. They did what he told them because they knew he always tried to be fair.

Every year the raja asked the villages to pay their taxes, and it was the job of the paharia to bring the money to the city of Burdwan, where the raja lived.

The paharia made ready for his journey. He cleaned his clothing, packed food and a blanket, and took a staff to lean upon if he grew tired. Then he kissed his wife and embraced his children and set out for the city of Burdwan.

It was a long way to travel.

The paharia met eleven others who were also going to Burdwan to pay their taxes, and they decided to travel together. When the sun grew hot, they rested in the shade of a tree. When they crossed a stream they washed their feet in the cool water.

Finally they entered the city and came to the palace of the raja. What a grand place it was! The paharia whispered to the others, "My whole village would fit inside the palace."

Each man came forward and bowed before the raja. "Great leader of all the people, here is the tribute of my village."

After they had paid their taxes, the raja gave a wonderful feast, where everyone ate whatever they wanted and enjoyed themselves very much. At the end, each man leaned back and shared stories. The paharia told a joke, and the raja laughed a deep laugh.

Late in the evening, the twelve men grew tired, so the raja sent them to a room to sleep. But the room held only one bed!

"Well, who should sleep in the bed?" asked one man.

"Eleven of us must sleep on the floor," said another.

"But that hardly seems fair, for only one to have the bed."

"It would also be ridiculous for no one to use it."

"I know," exclaimed the paharia. "We will all lie upon the floor and put our feet upon the bed."

"A good idea," agreed the first man. "That way we shall each have an equal share."

So they pulled out their blankets and spread them on the floor and lay down, all around the one bed.

"Ah," the paharia sighed. "When one is so tired, it feels good to place even one's feet upon a bed in the raja's palace."

Before long, they were all snoring.

Early the next morning, the raja went to the room where he had sent the men. What a funny sight! He saw twelve men snoring in a circle. A ring of their feet lay on the bed.

"What is this?" he cried.

The twelve men awakened, stood, and bowed to the raja.

"Have we offended you?" they asked.

"Not at all," replied the raja. "I was simply amazed at the strange sight. I had sent the bed for the man who is the most important among you. Don't you have any way of deciding who is the most important?"

"Not exactly," the paharia answered. "I suppose that we are each important in our own village because it is there we lead and try to serve our people. But this is a foreign land for us, far from our villages. Away from home, we are all equal."

The raja nodded with satisfaction.

"It is good to know," he answered, "that the leaders of my country's villages are so sensible and wise. I am pleased. If you treat each other with such respect, my country will remain at peace."

The twelve men gathered their belongings and took up their blankets. Servants came and filled their bags with food for their journey. They were glad to start the walk home, for they missed their families.

When they came to the place where they must part and travel to their own villages, they stopped and bowed to each other.

"What do you say?" asked the paharia. "Shall we travel together next year?"

"Yes, indeed," replied the others. "When the time comes to pay our tribute to the raja, it will be pleasant to have companions on the road."

The paharia hurried to his own village, where he greeted his family and friends. And each day he sat in the sun and tried to make wise decisions for his people.[1]

The Marriage of a Cat

This story is loosely adapted from a tale from Japan in which the protagonist is a rat whose parents wish to arrange a suitable marriage. There is a similar French version. A Hindu fable from India tells of a mouse magically turned into a girl for whom a mate is sought.

A truly remarkable cat once lived with a man. The man felt quite honored with the company of this feline and wished to find her the finest possible husband. He finally decided there was nothing greater than the sun, so he brought his cat to the sun and suggested an engagement. But the sun pointed out that because the clouds so often cover him, it might be fairer to the cat to marry her to the clouds.

The clouds complained about the wind blowing them away, so the man went to the wind, who grumbled about the walls that stop him from blowing through the houses. So, the man took the cat to his home and introduced her to a wall. Just then a neighbor came by and complained of the mice chewing through all her walls. The man declared himself a fool for seeking the wall when it was the mouse the cat should marry.

That very evening, the soon-to-be Mrs. Mouse sat on the man's lap, and he stroked her fur while he reflected on what a wonderful creature she was. Then to his ears came a faint scratching and a tiny squeak. He turned and saw a mouse emerging from a new hole chewed in the wall. The remarkable cat crouched, and sniffed, then pounced! She licked her lips over the delicious morsel.

"Auggghh!" the man exclaimed. "What a fool I am. The most wonderful thing in this world is the cat, and I suppose she must seek her own husband."[2]

The Brahman's Clothes

This story teaches wisdom about society's regard and comes from the Santal Parganas of India.

A Brahman once decided to go to the marketplace dressed only in some ragged clothing such as the poorest people wear. He wanted to see how people reacted. Everyone ignored him. He soon tired of this and hurried home to put on his best clothing. This time everyone bowed and made way for him; the shopkeepers gave him good things, and the people in the village gladly made gifts for him.

The Brahman went home, smiling to himself. He removed his clothes and put them in a heap and bowed before them three or four times, saying each time, "O source of wealth; O source of wealth! It is you, my clothing, that is honored in the world, not I."[3]

The Lion and the Ass

This story has been attributed to Aesop.

A conceited ass once had the impudence to bray forth some insulting speeches against the lion. The suddenness of the insult at first made the lion very angry. Then he turned his head and saw where the insult came from, so he shrugged and walked on without a word.[4]

Humanity's Two Bags

This fable has been attributed to Aesop.

It is said that when humans were made, they were given two bags, one for their neighbor's faults, the other for their own. The bags were thrown over humanity's shoulder, so that one hung in front and the other behind.

Unfortunately, the people kept the one in front for their neighbor's faults and the one behind for their own. That way, while the first was always under their nose, it took some trouble to see the latter.[5]

The Camel and the Pig

This story is from India. Its message is similar to the story from Africa, where fire and water argue over their relative merits.

A camel boasted, "There's nothing like being tall! See how tall I am!"

A pig who heard these words said, "There's nothing like being short; see how short I am!"

The camel said, "Well, I'll prove that what I say is true. If I don't, I'll give up my hump." The pig answered, "I shall prove my point instead. And if I fail to do so, I will give up my snout!"

Agreed!" said the camel.

"Just so!" replied the pig.

The two came to a garden enclosed by a low wall. The place was deserted, and the openings to the garden were filled with broken stone. The camel stood beside the wall and could reach the plants inside because of his long neck. He had a fine breakfast.

"Ha, ha!" he jeered at the pig, who had stood at the bottom of the wall and hadn't even had so much as a look at the good things in the garden. "Now," he said, "would you be tall or short?"

Next they came to another part of the garden and found just a small hole at the corner where the stones had fallen away. The pig was small enough to scramble thorough this hole and eat his fill of the vegetables gone wild in the garden.

Later he came out laughing at the poor camel, who had to stay outside because he was too tall to get through the hole.

"Now," said the pig, "would you rather be tall or short?"

The camel and the pig thought the matter over for some minutes, then came to the conclusion that the camel should keep his hump and the pig his snout.

They agreed:

"Tall is good, where tall would do;
Of short, again, 'tis also true!"[6]

The Rival Queens

This tale was adapted from a poem by John Godfrey Saxe. Another version of this story is "The Lily and the Rose," found in Part 1.

A deep red rose and pure white lily argued over which of them should be considered the queen of flowers. Some people preferred the lily, and others just as firmly declared their favor for the rose.

Their quarrel was long and bitter and loud. It's no wonder the rose grew proud and the lily grew vain. For many hateful days and weeks, they refused to speak to each other.

Then one golden morning in summer, the rose awakened and grew ashamed of her spiteful ways. "O lovely lily!" exclaimed the rose, "we are foolish to argue in this manner. Once upon a time, we were the dearest of friends."

"Ah," replied the lily, softening in turn, "it is a pity that pride should separate friends. And I've been thinking," she went on. "It is not by arrogant claims that nobility is shown, but in noble acts and goals."

"I agree," the rose nodded. "Also, I've been remembering that for all our personal pride, every flower has some quality that is uniquely special. The smallest flower in the field or garden has some beauty that we have not."[7]

The Sultan and the Man

Variations of this story may be found in the Middle East.

A sultan was out for a walk and enjoying his high, exalted status. He saw a poor man, deep in thought, sitting with a human skull in his lap. His attitude surprised the sultan, who demanded the reason.

"Sire," said the man, "this skull was given to me this morning; and I have been trying, without success, to discover whether it is the skull of a powerful king like Your Majesty, or a poor man like myself."[8]

The Sun's Waning Glory

This fable is Armenian or Turkish in background.

Each morning when he rose, the sun believed that he was a god. But at evening, when he set, he had to hide himself beneath the earth. So each night, he was forced to recognize his unimportance.[9]

The Hoopoe and the Bittern

Here, an ancient folktale is used to illustrate the dangers of extremism.
The story comes from Germany.

Which is your favorite pasture for your cows?" asked a gentleman of an old herdsman.

"Here, sir," was the answer, "where the grass is not too rich and not too poor; anywhere else would be useless."

"Why so?"

"We know this because of a story about a time when the bittern and the hoopoe kept cows. The bittern fed his herds on rich green pastures, where flowers grew in abundance. As a result, his cattle became wild and frisky. The hoopoe drove his cattle onto high and barren hills, where the wind blew the sand about in clouds, and the cattle got thinner and thinner, and lost all their strength.

"One day, toward evening, when the herdsmen were about to return home, the bittern could not get his cows together. They were mettlesome—frolicking and kicking up their heels all around him. He called them, but to no purpose; they would not listen. In contrast, the hoopoe could not make his cows stand up, for they were weak and tired. 'Up! up! up!' he cried, but it was of no use—there they lay on the ground and refused to stir.

"That is what happens," said the herdsman, "if you go to extremes."[10]

The Flies and the Honey Pot

This fable has been attributed to Aesop.

A jar of honey was spilled in the kitchen, and a number of flies were attracted to its sweetness. They settled into it and ate greedily. Their feet, however, became so smeared and stuck with the honey that even their wings couldn't lift them out of it. Just as they were dying, they cried, "Oh, what foolish creatures we are; for the sake of a little pleasure we have destroyed ourselves."[11]

The Story of the Peasant, the Snake, and King Solomon

This tale about King Solomon comes from Romania. A story from China also tells about a man who had pity on a snake, but the ending of the story varies, as the snake rewards the man because "good should repay good." A fable of Aesop also shows a man taking pity on a snake and warming it to save its life. An Armenian proverb hints at the possibility of a similar type of story in that culture: "Warm a frozen serpent, and it will sting you first." There are also Native American stories with the same message.

Once upon a time, when King Solomon the wise ruled over the people, a tree caught fire. A snake had crept onto that tree and now found himself in danger of perishing in the flames. The snake climbed to the very top of the tree and cried as loud as it could for help.

At that moment a man passed by and heard the shrieking of the snake. The man pitied the creature but was wary because it might hurt him. "If I help you," he said, "will you be good?"

"Oh, certainly!" the snake promised.

So the man cut a long stick and reached with it to the top of the tree so that the snake could glide down on it. But no sooner did the snake reach the neck of the man than it coiled itself around and around his neck! The man reminded the snake that he had saved its life, but the snake cared nothing for that.

Finding he could not get rid of the snake, the man went to King Solomon and laid his case before him.

"I am not going to judge between you," said Solomon, "unless you both first promise to abide by my word."

Both promised to do so.

Turning to the snake, King Solomon then said, "You must uncoil yourself and get down on the earth, for I cannot judge fairly between one who is standing on the ground and one who is riding."

So the snake uncoiled itself, glided down, and rested on the ground.

Turning to the man, Solomon said, "Don't you know that you must never trust a snake?"

The man at once understood what the king meant. He took up a stone and killed the snake. Thus justice was done.[12]

The Quail and the Fowler

Good sense and advice are easier to know than to follow in this story from India. Variants are found in Jewish and Turkish sources. The story was also recorded in the writings of Jacques De Vitry, who was born circa A.D. 1180.

A fowler once caught a quail. The quail said, "O fowler, I know four things that will be useful for you to know. If you release me, I will share them with you."

"Very well, what are they?" asked the man.

"Well," said the bird, "I don't mind telling you three of them now. The first is: Fast caught, fast keep; never let a thing go once you've got it. The second is: He is a fool that believes everything he hears. And the third is this: It's no use crying over spilt milk."

The fowler thought these very sensible ideas, if not very new ones. "Well," he said, "I've heard this before, so they are not very useful to me. What is the fourth?"

"Ah," said the quail, "you must set me free if you want to hear the fourth."

Hoping the fourth thing would be more helpful than the first three, the man set the quail free.

The bird flew into a tree and laughed. "Ah, so you've heard those things before and do not find them very useful! But you took no notice of what I told you. Fast caught, fast keep, I said; and yet you have let me go."

"Why, so I have," said the man, and scratched his head. "Well, never mind; what is the fourth thing? You promised to tell me, and I am sure an honorable quail will never break its word."

"The fourth thing I have to tell you is that in my body is a beautiful diamond, weighing ten pounds and larger than your head. If you hadn't let me go, you would have had that diamond, and you would have been rich."

"Oh dear, oh dear, what a fool I am!" cried the man. He fell on his face, clutched the grass, and began to weep.

"Ha, ha, ha!" laughed the quail. "He is a fool who believes everything he hears."

"What?" asked the man.

"Do you think a little body like mine can hold a diamond as big as your head?" asked the quail, roaring with laughter. "And even if it were true, what's the use of crying over spilt milk?"

The quail spread his wings. "Good-bye," he said. "Better luck next time, man. Knowing something is wise only if you practice it." He flew away, and the man went home with something to think about.[13]

The Stag Looking into the Pool

This fable has been attributed to Aesop.

A stag, drinking at a clear pool, admired the handsome look of his spreading antlers but was unhappy with the skinny and awkward appearance of his legs. "What a glorious pair of branching horns," he said. "How gracefully they hang over my forehead! But as for my spindle-shanks of legs, I am rather ashamed of them."

The words were hardly out of his mouth when he saw some huntsmen and a pack of hounds moving toward him. The legs he was ashamed of soon carried him quite a distance from danger while his horns did nothing to save him.[14]

The Hoopoe Birds and Their Crowns

This story may be English in origin.

King Solomon once journeyed across the desert and was fainting with heat, when a large flock of hoopoes came to his assistance. By flying between the sun and the monarch, they formed a heavy cloud with their wings and bodies.

Grateful for their help, Solomon asked what reward they would choose. They asked that each bird be decorated with a golden crown.

"I really don't think that is a good idea," Solomon told them.

"No, no!" cried the birds. "This is truly the reward we want."

For a few days they were proud of their golden decorations and strutted among the less favored birds and admired themselves in every stream or puddle. Then a fowler happened to catch one of them and discovered the value of its crown. From that hour the hoopoes had no rest.

Finally the birds sent two of the survivors to Solomon, full of repentance at their rejection of his advice. "We were fools. Please take back the golden crowns," they begged.

Solomon granted their request and removed the golden crowns from their heads. Yet, wishing to give them some mark of honor, he substituted a crown of feathers, and they returned home rejoicing.[15]

King Solomon and the Bees

In this tale from the Jewish Talmud, King Solomon was wise enough not to rely upon his own judgment. John Godfrey Saxe used this story for one of his poetical works.

The Queen of Sheba heard rumors about the wisdom of King Solomon of Israel, and she determined to test the truth of his reputation. She called her artists together and told them to make a bouquet of flowers that would look so real no one could tell the difference between the fake flowers and the genuine ones.

When the artists were finished, the queen realized something was missing, so she called the royal perfume maker and ordered him to create a scent exactly like the blossoms of the bouquet. Once everything was completed, she traveled to the court of Solomon and presented two bouquets, one real and one fake.

"In your wisdom, O Solomon," said the queen, "tell me which of these is real and which is a fake."

Solomon was terribly perplexed. As far as he could see, the two sets of flowers looked exactly alike. The scents that came from them couldn't be told apart.

Everyone in the royal court seemed to hold their breath. Who would win this contest? Would it be the Queen of Sheba and her difficult riddle, or the great lord?

While he studied the flowers, Solomon was disturbed by the buzzing of a bee at his window. He smiled and called his servant. "It is hot in here," he said. "Open the windows and let in some fresh air."

The servant opened the window. Unnoticed by everyone except Solomon, the little bee flew inside the room straight to one bouquet, where it buried itself deep in the blossoms. "Those are the real flowers," Solomon said, pointing to the one in which the bee was hidden.

Everyone "ooed" and "aahed," and the queen was deeply impressed. But Solomon privately knew the real wisdom was found in the tiny bee.[16]

The Oak and the Reeds

This fable has been attributed to Aesop.

A violent storm threw down a great oak tree that grew on the bank of a river. The oak floated across the stream until it was lodged against some reeds. It couldn't help asking them how they had escaped the fury of the storm that had torn the oak up by the roots.

"We bent our heads to the blast," they said, "and it passed over us. You stood stiff and stubborn until you could stand no longer."

Sometimes bending against the wind and compromising are a good idea.[17]

The Lion

In this tale from Oaxaca, Mexico, the animals wisely restrain their curiosity and desire to see an old enemy brought low—for they remember the danger and remain in safety.

A hungry lion chased a calf and a lamb who ran away and hid in a deep forest. The lion was weak from hunger. "Oh! Oh!" he shouted. "I am very sick!" He thought this would fool some animals and bring them to him.

Several animals were nearby, but they remembered that the lion was only sick because he was hungry and would eat anyone who came to see him. The fox was one of these. He came near the door of the lion's den, and when the lion saw him, he invited the fox to come inside as a special guest.

"I could come in," said the smart fox, "but I couldn't go out." The fox ran away in safety to the forest.[18]

The Foolish Turtle

This tale of irony is told by the Muskhogean and Creek people native to North America.

A turtle came out of the water and was sunning himself on a log. By and by he looked up and realized that rain was coming.

"Oh, no, it is going to wet me," he said to himself, and quickly jumped into the river.[19]

The Man and the Roadside Cheese

This tale comes from England.

A man of Gotham was riding from Nottingham when he saw a cheese that lay by the roadside. He attempted to pick it up with his sword, but the sword was too short. So he rode back to Nottingham to buy a longer blade. In the meantime, another rider saw the cheese, dismounted, and carried the cheese away.[20]

The Monkeys and the Moon

The danger of followers surrendering their brains to a leader
is illustrated in this tale from Tibet.

Long ago there lived a band of monkeys in a forest. As they wandered about they saw the reflection of the moon in a well. The leader of the band said, "Friends, the moon has fallen into the water. Let us pull it out."

The monkeys agreed to the venture and began to discuss how they were to accomplish their task. The leader suggested they form a chain and so draw out the moon.

Thus they formed a chain, the first monkey hanging on to the branch of a tree, and the second to the first monkey's tail, and a third one in its turn to the tail of the second. When a great number had been added to the chain, the branch began to bend. The water grew troubled; the reflection of the moon disappeared, the branch broke, and all the monkeys fell into the well and barely escaped with their lives.

It is said: "When the foolish have a foolish leader, they all go to ruin."[21]

The Marsh Antelope and the Forest Antelope

The foolishness of ignoring advice from experts
is illustrated in this tale from Africa.

The forest antelope said, "I am going down to the marsh." He set off, and along the way he met a marsh antelope.

"Where are you going?" asked the marsh antelope.

The forest antelope told him he was going to the marsh.

"The marsh is too wet," objected the other animal. "The rainy season has come; do not go there. I am coming up to the high land because it is too wet for me. If you go there you might be drowned."

The forest antelope went in spite of the words of his friend, but not long afterward he came running back, exclaiming, "The marsh is under water."

And so the saying "The marsh antelope tells you 'the marsh is under water'" is said to a person who doubts or contradicts the word of someone who has reason to know and is a reliable witness.[22]

A Man of Gotham

This story comes from England.

A man of Gotham went to market with two bushels of wheat. Being concerned about his horse, he carried the wheat upon his own shoulders when he rode so that his horse would not have to carry too heavy a burden.[23]

How Spider Caught the Tiger

This story is part of the Anansi tales of West Africa.

Spider wanted to catch a tiger. He took a needle and thread and sewed up one of his eyes, then set out for a den where he knew a tiger lived. As he approached the place he began to shout and sing so loudly that the tiger came out to see what was the matter.

"Can you not see?" said Spider. "My eye is sewn up and now I see such wonderful things that I must sing about them."

Now, the tiger should have known better and shouldn't have believed everything someone like Spider said. If he had used his brain, he would have been safe. But he was very foolish and thought Spider was telling the truth. "Sew up both my eyes," said the tiger. "Then I can see these surprising sights, too."

Spider did so, and when the tiger's eyes were sewn shut, he was helpless, and this is the way Spider caught his tiger.[24]

The Man and the Fly

This fable has been attributed to Aesop.

A man sat down after work on a hot summer's day, and a fly came buzzing around his nose. The man aimed a blow at the fly, but—whack—his palm struck his nose and it began to hurt.

The fly came again and bothered him, but this time the man was wiser and no longer tried to injure his tiny enemy at the cost of himself.[25]

The Sensible Ass

This story has been attributed to Aesop.

A man in time of war was allowing his ass to feed in a green meadow when he was alarmed by the sight of the enemy advancing upon him. He tried everything to urge the ass to run, but in vain. "The enemy is upon us," the man told him.

"And what will the enemy do?" inquired the ass. "Will they put two packs on my back instead of one?"

"No," answered the man.

"Well, then," replied the ass, "I can't see any reason to run away. I am born to be a slave, and my greatest enemy is the one who gives me the most to carry."[26]

The Reeds and the Oak

This fable is almost identical to "The Oak and the Reeds" (Part 6) except it teaches a different lesson. This variation, possibly by French poet Jean La Fontaine, suggests that to compromise too easily is sometimes a greater evil than to fall. Wisdom is found in knowing when to bend and when to stand firm.

A violent storm arose and beat against the forest. The oak on the riverbank stood firm against the howling wind for a long time, but the wind finally proved stronger than he. Uprooted, the oak floated across the water and came to rest against some reeds.

"Isn't that like an oak tree," sneered the reeds. "He is so stiff and stubborn, he'd rather be uprooted than bend."

"Perhaps," answered the oak. "But perhaps it is better to be an oak who will not bend than to be one who will go in any direction the wind blows."

Sometimes standing firm, even if we fall, is the higher choice.[27]

Wisdom and Selfishness

This allegory was adapted from a poem by John Godfrey Saxe.

Once upon a time, Wisdom was a lovely young woman, and one day she went for a walk. When she passed the cottage of Selfishness, he thought she was very beautiful, so he kidnapped Wisdom and forced her to marry him.

Such a marriage was doomed to failure, and Wisdom finally secured a divorce. But as it happened, she had a child. Now, the child's character and personality were almost exactly like those of his father, Selfishness; only in his face were a few echoes of his mother's looks. When his father died, the son took his place.

Unfortunately, ever since then, people have been confused by Selfishness. They catch the vague images of Wisdom in his features and fool themselves into thinking that following the example of Selfishness is wise.[28]

The Power of Story

This story is from Greece.

A famous Greek orator addressed an assembly at Athens and tried in vain to get the attention of his audience. They laughed among themselves, watched the children playing, and in many other ways showed their lack of interest.

After a short pause the orator said: "Once upon a time, Ceres journeyed in company with a swallow and an eel until they came to a river." At these words, the entire company settled down and paid close attention to what the man had to say.[29]

The Bramble-Bush King

This tale comes from Biblical Judaism.

Once upon a time the trees gathered together to choose a king to rule over them. First they invited the olive tree, but the olive tree said it was too busy bearing fruit. Then they asked the fig tree to be king, but the fig tree had its work to do and also declined. Next they invited the vine to become royal, but like the others, it did not wish to be their king.

Finally the trees asked the bramble to accept the position, and the bramble gladly agreed. The first order it gave was for all the trees to take shelter under its branches or be burned with fire.

When you give power to people who are petty, don't be surprised when they use their power to oppress or harm.[30]

How People Suffer Because They Resist a Change

This story comes from the Bulu people of West Africa.

One day a young man became lost from his village in the forest. After three nights he came to a town that was unknown to him. The people of this village were all very thin and dry.

"Ah, friends," the young man asked the people, "what sort of food is it that you eat?"

"We have only mushrooms. We have no fire. We do not cook. The whole village eats only raw mushrooms."

The young man felt great pity for them. "Come," he said. "You all should come to my village!"

"No," they declared. "It might be that you will be cruel to us when we arrive there."

"Please," said the young man. "We will be good to you and share what we have."

But the people would not listen, and the young man went away toward his own town. Yet two people of the village secretly followed him. When they arrived at his home, the young man called all the people together to see the Dry People. The villagers said, "Give these dry men food."

Then the two men ate and became healthy like the rest of the village and found it a place of great friendship.

"We must go home," the two dry men said. "We must bring our people back here." So they returned to their dry village. "Let us move to a real town! There is plenty of food and good friends for neighbors."

But the townspeople refused; they could hear only the fear and doubt in their own hearts. This is why they are still the tribe of the Dry People.[31]

Borrowing Trouble

A man "borrows trouble" in this tale from China.

A certain rich man had lived to an extreme age. He invited all of his children and grandchildren to celebrate his birthday. Although it was supposed to be a festive party, and all of his family were happily wishing him happiness, the man looked quite worried and upset. Finally they asked him what was the problem.

"Nothing, really," he replied. "I was just thinking about the trouble I would have inviting my guests when my two-hundredth birthday came around."[32]

The Origin of Fire

Laughter is the key in this story from Australia.

At one time the adder snake was the only one who had fire. He kept it in his insides. All the birds tried to get it, but nothing worked. Then the small hawk came along and started fooling around. He looked so ridiculous that the adder began to laugh. The fire escaped, and then it belonged to everyone.[33]

The Fox Without a Tail

This story has been attributed to Aesop.

A fox once caught his tail in a trap, and to get away he was forced to leave it behind. Knowing that without a tail he would be laughed at by all his fellow foxes, he decided to convince them to part with their own tails. At the next assembly of foxes he made a speech on the low value of tails in general, and the inconvenience of a fox's tail in particular. He added that he had never felt so comfortable since he had given up his own.

When he sat down, a wise old fellow stood, waved his long bushy tail, and said: "If I had lost my tail like brother fox here, I would not need to be convinced that tails should be discarded. But until such time, I will certainly vote in favor of tails. I distrust those who have something to gain by my following their advice."[34]

The Hungry Elephant

When the elephant uses more brawn than sense,
it is the frog who helps him in this Bulu tale from West Africa.

Once upon a time there lived an elephant who said to himself, "I am very hungry." So he walked down a path of the forest and found a bamboo palm standing in a swamp. He rushed over, broke down the palm, and found its tender bud of palm leaves. Being greedy, he hurried to eat it, and it fell into the water.

The elephant hunted and hunted for it, but he could not find the palm bud because he had stirred up the water and it blinded his eyes.

A frog saw this. "Listen!" said the frog.

The elephant paid no attention but hunted even harder.

"Listen!" the frog called again very loudly. "Wait!"

Then the elephant stood perfectly still. The water became clear again, so that he found the palm bud and ate it.[35]

The Monster in the Sun

This story is attributed to Aesop.

An astronomer observed the sun through a telescope in order to make a drawing of the several spots that appear on its face. While he was in the midst of his task, he was surprised by an astounding appearance: A large portion of the sun was suddenly covered by a monster of enormous size and form. It had huge wings, a great many legs, and a long nose. The astronomer knew it was alive because he could see its movements.

The man made some calculations and learned the size of the animal would cover half of the earth's hemisphere and that it was seven or eight times as big as the moon. It was also astonishing what heat it could bear as it crawled upon the sun.

The astronomer gathered many of his colleagues, and they were astounded by the accuracy of his observations. Yet, there was one that was more cautious than the rest, and before making the news public he wanted to investigate further. He opened the telescope and found a small fly trapped inside. Thus the monster was eliminated from the sun.[36]

The Fool's Axe

This story was told by Jacques De Vitry of France in the thirteenth century.

A fool's axe fell into the river one day. The owner stood on the bridge and waited for all the water to flow by so he could retrieve his axe.[37]

Caught in His Own Trap

In this tale from Poland, a mimic is caught by his own devices. The story's conclusion is reminiscent of the proverb that "the one who digs a pit falls into it."

A certain mimic's talent was hard to overestimate. He could bark like a dog; he could grunt like a hog. He could croak like a frog. Perhaps birds were his greatest imitations. He often went out to trap birds by chirping the chaffinch's tone.

The goldfinch and thrush would cry, "Hush! Our brothers and sisters are singing yonder. They flew to join the chorus and were caught by the mimic."

But it happened one day that the mimic gave one bird call too many. Another man was seeking partridges and thought the mimic was one. Netted and caught, he ruefully said, "Who prepares a trap for others should beware. Sooner or later they fall into their own snare!"[38]

The Dog and the Crocodile

This story has been attributed to Aesop.

A dog ran along the banks of the Nile and grew thirsty, but because he feared being seized by the monsters of that river, he didn't stop, but lapped as much as he could while he ran.

A crocodile raised his head above the surface of the water and asked him why he was in such a hurry. "I have often wanted a friend such as you, and if you would pause we could pursue our acquaintance," said the wily crocodile.

"You do me great honor," replied the dog, "but it is to avoid such friends as you that I am in such a hurry."[39]

The Buffoon and the Man

This fable has been attributed to Aesop.

At a country fair a man made the people laugh by imitating the sounds of different animals. He finished off by squeaking so much like a pig that the audience thought he must certainly have one hidden under his coat.

But one man in the audience disagreed. "Do you call that a pig's squeak? It's not even close. Wait until tomorrow, and I will show you what a pig really sounds like."

The people laughed, but the next day the man came to the stage. He put his head down and squealed. The audience hissed and booed. "Not half as good—not half as good!" they cried.

"You aren't very good judges," said the man. He took a live pig out from under his coat. "This is the performer you condemn."

People often applaud an imitation and hiss the real thing.[40]

The Best Path

This tale comes from the Ibo people of Nigeria.

A pig and a deer started on a journey together. They reached a spot where the path forked and began to argue concerning which road they should follow. The pig thought the longer path would be the best, but the deer wanted the shorter and easier way. They quarreled so much they decided to go separate ways.

The pig traveled by the longer path and arrived safely. The deer went by the easier road but had only gone a short distance when he was shot and killed.

Moral: The easiest is not always the best.[41]

The Travelers and the Crow

The folly of superstition is revealed in this fable attributed to Aesop.

Some travelers had set out on a journey and had not gone far when a one-eyed crow flew across their path. The superstitious people thought it was a bad omen and decided to give up their plan for that day at least.

But one man objected. "What nonsense!" he said. "If this crow could foresee what is to happen to us, he would also know the future for himself; and in that case, do you think he would have been silly enough to go where his eye would be knocked out of his head?"[42]

The Antelope Procrastinates

Procrastination costs the antelope his life in this story from Africa.

The elders of the village went out to hunt monkeys. They set up the nets and were shouting to each other. The monkey was sitting in a tree, eating fruit and throwing some of it onto the ground.

An antelope was under the monkey's tree eating the fruit that he was throwing onto the ground. The antelope heard the noise of the men setting up their nets but said, "So what? I have legs. I can run away soon!" He went on eating and listening to the people talking. But he said again, "So what? I have legs. I can run away soon!" He went on eating and thinking he would run away before long. Soon, however, the noise became greater, and the antelope was surrounded by the hunting nets. The antelope said, "Now I will run away. I'm off!" He leapt—straight into the net, and he was caught.[43]

A Rose Leaf

Although the setting is Babylon, this tale comes from Denmark.

Silence prevailed in the High Council of Babylon. The elders of the city were considering a great problem; they had received a letter stating, "Abdul Kader asks Babylon to show him hospitality."

Abdul Kader was the wisest among wise men. Now he stood before them and asked the city to let him stay—in Babylon, where hundreds of thousands already crowded the streets. If they let him in, who might follow? Tens, hundreds, perhaps thousands? However, this honorable gentleman could not be rejected. Suddenly the doors were opened, and Soleiman the Elder entered the room. He was also a wise man. When he saw the letter, he remained standing in the middle of the hall for a long time, then a light came into his eyes. He seized a golden cup and told the council, "Follow me."

They all followed him to the fountain near the gate of the city. Soleiman filled the cup with water, and when it was unable to hold another drop, he lifted it toward Abdul Kader as if to say, "Behold! Babylon is like this cup, which cannot hold another drop of water; the city has no room for another."

But Abdul Kader smiled and reached for a rose leaf upon the ground. Cautiously he placed it on the surface of the water in the cup, and not a drop overflowed. Silently, they all returned to the council hall. Abdul Kader had solved the problem.

Wise individuals are like the rose leaf on the water. The leaf floats on the surface without exerting any pressure; those with wisdom will be no source of trouble to a community, but will give it beauty.[44]

The Kite and the Pigeons

This fable has been attributed to Aesop.

A kite (a small hawk) flew around a dovecote for many days without being able to catch one dove for his dinner. So, he came to the doves in his kindest way and tried to show them how much better they would find themselves if they had a firm king. He explained how his protection would keep them safe from the attacks of the large hawks.

The doves foolishly believed him and gave him entrance to their home as their king. They found, however, that he also thought it was one of his kingly rights to eat one of them every day, and they were sorry for their stupidity.[45]

The Folly of Avarice

Found in the Middle East as well, this version of the story comes from China.

A rich man had hoarded a fine collection of jewels of which he was extremely proud. One day he invited a friend to see them, and this man enjoyed their glitter and glowing colors.

When he left, the friend said, "Thank you for the jewels."

"What?" cried the rich man. "I haven't given them to you! Why do you thank me?"

"Well," answered the friend, "I have had at least as much pleasure from seeing them as you have. The only difference between us, that I can see, is that you have the trouble of guarding them."[46]

The Peddler of Swaffham

This tale about a believer in dreams goes back at least to the eighteenth century in England.

In former times in Swaffham within Norfolk, a certain peddler dreamed that if he went to London Bridge and stood there, he would hear joyful news. At first he ignored this, but as the dreams continued and increased in intensity, he decided to give it a try.

He went to London and for two or three days stood on the bridge looking around him, but he heard nothing that could give him comfort. A shopkeeper noticed him lingering and wanted to know what his business was. The peddler told him of his dream.

The shopkeeper laughed heartily and asked why he was such a fool as to take a journey for such a silly reason. "I'll tell you, country fellow; last night I dreamed I was at Swaffham, in Norfolk, a place completely unknown to me. There, behind a peddler's house in a certain orchard and under a great oak tree, I dreamt that if I digged I would find a vast treasure. Now, do you think," he asked, "that I am such a fool to take such a long journey just because of a silly dream? No, I am wiser than that."

The peddler returned home, dug in his orchard, and found an enormous treasure.[47]

The Trees and the Woodsman

This fable has been attributed to Aesop.

One day a woodsman entered the forest and started searching. The trees asked what it was he wanted. He answered that he wanted a piece of wood. The trees were reluctant to give him such, but they finally granted him a branch, thinking he would take it and go away. But the woodsman used the branch to make a handle for his axe and then started chopping down the forest. The oak is said to have whispered to the beech tree, "It is our own fault. We ourselves gave him the tool to destroy us."[48]

Freedom and Responsibility

Freedom is paired with inevitable limits and responsibility in this tale from Greek mythology.

Daedalus and his son, Icarus, were imprisoned upon an island. They longed to be free, and Daedalus had a plan. Slowly, father and son collected the feathers that fell from the birds. After many months, they had enough. Daedalus fashioned thin wooden strips into the shape of wings. Then he made a wide expanse of feathers and secured them in place with softened wax. After the wax hardened, the wings could be strapped onto their bodies, and away from the island they would fly.

The day came for their escape.

"Be careful!" Daedalus warned his son. "The wings are held together by wax. Fly straight and even—don't get too high, where the sunshine is hot."

They set out across the sea. The wings were marvelous. Daedalus and Icarus soared above the waves and exulted in their freedom. "I'm free," Icarus whispered to himself. "I'm free!" He experimented with his wings—up, down. He saw a seabird and flapped his arms to outdistance it. Higher and higher he flew. "I'm free!" he exulted.

Alas! Icarus flew so high the sunshine grew hot and the wax began to soften. Still, the boy stroked higher, ignoring his father's frantic pleas to come down.

Finally, the weakened wings could no longer bear his weight; the feathers loosened and fell. But they drifted slower than Icarus, who plunged into the sea and was lost.[49]

Thirty-Two Teeth

This story comes from a Turkish fable.

Two men argued, and the younger finally said, "Before long, I'll knock your thirty-two teeth from your head!"

The older man returned quickly to his home in astonishment and said to his wife, "Quickly, wife, light a candle and count how many teeth I have."

She counted the teeth and said, "Thirty-two."

The older man returned to the young man and said, "How did you learn the number of my teeth? And who told you?"

"Sir," replied the younger, "I learned the number of your teeth from the number of my own."[50]

Anansi the Blind Fisherman

This tale comes from West Africa, but the stories of Anansi the trickster are common in many parts of Africa and have migrated to America as well. This particular story has a poignant edge as it shows the frustrations of aging and disablement as well as the frustrations of caregivers.

Anansi in his old age became a fisherman, but soon after that his sight failed and he was blind. He continued fishing with the help of two men. These men were very kind and helped him in every possible way. They led him to the canoe each day and told him where to spread his net and when it was full. When they returned to land they told him just where and when to step out, so he never got wet.

After a while, instead of being grateful to the men, Anansi behaved very badly. When they told him where to spread his net, he would reply sharply, "I know. I was just about to put it there." When they were telling him how to get out of the boat, he would say, "Oh, I know perfectly well we are at the beach. I was just getting ready to step out."

He got ruder and ruder until the men decided to teach him a lesson. One day, when the canoe was full of fish, they turned to paddle home. When they had gone a little way, they stopped. "Here we are at the beach."

He promptly told them they were very foolish to tell him a thing he knew so well. He made many rude and insulting remarks, then jumped out, expecting to land on the beach. Instead he found himself sinking in deep water, where, because he couldn't see which way it was to shore, he swam in circles for a long time.[51]

The Golden Purse and the Seeing Eyes

The cultural source of this story is unknown.

There was a poor woodcutter who had two sons. When he died he left them only a small hut on the edge of the forest. They had very little to eat or live on. Even so, the younger son always left half of his supper in his blue porridge bowl and placed it on the doorstep for the elves.

The older brother ate every bite of his own food. "That's what smart people do," he said. "Someday I shall be rich."

One day the younger son went into the forest to cut wood. He carried an apple and a piece of bread in his pocket for lunch. While he was eating his bread, he remembered there was a fairy ring nearby. "Oh," he exclaimed, "I will take my apple to the fairy ring and drop it there. It will make a fine feast for the Little People when they come to dance tonight."

Right after he dropped the apple into the fairy ring, a tiny man popped out of a fern. "Friend," he said, "the Little People thank you for your many gifts. One doesn't pay back love, but the fairies wish to give you a gift of their own love, and so they have sent the best they have. It is called the Seeing Eyes. It is an invisible gift, but it is worth more than wealth."

So the younger son thanked the elf and hurried home. All along the way he saw new wonders in the trees and flowers. It seemed as though he understood the song of the birds and the singing of the brooks of water he passed.

When he told his brother what had happened, his brother laughed at him. "Your eyes look to me just like they always did! Why didn't you ask for something worthwhile? You should have asked for a purse of gold!"

That night the older brother also put his bowl on the doorstep because he wanted to ask the Little People for a gift. After six nights, he went into the woods and dropped an apple into the fairy ring.

The tiny man popped out from the ferns. "Why did you drop your apple into our fairy ring?"

"It is my seventh gift to the Little People," said the older son. "In return for my gifts I ask for a purse of gold that will never be empty."

"Well," replied the elf, "such a purse is not worth very much in the opinion of the fairies. There are too many important things that money cannot buy. Happiness does not go with the purse, unless you already know how to be happy."

"I want it anyway," insisted the older brother.

So the tiny man gave the brother the purse, and hardly saying thank you, the elder brother grabbed it and started for the city. He couldn't wait to see what he could buy, and he bought everything he could when he got there.

Still, the elder brother found the elf had spoken the truth. There were many things his money wouldn't buy. He had no love, because it couldn't be bought. He had no peace, because he was always thinking about what he owned and how to protect it. He had no true friends, only people who hung on to him for the sake of his gold. The elder brother was very unhappy. He thought of nobody except himself from morning to evening, and he did no good for anyone.

As for the younger son, he lived on in the little hut on the edge of the forest. He shared what he could, and even when he had nothing to share, everyone loved him. In time he married, and he and his wife loved each other very much. Wherever the younger son went, he carried the magic of the fairies' gift. Every day he was newly surprised by the beauty of flowers and fields, trees and clouds. He lived happily ever after.[52]

Offering a White Pig to the Emperor

In this story about an attempted gift from Korea to China, something goes awry.

Pigs in Korea were usually black, but one day a white one was born. When the king heard of this rare animal, he thought it would make a gift special enough to send to the Chinese emperor. He purchased the pig, then called his ambassadors together and sent them to China with the pig.

When the travelers reached Peking, they saw an amazing sight. Pigs. White pigs. White pigs everywhere! The ambassadors realized it would be ridiculous to carry out their mission. So they carried the pig back to Korea.[53]

The Fox and the Icicle

"Don't judge by appearances" is the moral in this Turkish fable.

A hungry fox searched for food one winter day and came across a long icicle that was shaped very much like a bone. He began to chew on it eagerly. But after a time he exclaimed, "A plague on it! There is a sound of a bone in my ears, and the feel of a bone between my teeth, but not a scrap of it in my stomach!"[54]

The Lion and the Statue

This story has been identified as a Turkish fable, but some sources attribute a version to Aesop. The Turkish version concludes that artists base their creations on ideas rather than realities of life. The Aesop variation concludes that "we can easily represent things as we want them to be."

A man and a lion, traveling together as friends, passed the time by boasting of their own merits. Along the road they came to a great monument where carved in marble was a man trampling a lion under his feet.

The man called the lion's attention to the sculpture. "I need not say anything more," he remarked. "This is enough to prove that humans surpass the lion in strength and vigor."

"The chisel was in the hands of a man," replied the lion, "so of course he represented whatever he liked. If a lion had carved the stone, you would see a different view of our strength."[55]

Where Truth Lives

This brief tale is by Ernest Thompson Seton of the United States.

It's my opinion," said the frog as he sat in the well, "that the size of the ocean is greatly overrated."[56]

The Lion and the Elephant

This fable has been attributed to Aesop.

One day the lion complained sadly that a beast with such claws, teeth, and strength as he possessed should still be made so afraid by the crowing of a cock. "Can life be worth having when such a lowly creature has the power to rob it of its pleasure?"

Just then a huge elephant came along, flapping his ears back and forth with alarm.

"What troubles you so much?" asked the lion. "How can anything have the power to harm a beast of your great size and strength?"

"Don't you see this little buzzing gnat?" answered the elephant. "If he stings the inside of my ear, I'm sure I shall go crazy with pain."

So the lion took heart again, realizing that every created thing has problems, and he decided not to let troubles blind him to what was pleasant in life.[57]

The Raindrop

This story from Hindu sources looks at the potential of even the smallest things.

A raindrop fell from a dark spring cloud, and when it saw the wide expanse of the ocean it felt ashamed. "At best," it said, "I am only a drop of rain, the tiniest measure of moisture. Compared with the ocean I am nothing at all!"

But just at the moment when the little raindrop judged itself so humbly, an oyster swallowed the raindrop. In time, the oyster shaped the drop of rain into a royal pearl.[58]

The Blind Men and the Elephant

The following story is adapted from a poem by John Godfrey Saxe, which he retold from a Hindu fable.

Once upon a time there were six men who had studied much about the world and constantly sought to learn more. One day they decided to learn more about the creature known as the elephant. None had seen such a creature, for they were all blind. But by hand and touch, they believed it possible to determine the nature of the elephant.

The first man approached the elephant and happened to fall against his broad and sturdy side. "Aha," he exclaimed, "the elephant is very like a wall."

The second came to the ivory tusk and felt how round and smooth and sharp it was. "It is clear," he said, "that the elephant is like a spear."

The third man disagreed, for he came upon the creature from the front and took the squirming trunk in his hands. He declared, "The elephant is very like a snake!"

With an eager hand, the fourth blind man rushed forward and felt against the elephant's leg. "It is plain," he announced, "that this marvelous beast is like a tree."

The fifth gentleman stepped forward to take his turn and chanced to grasp the ear. He told the rest, "It is clear that even the blindest man can know that this marvel of an elephant is very like a fan."

The sixth and final blind man approached the elephant from behind and reached a groping hand to seize the swinging tail. "I have it now," he declared. "The elephant is quite like a rope."

The six blind men of Indostan argued long and loud. Each had groped and touched and felt. "I am right," each man declared. None would budge, and they long disputed the nature of the elephant. Not one would accept that each was partly right, and all were wrong.[59]

The Spectacles

This story has been adapted from an English fable.

The King of Fairies decided to give humans a gift and sent his right-hand fairy to deliver it. The messenger came to the world and called for the humans to come. "It is true," she said, "that you are all a bit shortsighted, but to help that inconvenience, the king has sent you a gift."

She opened an enormous bundle, and a great number of spectacles tumbled out. The people seized them with great eagerness. Soon, all the humans sported their own pair of fairy spectacles.

However, the people didn't always see the same things out of the spectacles, for one pair was purple, another blue, one was white, and another black; some of the glasses were red, some green, and some yellow. There were all colors and every shade of color.

The odd thing was that each person was delighted with his or her own pair and believed it was the very best. How strange it is that all humans differ in their opinions and how strongly they are attached to their own![60]

A Boar Challenges an Ass

Aesop's humor is shown in this tale.

An argument began between a boar and an ass, and they challenged each other to a fight. The boar prided himself on his tusks, and when he compared his head with the ass's, he looked forward to winning the battle easily.

The time for the fight arrived.

The two came toward each other. The boar rushed upon the ass, who suddenly turned around and let his hooves fly with all their might right in the jaws of the boar.

The boar staggered back. "Well," he said with aching face, "who could have expected an attack from that end?"[61]

Fire and Water

Competition between fire and water over relative strength ends with the conclusion that if both are of sufficient power for their respective responsibilities, they are equal. The story comes from the Batanga tribe of East Africa.

Fire and Water were neighbors. Fire said to Water, "I am stronger than you. Without me, you could not cook food; without me, people could never survive."

"No," said Water. "I have greater power. Without me, what would people drink?"

These two kept on arguing about their power. Wherever they met, they argued in the same way. Their neighbors became tired of their discussions and held a council to settle the matter.

They announced their decision: "You each have sufficient power." Thus it was settled. Neither one was greater than the other. They were of equal power and must end their argument.[62]

The Gnat and the Bull

This fable has been attributed to Aesop, with a variant by Phaedrus.

A strong bull tried to escape the heat of the weather by wading in a cool, swift-running stream. He had not been there long when a gnat landed upon one of his horns. "My dear fellow," said the gnat, with as great a buzz as he could manage, "please excuse me. If I am too heavy, just say so, and I will go and rest upon the poplar tree that grows by the edge of the stream."

"Stay or go, it makes no difference to me," answered the bull. "If it hadn't been for your buzz I wouldn't have even known you were there."[63]

The Story of Long-Legs

In this tale from Mexico, Long-Legs is a mosquito. Some of the story's progression is reminiscent of "The Marriage of a Cat" (Part 6).

Long-Legs went to sleep one day in the leaves of the tree, and when the frost came, his foot was broken. "Frost, frost, how strong you are, you who have broken my foot!" he wailed. Then the frost said, "But stronger is the sun, because he heats me."

Long-Legs went to the sun. "Sun, how strong you are, sun that heats frost, frost that broke my foot!"

"But stronger is the cloud, because it covers me," replied the sun.

So Long-Legs went to the clouds and spoke. "Cloud, how strong you are, cloud that covers sun, sun that heats frost, frost that broke my foot!"

"But stronger is the wind, because it blows me away," replied the cloud.

Long-Legs next addressed the wind: "Wind, how strong you are, wind that blows away cloud, cloud that covers sun, sun that heats frost, frost that broke my foot!"

"But stronger is the wall, because it resists me," replied the wind.

And so Long-Legs spoke to the wall: "Wall, how strong you are, wall that resists wind, wind that blows away cloud, cloud that covers sun, sun that heats frost, frost that broke my foot!"

"But stronger is the mouse because he chews holes in me," replied the wall.

Now the little mosquito went to find the mouse. "Mouse, how strong you are, mouse that chews holes in wall, wall that resists wind, wind that blows away cloud, cloud that covers sun, sun that heats frost, frost that broke my foot!"

"But stronger is the cat, because he eats me," said the mouse.

To the cat, Long-Legs said: "Cat, how strong you are, cat that eats mouse, mouse that chews holes in wall, wall that resists wind, wind that blows away cloud, cloud that covers sun, sun that heats frost, frost that broke my foot!"

"But stronger is the stick, because it frightens me," replied the cat.

Next it was the stick's turn to hear Long-Legs' words: "Stick, how strong you are, stick that frightens cat, cat that eats mouse, mouse that chews holes in wall, wall that resists wind, wind that blows away cloud, cloud that covers sun, sun that heats frost, frost that broke my foot!"

"But stronger is the fire, because it burns me," replied the stick.

Long-Legs found the fire and said to it, "Fire, how strong you are, fire that burns stick, stick that frightens cat, cat that eats mouse, mouse that chews holes in wall, wall that resists wind, wind that blows away cloud, cloud that covers sun, sun that heats frost, frost that broke my foot!"

Fire responded, "But stronger is the water, because it puts me out."

So Long-Legs told the water, "Water, how strong you are, water that puts out fire, fire that burns stick, stick that frightens cat, cat that eats mouse, mouse that chews holes in wall, wall that resists wind, wind that blows away cloud, cloud that covers sun, sun that heats frost, frost that broke my foot!"

"But stronger is the cow who drinks me," the water replied.

Long-Legs spoke to the cow: "Cow, how strong you are, cow who drinks water, water that puts out fire, fire that burns stick, stick that frightens cat, cat that eats mouse, mouse that chews holes in wall, wall that resists wind, wind that blows away cloud, cloud that covers sun, sun that heats frost, frost that broke my foot!"

"But stronger is the knife, because it kills me," said the cow. Long-Legs looked about and came upon a knife lying in the field.

"Knife, how strong you are, knife that kills cow, cow that drinks water, water that puts out fire, fire that burns stick, stick that frightens cat, cat that eats mouse, mouse that chews holes in wall, wall that resists wind, wind that blows away cloud, cloud that covers sun, sun that heats frost, frost that broke my foot!"

"But stronger is the blacksmith," said the knife, "because he makes me."

The tired mosquito searched the area and found a blacksmith toiling in his smithy. "Blacksmith," he said, "how strong you are, blacksmith who makes knife, knife that kills cow, cow that drinks water, water that puts out fire, fire that burns stick, stick that frightens cat, cat that eats mouse, mouse that chews holes in wall, wall that resists wind, wind that blows away cloud, cloud that covers sun, sun that heats frost, frost that broke my foot!"

"But stronger is Death, because it kills me," answered the blacksmith.

Long-Legs went to Death and said, "Death, how strong you are, death that kills blacksmith, blacksmith who makes knife, knife that kills cow, cow that drinks water, water that puts out fire, fire that burns stick, stick that frightens cat, cat that eats mouse, mouse that chews holes in wall, wall that resists wind, wind that blows away cloud, cloud that covers sun, sun that heats frost, frost that broke my foot!"

"But stronger is God, who rules over even me," admitted Death.

Long-Legs looked up and all about and cried out, "God, how strong you are, God who rules over Death, death that kills blacksmith, blacksmith who makes knife, knife that kills cow, cow that drinks water, water that puts out fire, fire that burns stick, stick that frightens cat, cat that eats mouse, mouse that chews holes in wall, wall that resists wind, wind that blows away cloud, cloud that covers sun, sun that heats frost, frost that broke my foot! God, how strong you are!"[64]

The Kingfisher and the Sparrow

This is an English fable.

A kingfisher was perched in a shady spot on the bank of a river when she was surprised by the arrival of a sparrow, who had flown out from town to visit her. After the first greetings, the sparrow asked, "How is it possible that a bird so finely feathered should spend all her days in such an obscure location? The golden plumage of your breast, the shining azure of your wings were not given to you for hiding, but to attract the admiration of all who behold you. Why don't you travel and see the world? Why don't you become famous and admired?"

"You are very kind," replied the kingfisher. "You flatter me to assume that I only need to be known to be admired. But even in this lonesome valley, I have sometimes heard of beauty that has been neglected, and of true worth that has been despised. I have learned, besides, not to base my happiness on what others think of me, but on the approval of my own conscience. It may be a joy to a sparrow to indulge his curiosity and display his eloquence. But I am a kingfisher. These woods and streams are my delight, and I am perfectly content with my situation."[65]

The Man and the Nose of His Camel

This story comes from the Arab Middle East.

One cold night as a man sat in his tent, his camel thrust aside the flap of the tent and looked inside. "I pray thee, master," he said, "let me put my nose inside the tent, because it is quite cold outside."

"Well, all right," said the man, "if it is only your nose, for it is not a very large tent and there is not very much room."

So the camel edged his nose inside the tent.

"Perhaps," said the camel, "I could also warm my head?"

"Hmmm," said the man, "perhaps you could."

Before long, the man felt a nudge against his side. "I'm sure you won't mind," said the camel, "if I warm my neck inside the tent as well."

"If you must," grumbled the man. "But there is not much room in here."

Another nudge. "It is very difficult standing outside of the tent," said the camel. "Can't I put my forelegs inside?"

The man sighed. "All right," he said, and moved to make more room. But it wasn't long before he felt another sharp nudge, and the camel stood completely inside the tent.

The tent was very small, and there wasn't sufficient room for both the man and the camel. "I think," said the camel, "that there is not enough room for both of us here. It will be best for you to stand outside, because you are the smallest. Then there will be plenty of room for me." With those words, the camel pushed the man a bit more until he was outside of the tent.

It is a wise rule to resist the beginnings of evil.[66]

Premature

In this story from Liberia, a father tells his son a proverb to teach him about premature words.

A man took his son in a canoe to teach him to fish. The fishing was poor, but as they were about to return to the beach, the boy felt a bite. "I've got a big one!" cried the boy, and they saw the head of a large fish. "He's mine, he's all mine!" the boy shouted.

Just then, the fish jerked and the hook broke. "Oh!" the boy wailed. "I'm so angry; I thought I had him for sure!"

The father told him, "You should never curse the crocodile, my son, until you have crossed the river."[67]

The Close Alliance

This story from India tells us that it's a bad idea to ally yourself too closely with a coward.

A jackal was servant to a tiger. The reward of his service was the generous helping of bones he received after the tiger had finished his meals.

One day the tiger approached a man who was caring for a herd of bulls. "I will have one of those for my meal," the tiger announced, and the man was so frightened by the fearsome animal that he could only watch while the tiger dragged a bull away. Then he faced the difficult task of going home and telling the woman who employed him what had happened.

"Well!" was her reply. "We'll just see about this." She dressed herself in the clothing of a hunter and the next morning jumped upon a pony and went to where the man was herding the bulls. Out of the corner of her eye she saw the striped beast approaching. "I hope," she announced loudly, "that I may find a tiger in this place. I haven't tasted tiger's meat since yesterday, when I had three for breakfast."

When he heard this, the tiger turned tail and ran away into the forest, nearly running down the jackal in his hurry. "Run," he gasped. "A great hunter is looking for tiger meat."

"Don't fear the hunter," the jackal said. "Didn't you notice the long hair down the back? That hunter is a woman; surely she can't overcome such a powerful creature as yourself."

The cowardly tiger was afraid to return, and the jackal began to fear he would miss out on the bones he had expected for his dinner. "There's nothing to fear," he insisted to the tiger again and again.

"But," objected the tiger, "she might have bribed you to say that. Perhaps you plan to betray me into her hands."

"We'll go together," promised the gallant jackal.

"What if that is your plan?" worried the tiger. "You'll lead me to her and then run away."

"If that is your fear," said the jackal, who didn't want to lose his bones, "let us tie our tails together. Then I can't run away from you."

On this condition, the tiger agreed to return to the herd of bulls. He and the jackal tied their tails together tightly and marched forward. The tiger was quaking, the jackal cheerful.

Now, the woman and her herdsman had remained in the field laughing over the trick she had played on the tiger. The tiger and the jackal came in sight.

"We are lost!" the man cried in terror. "The bulls shall be eaten, and then we shall provide their dessert."

"Nothing of the kind," answered the woman. "Hush and let me think without your babbling." In a moment she smiled, then turned and faced the pair of animals coming toward them. "How nice of you, Mr. Jackal," she called out politely. "Thank you for bringing me such a nice fat tiger! I won't be a moment finishing my share of him, and then you can have the bones."

At these words the tiger became wild with fright and ran away, dragging the jackal behind him, who bumped and crashed against the rocky ground. "Stop, stop," moaned the jackal. But the noise behind him frightened the cowardly tiger all the more, and he dashed helter-skelter until he was so tired he was nearly dead and the jackal was almost dead from his bumps and bruises.

It's a bad idea to tie your tail to that of a coward.[68]

The Sillies

People often worry over silly things—as did the family in this story adapted from an English tale.

Once upon a time there was a farmer and his wife who had one daughter. She was being courted by a young man who came every evening to visit her and eat supper at the farmhouse.

One evening the daughter went down to the cellar to get a pitcher of cider, and she happened to look up at the ceiling while she was pouring the cider. In the ceiling beam, she saw an axe stuck into the wood. It must have been there for a very long time, but somehow or other she had never before noticed it. She began to think that it was very dangerous to have that axe there. She said to herself, "Suppose the gentleman and I get married, and we have a son, and he grows up to be a man and comes down into the cellar to draw the cider as I am doing now. And what if the axe fell down on his head and killed him! What a dreadful thing that would be!"

At this the daughter put down her candle and the jug and sat down to begin crying.

Upstairs, it was taking so long for the daughter to get the cider that her mother went down to find out what was happening. She found her daughter sitting on the ground crying while the cider ran onto the cellar floor from the barrel.

"What is the matter?" asked the mother.

"Oh, Mother!" cried the daughter. "Just look at that horrid axe! Suppose the gentleman and I were to marry and we had a son who grew up and came down here to get cider, and what if the axe fell down on his head and killed him? Wouldn't that be terrible?"

"Oh dear, oh dear!" the mother cried. "What a dreadful thing that would be!" She sat down before her daughter and began to sob.

Upstairs, the father began to wonder what was taking his wife so long, so he also went down into the cellar to find her. There he found his wife and his daughter sitting on the floor weeping, with the cider still running out of the barrel.

"Whatever is the matter?" he exclaimed.

"Why, don't you see?" said the mother. "Look at that horrid axe. Just suppose if our daughter and her sweetheart were to be married, and were to have a son, and he were to grow up and then came down into the cellar to get the cider, and the axe were to fall on his head and kill him. Would that be a dreadful thing to happen?"

"Oh dear, oh dear!" cried the father. "So it would, just terrible, terrible." Then he sat down on the floor beside his wife and daughter. They wept and wailed together.

Upstairs, the gentleman was sitting alone and couldn't understand what was taking so long, so he finally decided to go into the cellar and discover the problem. He found the three of them wailing side by side and the cider running all over the floor.

The first thing the gentleman did was turn the tap to stop the cider from pouring out of the barrel. Then he asked, "Whatever are you three doing, sitting there crying and letting the cider run everywhere?"

"Oh, oooooooh!" said the father. "Look at that horrid axe! Suppose you and our daughter were married, and were to have a son, and he were to grow up and then came down into the cellar to draw the cider, and the axe fell on his head and killed him!" He could barely get the words out of his mouth as he sobbed over the tragedy. And all three of them moaned and wept.

But the gentleman burst out laughing. He reached up, pulled out the axe, and said, "I've traveled many miles and I've seen many things, but I've never met three such big sillies as the three of you!"

With that he left and may never have returned to such a silly household.[69]

A Bird in the Hand

This fable is of United States origin.

A family was picnicking in the woods, and the younger of their two sons was somehow able to capture a bird. He held it carefully between his fingers and ran to show his older brother. On the way, he saw a large number of birds in the surrounding bushes. Having had success in his first attempt, the boy started forward, intent on gaining a second bird, and perhaps a third.

"I don't think that's a good idea," advised his brother with a laugh. "If you try to get more, you might lose the one you have. Besides, you know what people say."

"What's that?" the younger child asked.

"A bird in the hand is worth two in the bush."

At this point, the mother of the boys joined the conversation.

"I've heard that too," she said, while she gently opened her son's fingers to let the first bird go free. "But that all depends upon where you want your birds to be."[70]

Watching a Stump

This story from Japan, with cultural influences from China, gave rise to the proverb "Like watching a stump to catch a rabbit."

One day a rabbit was running at full speed through the meadow when he struck his head against a stump and killed himself. Not long after, a farmer found the dead animal and rejoiced at his good fortune. From that time forward, the farmer spent all his time in watching the stump, expecting to get another rabbit.[71]

Opossum Fools Puma

This story from Mexico tells us about the foolishness both of not checking things for yourself and of believing someone who isn't trustworthy.

Puma and Opossum came to a rock. Opossum said to Puma, "See! This rock is moving and cutting through the clouds! Who knows what damage will be done. Hold onto it until I get back."

Puma saw the clouds passing over the top of the rock and believed that Opossum had told the truth, which wasn't very smart, because Opossum had lied to him about many other things.

Puma closed his eyes and held onto the rock while Opossum ran away. He waited a long time for Opossum to return but finally opened his eyes and saw that the rock was not moving at all; the clouds were only passing over it.[72]

Endnotes

1
Community

1. Ruskin, Edward A., *Mongo Proverbs and Fables* (Bongandanga: Congo Balolo Mission Press, 1921), 69.
2. Cooper, Frederic Taber, *An Argosy of Fables* (New York: Frederick A. Stokes, 1921), 149.
3. Adapted from the Ariadne and Theseus myth: Gayley, Charles Mills, *The Classic Myths in English Literature and in Art* (Boston: Ginn, 1911), 252–253.
4. This fable by Aesop was also told by Tolstoy. Because of cowardice and indifference the bat was not accepted in either the animal or the bird community. He had chosen neutrality not in order to seek peace, but to save himself. An African variant has a different conclusion, for after ten years of prison, the bat argues his case and the judge decides that because he has the characteristics of both birds and animals, he should be allowed to proclaim his loyalties as he chooses. Phaedrus version: Cooper, Frederic Taber, *An Argosy of Fables* (New York: Frederick A. Stokes, 1921), 151. Aesop variant: Eliot, Charles W., ed., *The Harvard Classics: Folk-Lore and Fable*, Volume 17 (New York: P. F. Collier & Son, 1909), 20. African variant found in Basden, G. T., *Among the Ibos of Nigeria* (Philadelphia: J. B. Lippincott, 1921), 281–282. Native American variant: Curtin, Jeremiah, *Myths of the Modocs* (Boston: Little, Brown, 1912), 213.
5. Knatchbull, Wyndham, trans., *Kalila and Dimna* or *The Fables of Bidpai* (Oxford: W. Baxter, for J. Parker and Messrs. Longman, Hurst, Rees, Orme, and Brown, 1819), 193–196. Variant: Cooper, Frederic Taber, *An Argosy of Fables* (New York: Frederick A. Stokes, 1921), 181–182.
6. This story could be told in completion or could end with the gratitude of the other birds, depending upon which message is desired. Swainson, Charles, *The Folk Lore of British Birds* (London: Elliot Stock, 1886), 124.
7. *Fables of Aesop* (New York: A. L. Burt, 1890), 111–112.
8. *Fables of Aesop* (New York: A. L. Burt, 1890), 64.
9. Basden, G. T., *Among the Ibos of Nigeria* (Philadelphia: J. B. Lippincott, 1921), 282–283.
10. Thorpe, Benjamin, *Yule Tide Stories* (London and New York: George Bell & Sons, 1892), 355–359.
11. Hartland, Edwin Sydney, *English Folk and Fairy Tales* (London: W. Scott, 1890), page number unnoted. Hartland cites Keightley, T., *The Fairy Mythology*, p. 293, quoting Aubrey's *Natural History of Surrey*.
12. This is a variation of Breton and Norman legends of the wren. Many cultures tell stories of heroes who have sacrificed to bring fire, such as the Greek story of Prometheus. Prometheus stole fire from Olympus to save human beings. As punishment he was bound to a rock to have his liver eternally eaten by a bird of prey. Swainson, Charles, *The Folk Lore of British Birds* (London: Elliot Stock, 1886), 42.
13. Judd, Mary Catherine, *Wigwam Stories* (Boston: Athenaeum Press, 1905), 130–132. Variant: Tanner, Dorothy, *Legends from the Red Man's Forest* (Chicago: A. Flanagan, 1895), 123–125.
14. Eliot, Charles W., ed., *The Harvard Classics: Folk-Lore and Fable*, Volume 17 (New York: P. F. Collier & Son, 1909), 22.
15. *Fables of Aesop* (New York: A. L. Burt, 1890), 76–78.
16. *Fables of Aesop* (New York: A. L. Burt, 1890), 185.
17. Redesdale, Lord, *Tales of Old Japan* (London: MacMillan, 1908), 191–192.
18. Tolstoi, Lyof N., *The Long Exile* (New York: Charles Scribner's Sons, 1907), 142–143; Dadmun, Frances M., *Living Together* (Boston: Beacon Press, 1915), 119–122.
19. Ruskin, Edward A., *Mongo Proverbs and Fables* (Bongandanga: Congo Balolo Mission Press, 1921), 63–64.
20. Hanauer, James Edward, *Folk-Lore of the Holy Land* (London: Duckworth, 1907), 161–162.
21. Curry, Charles Madison, and Erle Elsworth Clippinger, *Children's Literature* (New York: Rand McNally, 1921), 288.
22. Cooper, Frederic Taber, *An Argosy of Fables* (New York: Frederick A. Stokes, 1921), 293.
23. Swainson, Charles, *The Folk Lore of British Birds* (London: Elliot Stock, 1886), 108.
24. Swainson, Charles, *The Folk Lore of British Birds* (London: Elliot Stock, 1886), 17.
25. Barker, W. H., and Cecilia Sinclair, *West African Folk-Tales* (London: George G. Harrap, 1917), 167–169.
26. There is a variant found in a story from the Middle East, where the condemned man begged for three days to take care of family arrangements. A stranger offered himself in the man's place but was saved by the last-minute return of the condemned man. When asked why he returned, he said it was to prove that virtue and truth had not died out. Lowe, Samuel E., and Viola E. Jacobson, *Fifty Famous Stories* (Racine,

Wisc.: Whitman Publishing, 1920), pages unnumbered. Middle East variant: Hanauer, James Edward, *Folk-Lore of the Holy Land* (London: Duckworth, 1907), 171–176.

27. This story is reminiscent of the story of Nathan, who confronted David over his sins concerning Bathsheba and Uriah in the Bible. *The Poetical Works of John Godfrey Saxe* (Boston and New York: Houghton, Mifflin, 1887), 158. Variant: Hanauer, James Edward, *Folk-Lore of the Holy Land* (London: Duckworth, 1907), 170–171.
28. Dennys, N. B., *The Folk-Lore of China* (London: Trachner, 1876), 147.
29. *Fables of Aesop* (New York: A. L. Burt, 1890), 28.
30. Cooper, Frederic Taber, *An Argosy of Fables* (New York: Frederick A. Stokes, 1921), 361.
31. Buck, Charles, *Anecdotes* (Boston: Otis, Broaders, 1843), 245.
32. The paralyzing nature of fear was also expressed in *The Fables of Bidpai*. In both cases, the danger was imaginary, conjured by the dishonesty of a trickster. Cooper, Frederic Taber, *An Argosy of Fables* (New York: Frederick A. Stokes, 1921), 131–132; *Fables of Aesop* (New York: A. L. Burt, 1890), 40–41; Tolstoi, Lyof N., *The Works of Lyof N. Tolstoi* (New York: Thomas Y. Crowell, 1899), 161.
33. *Fables of Aesop* (New York: A. L. Burt, 1890), 294–295.
34. Eliot, Charles W., ed., *The Harvard Classics: Folk-Lore and Fable*, Volume 17 (New York: P. F. Collier & Son, 1909), 23–24.
35. Schiefner, F. Anton, and W.R.S. Ralston, trans., *Tibetan Tales* (London: Trubner, 1882), 358–359. Variant: Cooper, Frederic Taber, *An Argosy of Fables* (New York: Frederick A. Stokes, 1921), 224–225.
36. Cooper, Frederic Taber, *An Argosy of Fables* (New York: Frederick A. Stokes, 1921), 381–383.
37. Cooper, Frederic Taber, *An Argosy of Fables* (New York: Frederick A. Stokes, 1921), 304–305.
38. *The Poetical Works of John Godfrey Saxe* (Boston and New York: Houghton, Mifflin, 1887), 108–109.
39. This story is adapted from motifs of the Magyar (Hungary) folktales, where the grieving father is approached by his sons only to have spoon, fork, and knife thrown at them.
40. Buck, Charles, *Anecdotes* (Boston: Otis, Broaders, 1843), 236.
41. Two versions of the story can be found in Skinner, Alanson, and John V. Satterlee, "Menomini Folklore," *Anthropological Papers of the American Museum of Natural History* 13, Part 3 (1915): 412–413.
42. Quinn, Vernon, *Beautiful Mexico* (New York: Frederick A. Stokes, 1924), 34–35, 67–68.
43. Nezahualcoyotl also tried to stop human sacrifice and dedicated a temple to the Unknown God. Quinn, Vernon, *Beautiful Mexico* (New York: Frederick A. Stokes, 1924), 74–77.
44. Schwab, George, "Bulu Folk-Tales," *Journal of American Folk-Lore* 27, No. 105, July–Sept. (1914): 279–280.
45. Teit, James A., "Tahltan Tales," *Journal of American Folk-Lore* 33, No. 124, April–June (1919): 238.
46. Schwab, George, "Bulu Tales," *Journal of American Folk-Lore* 33, No. 125, July–Sept. (1919): 431–432. Variant: Krug, Adolph N., "Bulu Tales from Kamerun, West Africa," *Journal of American Folk-Lore* 25, No. 96, April–June (1912): 118–119.
47. Schwab, George, "Bulu Tales," *Journal of American Folk-Lore* 33, No. 125, July–Sept. (1919): 435.
48. Krug, Adolph N., "Bulu Tales from Kamerun, West Africa," *Journal of American Folk-Lore* 25, No. 96, April–June (1912): 119–120.
49. Davis, Henry C., "Negro Folk-Lore in South Carolina," *Journal of American Folk-Lore* 27, No. 105, July–Sept. (1914): 243.
50. Spence, Lewis, *Hero Tales and Legends of the Rhine* (New York: Farrar & Rinehart, 1915), 7–12.
51. *Fables of Aesop* (New York: A. L. Burt, 1890), 300–301.
52. Cooper, Frederic Taber, *An Argosy of Fables* (New York: Frederick A. Stokes, 1921), 299–302. See also *Fables of Aesop* (New York: A. L Burt, 1890), 237–238.
53. Dennett, R. E., *Notes on the Folklore of the Fjort* (London: David Nutt, 1898), 106–107.
54. This is the shortened end of a long narrative that tells of the brave and futile struggle of the Cubans against the cruel invaders. The notation about the death of the two children comes from another story about the initial invasion. These stories have been passed down for many generations. Stoddard, Florence Jackson, *As Old as the Moon* (New York: Doubleday, Page, 1909), 119–121.
55. Dixon, Roland, "Some Coyote Stories from the Maidu Indians," *Journal of American Folk-Lore* 13, No. 51, Oct.–Dec. (1900): 268–269.

2
Love & Family

1. The mother moon's Pueblo name was P'ah-hlee-oh. The moon maiden was the Tee-wahn Eve and was honored in almost every detail of the Pueblo ceremonies. It was believed that she was created by the Trues

to be the wife of the sun, T-hoor-i-deh, who was to be the father of all things. From them (sun and moon) began the world and all that is in it. Lummis, Charles F., *The Man Who Married the Moon (and Other Pueblo Indian Folk-Stories)* (New York: Century, 1894), 71–73.

2. Jacobs, Joseph, *English Fairy Tales* (New York: G. P. Putnam's Sons, 1902), 51–56. See also Addy, Sidney A., *Household Tales* (London: David Nutt, 1895); Cox, Marian R., *Cinderella* (London: Folk-Lore Society, 1892).
3. Barker, W. H., and Cecilia Sinclair, *West African Folk-Tales* (London: George G. Harrap, 1917), 85–86.
4. Batchelor, John, *The Ainu and Their Folklore* (London: Religious Tract Society, 1901), 450–451.
5. Children enjoy this story, especially when the proposal of the king is elaborated upon with great ceremony; then the blunt and bored "no" of the witch becomes amusing. It often also helps, for oral telling, to add the traditional ending, for example, "They went back to the castle and lived happily ever after." This is an original story by Linda M. Ford, inspired by several folk motifs.
6. A similar theme is found in a Czechoslovakian tale, but the focus of that story is less about love and more about the clever justice of the wife. See "Clever Manka," this volume. Petrovitch, Woislav M., *Hero Tales and Legends of the Serbians* (London: George G. Harrap, 1914), 287–291.
7. This can be a very dramatic story to tell when the struggle with the fairy during her transformations is acted out. Similar motifs can be found in varied fairy and folk tales, such as from Rugen, where in trying to escape the heroine turns herself into a lion, tiger, serpent, scorpion, tarantula, and dragon. Another story, of the Shans (India and China), tells how a fairy is captured and married to the prince. At first unhappy, she found her husband's love was "greater than the sun; it was so great that she forgot her sisters and her home on the silver mountain." Story by Linda M. Ford.
8. Boyajian, Zabelle C., *Armenian Legends and Poems* (London: J. M. Dent & Sons; New York: E. P. Dutton, 1916), 137.
9. Hanauer, James Edward, *Folk-Lore of the Holy Land* (London: Duckworth, 1907), 167–168.
10. This adaptation of the story is mostly from the notes of Clifford Ford and may have been told in the mountains of Tennessee during the early part of the century, but its origins were probably European or Russian. A variant of the tale appears in Ukrainian sources and in a fable by Leo Tolstoy. See Tolstoi, Lyof N., *The Works of Lyof N. Tolstoi* (New York: Thomas Y. Crowell, 1899), 158.
11. Curry, Charles Madison, and Erle Elsworth Clippinger, eds., *Children's Literature* (New York:: Rand McNally, 1921), 156–158. Variant: Whitehorn, Alan Leslie, *Wonder Tales of Old Japan* (London & Edinburgh: P. C. & E. C. Jack, 1911), 42–48. See also Davis, F. Hadland, *Myths and Legends, Japan* (Boston: David D. Nickerson, before 1918), 196–198.
12. Matthew, Cornelius, *Indian Fairy Book* (New York: Allen Brothers, 1869), 83–89.
13. This was adapted from a story of the Angami Nagas, a people living at the eastern end of the Himalayas in the area of old Assam, Bengal, and Burma. Hutton, J. H., *The Angami Nagas* (London: Macmillan, 1921), 95–96.
14. Judd, Mary Catherine, *Wigwam Stories* (Boston: Athenaeum Press, 1905), 208–210. Variant: Swainson, Charles, *The Folk Lore of British Birds* (London: Elliot Stock, 1886), 13–14. The robin, unlike many birds, has an almost universally popular reputation in folklore, although as a result, folklore also suggests dire consequences for the individual (sometimes the family) of one who harms a robin or disturbs its nest. Variant: Tanner, Dorothy, *Legends of the Red Man's Forest* (Chicago: A. Flanagan, 1895), 113–114.
15. Liberian version: Bundy, Richard C., "Folk Tales from Liberia," *Journal of American Folk-Lore* 32, No. 125, July–Sept. (1919): 425. Variant: *Fables of Aesop* (New York: A. L. Burt, 1890), 34.
16. Gaster, M., *Rumanian Bird and Beast Stories* (London: Sidgwick & Jackson, 1915), 170–171.
17. Grundtvig, Svend, E. T. Kristensen, and Ingvor Bondesen, *Danish Fairy and Folk Tales*, J. Christian Bay, trans. (New York and London: Harper and Bros., 1899), 81–83.
18. Swainson, Charles, *The Folk Lore of British Birds* (London: Elliot Stock, 1886), 107–108.
19. Filmore, Parker, *The Shoemaker's Apron* (New York: Harcourt, Brace, 1920), 167–176.
20. Wilson, Epiphanius, *Turkish Literature* (New York: P. F. Collier & Son, 1901), 5–6.
21. Wardrop, Marjory, trans., *Georgian Folk Tales* (London: David Nutt, 1894), 171–172.
22. Variations of this story can be found in several cultures, including Ireland and Germany, but those in Europe may have been an importation from the Orient. Filial respect, love, and/or obedience is a favorite theme in the folktales of cultures around the world. It is worth noting, however, that folktales also relate the wickedness of parents toward children and show such parents generally receiving a harsh justice. See also "The Old Man and His Son," this volume. Knowles, J. Hinton, *Folk-Tales of Kashmir* (London: Kegan Paul, Trench, Trubner, 1893), 241–243. A Russian Cossack variant can be found in Bain, R. Nisbet, *Cossack Fairy Tales and Folk-Tales* (New York: A. L. Burt, 1894), 261– 272. See Jacobs, Joseph, *Indian Fairy Tales* (New York and London: G. P. Putnam's Sons, 1892), 268–269.

23. *The Poetical Works of John Godfrey Saxe* (Boston and New York: Houghton, Mifflin, 1887), 150–151.
24. *Fables of Aesop* (New York: A. L. Burt, 1890), 31.
25. Pitman, Norman Hinsdale, *Chinese Wonder Book* (New York: Dutton, 1919), 21–38.
26. *The Poetical Works of John Godfrey Saxe* (Boston and New York: Houghton, Mifflin, 1887), 156–157.
27. Powell, J. W., *Sixth Annual Report of the Bureau of Ethnology* (Washington, D.C.: Government Printing Office, 1888), 638–639.
28. Nassau, R. H., "Batanga Tales," *Journal of American Folk-Lore* 28, No. 112, Jan.–March (1915): 38–41.
29. Sapir, Edward, and Hsu Tsan Hwa, "Two Chinese Folk-Tales," *Journal of American Folk-Lore* 36, no. 139, Jan.–March (1923): 30.
30. *Fables of Aesop* (New York: A. L. Burt, 1890), 150–151.
31. Allan, Horace Newton, *Korean Tales* (New York and London: G. P. Putnam's Sons, Knickerbocker Press, 1889), 33.
32. Wait, Frona Eunice, *The Stories of El Dorado* (San Francisco: Sunset Press, 1904), 11–17.
33. Lowe, Samuel E., and Viola E. Jacobson, *Fifty Famous Stories* (Racine, Wisc.: Whitman Publishing, 1920), unnumbered pages.
34. Thorne-Thomsen, Gudrun, *East o' the Sun and West o' the Moon* (Chicago: Row, Peterson, 1912), 199–203.

3
Resources

1. Tanner, Dorothy, *Legends from the Red Man's Forest* (Chicago: A. Flanagan, 1895), 44–45.
2. The Moqui (pronounced Moh-kee) pueblo is Native American Hopi. "The Moqui Boy and the Eagle" is similar to a Native American story of the Northwest where a boy learns respect and sympathy for the Salmon people after visiting their home. This story could also be used to teach respect for people of different cultures. Lummis, Charles F., *The Man Who Married the Moon* (New York: Century, 1894), 122–126.
3. Russell, Frank, "Myths of the Jicarilla Apaches," *Journal of American Folk-Lore* 11, No. 43, Oct.–Dec. (1898): 258.
4. Judd, Mary Catherine, *Wigwam Stories* (Boston: Athenaeum Press, 1905), 108–109.
5. The Ainu of Japan have numerous stories to explain the characteristics of certain birds or animals. Batchelor, John, *The Ainu and Their Folklore* (London: Religious Tract Society, 1901), 441–442.
6. This was adapted from a longer story of the Thompson River Native Americans of British Columbia. The coyote is a common figure within many Native American folk stories. In the Northwest he shares a mixed reputation with the raven; both are tricksters, sometimes doing good, more often not. Coyote can be both crafty and foolish. He is also known for his romantic exploits. Unfortunately, Coyote rarely learns from his mistakes. This is the second of three similar incidents, during the last of which Coyote is nearly killed. Teit, James, *Thompson River Indians of British Columbia*, introduction by Franz Boas (Boston and New York: Houghton, Mifflin, 1898), 41. In a variant found in the Native American Salishan tribe, the kingfisher and the coyote are protagonists. See Boas, Franz, ed., *Folk-Tales of Salishan and Sahaptin Tribes* (Lancaster, Pa., and New York: G. E. Stechert, 1917), 6.
7. Armenians also have a story in which heart and mind come to the same conclusion. Original story by Linda M. Ford.
8. Eliot, Charles W., ed., *The Harvard Classics: Folk-Lore and Fable*, Volume 17 (New York: P. F. Collier & Son, 1909), 32.
9. Judson, Katharine B., *Myths and Legends of the Mississippi Valley and the Great Lakes* (Chicago: A. C. McClurg, 1914), 144. Aesop versions: Eliot, Charles W., ed., *The Harvard Classics: Folk-Lore and Fable*, Volume 17 (New York: P. F. Collier & Son, 1909), 25. Variant: *Fables of Aesop* (New York: A. L. Burt, 1890), 132.
10. *Fables of Aesop* (New York: A. L. Burt, 1890), 82.
11. *Fables of Aesop* (New York: A. L. Burt, 1890), 58–59.
12. *Fables of Aesop* (New York: A. L. Burt, 1890), 198–199.
13. *Fables of Aesop* (New York: A. L. Burt, 1890), 116–117.
14. *Fables of Aesop* (New York: A. L. Burt, 1890), 219–220.
15. *Fables of Aesop* (New York: A. L. Burt, 1890), 230–231.
16. Wiggins, Kate Douglas, and Nora Archibald Smith, *Tales of Laughter* (New York: Doubleday, 1908), 152. Variant: *Fables of Aesop* (New York: A. L. Burt, 1890), 245.
17. *Fables of Aesop* (New York: A. L., 1890), 318.
18. *Fables of Aesop* (New York: A. L. Burt, 1890), 318–319.

19. This fable has also been incorporated in another story from India, whereby a king on his way to war to gain more territory and glory observed the monkey and realized he was being just as foolish. Tolstoi, Lyof N., *The Long Exile* (New York: Charles Scribner's Sons, 1907), 136. A variant may be found in Knatchbull, Wyndham, trans., *Kalila and Dimna* or *The Fables of Bidpai* (Oxford, London: W. Baxter, for J. Parker and Messrs. Longman, Hurst, Rees, Orme, and Brown, 1819), 332–333.
20. Tolstoi, Lyof N., *The Long Exile* (New York: Charles Scribner's Sons, 1907), 136.
21. Adapted from the creation myths of the Santal Parganas in India (see notes on "The Raja Who Went to Heaven"). Bompas, Cecil Henry, trans., *Folklore of the Santal Parganas* (London: David Nutt, 1909), 401–402. Filipino variant: Fansler, Dean S., *Filipino Popular Tales* (Lancaster and New York: G. E. Stechert, 1921), 426–427.
22. Original story by Linda M. Ford.
23. Petrovitch, Woislav M., *Hero Tales and Legends of the Serbians* (London: George G. Harrap, 1914), 366–369.
24. This folktale comes from the part of western Africa once known as the Gold Coast. Cardinall, A. W., *The Natives of the Northern Territories of the Gold Coast* (London: George Routledge & Sons; New York: E. P. Dutton, 1920), 22–23.
25. This story is adapted from an Icelandic fairy tale recorded in 1897. People of good conscience have long been asked to examine the mixed motives of their own generosity. The modern world rejects "paternalism," which implies the average person needs to have his or her decisions made by someone of higher rank, education, or religion. This does not negate the responsibility of the giver to give with discrimination. Hall, Mrs. Angus W., trans., ed., *Icelandic Fairy Tales* (London and New York: Frederick Warne, 1897), 46–49.
26. Adapted from a narrative of Soviet Georgia. While this story retains the impression of the inherent qualities of social classes, as a fairy/folk tale it is useful for considering the characteristics of those who are the true children of creation. Wardrop, Marjorie, trans., *Georgian Folk Tales* (London: David Nutt, 1894), 162–163.
27. Chatelain, Heli, ed., *Folk-Tales of Angola* (Boston and New York: G. E. Stechart, 1894), 247.
28. *The Poetical Works of John Godfrey Saxe* (Boston and New York: Houghton, Mifflin, 1887), 153–154.
29. Fielde, Adele M., *Chinese Nights' Entertainment* (New York and London: G. P. Putnam's Sons, Knickerbocker Press, 1893), 181–182.
30. This story of how creatures who are small but many, and how they work together, is somewhat reminiscent of the tale from India (Santal Parganas) where the elephant thinks the ant is too small to bother with or to show courtesy or consideration to. Lummis, Charles F., *The Man Who Married the Moon* (New York: Century, 1894), 147–160.
31. Also see notes on "The Raja Who Went to Heaven." The original story ended with these comments: "This story teaches us not to despise the poor man, because one day he may have an opportunity to put us to shame. From this story of the elephant we should learn this lesson; the Creator knows why He made some animals big and some small and why He made some men fools; so we should neither bully nor cheat men who happen to be born stupid." Bompas, Cecil Henry, trans., *Folklore of the Santal Parganas* (London: David Nutt, 1909), 328–329.
32. As with many stories, the familiarity of this one need not preclude its use. *Fables of Aesop* (New York: A. L. Burt, 1890), 106–107.
33. *Fables of Aesop* (New York: A. L. Burt, 1890), 262.
34. This is one of two similar stories from the Arikara people where a boy exhibits kindness toward an animal in his youth and is given great power as a result. Unfortunately, in both cases, the boys grow into men who abuse their abilities and powers, which results in the deaths. The Native American Arikara belong to the Caddoan linguistic group and were once closely allied with the Skidi band of Pawnee, from which tribe they separated in about 1832. After that time they made their home at various points along the Missouri River until, in 1854, they were placed at Fort Berthold Reservation in North Dakota along with the Mandan and Minitaree or Grosventres, the latter two tribes being of Sioux origin. Dorsey, George A., *Traditions of the Arikara* (Washington, D.C.: Carnegie Institution, 1904), 83–84.
35. This story gives a positive message in contrast to the European stories of how the wren became king by the same strategy. In the Ojibwa tale, we could see the wren/linnet as typical of us all, because no one flies alone and we all fly higher because of the efforts of those around us. The Ojibwa legend has a nice twist because the birds acknowledge the contribution of the eagle. Of interest also in relation to this story may be the discovery that the flight formation of Canada geese makes it aerodynamically easier for those behind the leader—the leader takes the hardest job for the sake of the others. Swainson, Charles, *The Folk Lore of British Birds* (London: Elliot Stock, 1886), 65. Variant: Tanner, Dorothy, *Legends from the Red Man's Forest* (Chicago: A. Flanagan, 1895), 49–50.

36. Fillmore, Parker, *Mighty Mikko* (New York: Harcourt, Brace, 1922), 307–308. Variant: *Fables of Aesop* (New York: A. L. Burt, 1890), 34–35.
37. Schwab, George, "Bulu Folk-Tales," *Journal of American Folk-Lore* 27, No. 105, July–Sept. (1890): 282.
38. The American poet John Hay has a delightful rendition of this story entitled "The Enchanted Shirt." *Poems by John Hay* (Boston and New York: Houghton, Mifflin, 1899), 67–72.
39. Hofberg, Herman, *Swedish Folklore*, W. H. Myers, trans. (Chicago: Belford Clark, 1888), 71–74.
40. A West African story has a similar conclusion: The leopard was a poor hunter and went to the cat to teach him. She gave him his first lessons about hiding beside the trail and how to strike with his left paw. One day the leopard found nothing to eat and ate the cat's kittens. For his lack of gratitude and cruelty, the cat refused to give him any more lessons, so the leopard only knows how to hunt with his left paw. Swainson, Charles, *The Folk Lore of British Birds* (London: Elliot Stock, 1886), 80.
41. Gaster, M., *Rumanian Bird and Beast Stories* (London: Sidgwick and Jackson, 1915), 69–70.
42. *Fables of Aesop* (New York: A. L. Burt, 1890), 78–79.
43. This is reminiscent of how the Swiss Family Robinson captured apes that were destroying their property. The apes wouldn't let go of the treat they had grasped and so were held by their own greed until the family arrived to deal with them. *Fables of Aesop* (New York: A. L. Burt, 1890), 259.
44. Teit, James A., "Tahltan Tales," *Journal of American Folk-Lore* 34, No. 133, July–Sept. (1921): 225.
45. Krug, Adolph N., "Bulu Tales from Kamerun, West Africa," *Journal of American Folk-Lore* 25, No. 96, April–June (1922): 113.
46. Bell, William C., "Umbundu Tales, Angola, Southwest Africa," *Journal of American Folk-Lore* 35, No. 136, April–June (1922): 148.
47. Boas, Frank, and C. Kamba Simango, "Tales and Proverbs of the Vandau of Portuguese South Africa," *Journal of American Folk-Lore* 35, No. 136, April–June (1922): 182.
48. *Fables of Aesop* (New York: A. L. Burt, 1890), 147–148.
49. *Fables of Aesop* (New York: A. L. Burt, 1890), 17.
50. Spence, Lewis, *Myths and Legends: The North American Indians* (Boston: David D. Nickerson, 1914), 249–252.
51. Chidley, Howard J., *Fifty-Two Story Talks to Boys and Girls* (New York: George H. Doran, 1914), 9.
52. Krug, Adolph N., "Bulu Tales from Kamerun, West Africa," *Journal of American Folk-Lore* 25, No. 106, April–June (1922): 120–121.
53. *Fables of Aesop* (New York: A. L. Burt, 1890), 178–179. For a Mexican variant see Brenner, Anita, *The Boy Who Could Do Anything and Other Mexican Folk Tales* (New York: William R. Scott, 1942), 18–19. Jacobs, Joseph, *Indian Fairy Tales* (New York and London: G. P. Putnam's Sons, 1892), 49–50.
54. Teasdale, Sara, *Rainbow Gold* (New York: Macmillan, 1922), 140.
55. Ridpath, John Clark, ed., *The Ridpath Library of Universal Literature,* Volume 15 (New York: Fifth Avenue Library Society, 1910), 109.
56. *The Poetical Works of John Godfrey Saxe* (Boston and New York: Houghton, Mifflin, 1887), 147–148.
57. This story was collected by Jeremiah Curtin and is from the Wasco culture. It is recorded in Sapir, Edward, *Wishram Texts* (Leyden: Late E. J. Brill Publishers and Printers, 1909), 257–259.
58. Bogaras, Waldemar, *Anthropological Papers of the American Museum of Natural History,* 20, Part 1, "Tales of Yukaghir, Lamut, and Russianized Natives of Eastern Siberia" (New York: American Museum of Natural History, 1918), 34–35.
59. Frere, M., *Old Deccan Days*, introduction and notes by Bartle Frere (Philadelphia: J. B. Lippincott, 1868), 161–163.
60. A similar story is told in the Philippines. Cardinall, A. W., *The Natives of the Northern Territories of the Gold Coast* (London: George Routledge & Sons; New York: E. P. Dutton, 1920), 23.

4
Room for Improvement

1. Dennett, R. E., *Notes on the Folklore of the Fjort* (London: David Nutt, 1898), 124.
2. Douglas, George B., *Scottish Fairy and Folktales* (London: Walter Scott, 1901), 29.
3. Ralston, W.R.S., *Russian Folktales* (London: Smith, Elder, 1873), 213–214.
4. Lummis, Charles F., *The Man Who Married the Moon* (New York: Century, 1894), 51–52.
5. Wilhem, R., ed., *The Chinese Fairy Book*, Frederick H. Martens, trans. (New York: Frederick A. Stokes, 1921), 29–30. A Filipino variant has a different moral to the story. In it the hawk, having stolen a piece of salted fish, is flattered into letting it drop from his mouth. A hero advises him concerning the future, not to

believe what others tell him, to think for himself, and to remember that ill-gotten gains never prosper. See Fansler, Dean S., *Filipino Popular Tales* (Lancaster and New York: G. E. Stechert, 1921), 395–396.

6. Cooper, Frederic Taber, *An Argosy of Fables* (New York: Frederick A. Stokes, 1921), 409–410.
7. Wilhem, R. ed., *The Chinese Fairy Book*, Frederick H. Martens, trans. (New York: Frederick A. Stokes, 1921), 10–11.
8. *Fables of Aesop* (New York: A. L. Burt, 1890), 31–32.
9. Cooper, Frederic Taber, *An Argosy of Fables* (New York: Frederick A. Stokes, 1921), 162.
10. Milne, Mrs. Leslie, *Shans at Home* (London: John Murray, 1910), 239.
11. Cooper, Frederic Taber, *An Argosy of Fables* (New York: Frederick A. Stokes, 1921), 295.
12. This story was adapted from a tale of the Thompson River Native Americans of British Columbia. In the original story, Coyote is fooled four times by the fox's flattery, until all his bones are used up. See Teit, James, *Thompson River Indians of British Columbia* (Boston and New York: Houghton, Mifflin; London: David Nutt, 1898), 29.
13. There are parallels in this tale with "The Story of the Peasant, the Snake, and King Solomon" in this volume. Smith, Herbert H., *Brazil, the Amazons, and the Coast* (New York: Charles Scribner's Sons, 1879), 553.
14. *Fables of Aesop* (New York: A. L. Burt, 1890), 35. African variant: Lomax, John A., "Stories of an African Prince," *Journal of American Folk-Lore* 26, No. 99, Jan.–March (1913): 7.
15. Chatelain, Heli, *Folk-Tales of Angola* (Boston and New York: G. E. Stechert, 1894), 211.
16. Barker, W. H., and Cecilia Sinclair, *West African Folk-Tales* (London: George G. Harrap, 1917), 69–72.
17. Swainson, Charles, *The Folk Lore of British Birds* (London: Elliot Stock: 1886), 7. Swainson repeated this story from a French folktale.
18. Note the parallels between this story from the Philippines and the fable of Aesop, "The Dog and His Shadow," where the dog was crossing the bridge with a bone and looked down to see another dog carrying a bone. He barked ferociously at the other dog, intending to take the bone, but it was only his reflection, and when he barked he lost the bone he already had. Aesop's moral of the fable was "Beware, lest you lose the substance by grasping at the shadow." Fansler, Dean S., *Filipino Popular Tales* (Lancaster and New York: G. E. Stechert, 1921), 391–392.
19. Adapted from *Fables of Aesop* (New York: A. L. Burt, 1890), 196.
20. *The Poetical Works of John Godfrey Saxe* (Boston and New York: Houghton, Mifflin, 1887), 148–149.
21. Arndt, Ernst Moritz, *Fairy Tales from the Isle of Rugen* Anna Dabis, trans. (London: David Nutt, 1896), 227–229.
22. Wilhem, R., ed., *The Chinese Fairy Book*, Frederick H. Martens, trans. (New York: Frederick A. Stokes, 1921), 184–186.
23. Cooper, Frederic Taber, *An Argosy of Fables* (New York: Frederick A. Stokes, 1921), 242.
24. If this fable is used with children in oral storytelling, some discussion about cruelty to animals would likely be in order. *Fables of Aesop* (New York: A. L. Burt, 1890), 105.
25. Drouse, W. H., *The Talking Thrush* (New York: E. P. Dutton; London: J. M. Dent, 1899), 139–144.
26. "Notes and Queries," *Journal of American Folk-Lore* 9, No. 34, June–Aug. (1896): 147.
27. Curry, Charles Madison, and Erle Elsworth Clippinger, *Children's Literature* (New York: Rand McNally, 1921), 178.
28. Milne, Mrs. Leslie, *Shans at Home* (London: John Murray, 1910), 273–275.
29. Swainson, Charles, *The Folk Lore of British Birds* (London: Elliot Stock, 1886), 124.
30. Barker, W. H., and Cecilia Sinclair, *West African Folk-Tales* (London: George G. Harrap, 1917), 89–94.
31. One sequel to the story says that after the wren had triumphantly proclaimed himself as king, the other birds allowed his claim, and he was duly elected to that office. But the eagle was so exasperated at the decision that he caught up the wren in a rage, flew up high in the air with his rival in his claws, and dropped him to the ground. The wren was more frightened than hurt, but he lost part of his tail in the fall and has ever since gone about with only half of that necessary appendage. A variation of this legend relates that the angry eagle gave the wren such a stroke with his wing as he came down that from that time he has never been able to fly higher than a hawthorn bush (or elder tree). The wren in folklore does not have quite the same unblemished reputation as the robin. Indeed, the wren is blamed for some acts of treachery toward St. Stephen. The wren's pride and conceit are at times viewed as obnoxious, though the wren is also seen as a homely, cheery bird and is connected with selflessness in some stories about bringing fire for the sake of humankind. The tradition of the sovereignty of the wren over the feathered race is widespread. (Greek, Latin, French, Spanish, Italian, and German names for the wren allude to this.) An almost identical story appeared in a Jewish collection of animal tales composed in the thirteenth century, and the tale is common to Ireland, France, Germany, Norway, and Scotland. A similar story, with the exception of the linnet (instead of the wren) being the hero, is told by the

Ojibwas of North America. Swainson, Charles, *The Folk Lore of British Birds* (London: Elliot Stock, 1886), 36. Scottish variant: Douglas, George B., *Scottish Fairy and Folktales* (London: Walter Scott, 1901), 28. Romanian variant: Gaster, M., *Rumanian Bird and Beast Stories* (London: Sidgwick & Jackson, 1915), 300–301. Another variant can be found in "Folk-lore Scrap Book," *Journal of American Folk-Lore* 12, No. 47, July–Aug. (1899): 229. German variant: Wiggins, Kate Douglas, and Nora Archibald Smith, *Tales of Laughter* (New York: Doubleday, 1908), 172–175.

32. Chatelain, Heli, *Folk-Tales of Angola* (Boston and New York: G. E. Stechert, 1894), 211.
33. This tale may be the source of the saying "I have a crow to pluck with you." In most folklore, the crow is a bird of the worst and most sinister character, representing either death, night, or winter. An exception is found in the Native American legends of the Northwest concerning the raven. The cultural source for the crow-plucking story may be British. Swainson, Charles, *The Folk Lore of British Birds* (London: Elliot Stock, 1886), 84.
34. Lorimer, D.L.R., and E. O. Lorimer, trans., *Persian Tales* (London: Macmillan, 1919), 304–305.
35. *Fables of Aesop* (New York: A. L. Burt, 1890), 65–66.
36. Drouse, W. H., *The Talking Thrush* (New York: E. P. Dutton; London: J. M. Dent, 1899), 33–35.
37. Cooper, Frederic Taber, *An Argosy of Fables* (New York: Frederick A. Stokes, 1921), 113. *Fables of Aesop* (New York: A. L. Burt, 1890), 25–27.
38. This story can be a lot of fun to tell when mimicking the boy's laughter and the disgruntlement of the townspeople. Care should be taken in doing so, however, to also emphasize the unhappy ending. *Fables of Aesop* (New York: A. L. Burt, 1890), 97–98. There is an African (Yoruba) variant in which a parrot is supposed to warn the householder of approaching danger, but crows at everything. The variant can be found in Lomax, John A., "Stories of an African Prince," *Journal of American Folk-Lore* 26, No. 99, Jan.–March (1913): 10.
39. *Fables of Aesop* (New York: A. L. Burt, 1890), 275–276.
40. Boas, Franz, "The Central Eskimo," *Sixth Annual Report of the Bureau of Ethnology* (Washington, D.C.: Government Printing Office, 1888), 641.
41. This story was adapted from an early-nineteenth-century translation of an Arabic manuscript, *The Fables of Bidpai,* which contains much of the wisdom and fables of India. Knatchbull, Wyndham, trans., *Kalila and Dimna* or *The Fables of Bidpai* (London: W. Baxter, for J. Parker and Messrs. Longman, Hurst, Rees, Orme, and Brown, 1819), 146–147. Chinese variant: Dennys, N. B., *The Folk-Lore of China* (London: Trachner, 1876), 149. North Carolina variant: Parsons, Elsie Clews, "Tales from Guilford County, North Carolina," *Journal of American Folk-Lore* 30, No. 116, April–June (1917): 198–199. Jacobs, Joseph, *Indian Fairy Tales* (New York and London: G. P. Putnam's Sons, 1892), 123–125.
42. *Fables of Aesop* (New York: A. L. Burt, 1890), 87.
43. *Fables of Aesop* (New York: A. L. Burt, 1890), 236–237.
44. *Fables of Aesop* (New York: A. L. Burt, 1890), 221–222.
45. Cooper, Frederic Taber, *An Argosy of Fables* (New York: Frederick A. Stokes, 1921), 273.
46. Knowles, J. Hinton, *Folk-Tales of Kashmir* (London: Kegaw Paul, Trench, Trubner, 1893), 257.
47. Teit, James A., "Tahltan Tales," *Journal of American Folk-Lore* 32, No. 124, April–June (1917): 243.
48. Cooper, Frederic Taber, *An Argosy of Fables* (New York: Frederick A. Stokes, 1921), 167.
49. Quetzalcoatl was seen as both lord of light (eastern) or the sun and of the winds, and many varied stories are told of him. Of interest is the fact that some of the early Spanish missionaries professed to see in Quetzalcoatl the apostle St. Thomas, who had journeyed to America to effect its conversion. Spence, Lewis, *The Myths of Mexico and Peru* (New York: Thomas Y. Crowell, 1913), 60–61.
50. *Fables of Aesop* (New York: A. L. Burt, 1890), 242–243.
51. Teit, James, "Traditions of the Lillooet Indians of British Columbia," *Journal of American Folk-Lore* 25, No. 98, Oct.–Dec. (1912): 311–312. Native American Tahltan variant: Teit, James A., "Tahltan Tales," *Journal of American Folk-Lore* 32, No. 124, April–June (1919): 243.
52. It is interesting to note that Native Americans of the Northwest have also told stories of how the raven was once white. These tales sometimes involve the vanity of the raven, but at least one tells how the raven became black in a task of service. *The Poetical Works of John Godfrey Saxe* (Boston and New York: Houghton, Mifflin, 1887), 142–143.
53. See notes on "The Raja Who Went to Heaven." Variations of this story can be found outside of India as well. Bompas, Cecil Henry, trans., *Folklore of the Santal Parganas* (London: David Nutt, 1909), 141–142.
54. *Fables of Aesop* (New York: A. L. Burt, 1890), 18.
55. *Fables of Aesop* (New York: A. L. Burt, 1890), 16–17.
56. *The Poetical Works of John Godfrey Saxe* (Boston and New York: Houghton, Mifflin, 1887), 171.
57. Powell, J.W., "Myths of the Cherokees," *Nineteenth Annual Report of the Bureau of American Ethnology* (Washington, D.C.: Government Printing Office, 1900), 257.

58. Lomax, John A., "Stories of an African Prince," *Journal of American Folk-Lore* 26, No. 99, Jan.–March (1913): 8.
59. Drouse, W. H., *The Talking Thrush* (New York: E. P. Dutton; London: J. M. Dent, 1899), 110–111.
60. Sapir, Edward, *Wishram Texts* (Leyden: Late E. J. Brill Publishers and Printers, 1909), 235.
61. Roth, Walter E. "An Inquiry into the Animism and Folk-Lore of the Guiana Indians," *Thirtieth Annual Report of the Bureau of Ethnology* (Washington, D.C.: Government Printing Office, 1915), 222.
62. Roth, Walter E. "An Inquiry into the Animism and Folk-Lore of the Guiana Indians," *Thirtieth Annual Report of the Bureau of Ethnology* (Washington, D.C.: Government Printing Office, 1915), 302–303.
63. This Navajo folktale tells the origin of why their Pueblo neighbors have finer corn crops than the Navajo themselves. Matthews, Washington, ed., *Navaho Legends* (Boston and New York: Houghton, Mifflin, 1897), 78.

5
Beauty & Virtue

1. Fielde, Adele M., *Chinese Nights' Entertainment* (New York and London: G. P. Putnam's Sons, Knickerbocker Press, 1893), 154–159.
2. A number of African fables also seem to deal with the concept of each creature as sufficient and appropriate in itself, with no need to feel better or less than another. See the stories in this volume titled "Fire and Water" and "The Canoe and the Paddle." For a Moorish variant, see McCarthy, Justin, Richard Henry Stoddard, Arthur Richmond Marsh, Paul Van Dyke, and Albert Ellery Bergh, eds., *The World's Great Classics: Moorish Literature*, introduction by Epiphanius Wilson (New York: Colonial Press, 1901), 266. An African variant can be found in Cooper, Frederic Taber, *An Argosy of Fables* (New York: Frederick A. Stokes, 1921), 452.
3. Dennys, N. B., *The Folk-Lore of China* (London: Trachner, 1876), 136.
4. *Fables of Aesop* (New York: A. L. Burt, 1890), 182.
5. Buck, Charles, *Anecdotes* (Boston: Otis, Broaders, 1843), 215.
6. This story is part of a longer narrative that tells how the King of Tonga heard about the shell of the great turtle and sent men to bring it to him to make fish hooks. When they eventually located the ancient grave, they dug it up and found the shell in thirteen pieces; they only delivered twelve to the king, and he sent them back to get the thirteenth. Because of their duplicity in keeping the final piece, they knew they could not return home or go to Samoa. So, they let the winds take them wherever they would and eventually landed in Fiji. The longer tale is called "How the Tongans Came to Fiji." Depending upon the desired message, the story could be told in full or end with the man landing on the beach. The first part could be used as a tale of faith or obedience—how the man obeyed the words of the Sky King and refused to look despite the voices that tempted him. The ending of the story is a tale of delayed gratitude. Fison, Lorimer, *Tales from Old Fiji* (London: De La More Press, 1904), 19–23.
7. *Fables of Aesop* (New York: A. L. Burt, 1890), 127–128.
8. It has been noted that Georgia lies between the worlds of the East and the West and has been influenced by both Christianity and Islam. The judgment of the shepherd in this tale is similar to stories throughout Asia and the Middle East. The unique background of the shepherd appears to be a special quality added by Georgian storytellers. Wardrop, Marjory, *Georgian Folk Tales* (London: David Nutt, 1894), 138–140.
9. Slossen, Annie Trumbull, *Story-Tell Lib* (New York: Charles Scribner's Sons, 1900), 75–79.
10. Readers may be interested to know that Henry M. Stanley (of Stanley and Livingstone fame) recorded a tale of creation by a member of the Basoka ("a tribe occupying the right bank of the Aruwimi River from its confluence with the Congo to within a short distance of the rapids of Yambuya and inland for a few marches"). In this story, the hare is not mentioned, but it is the moon that asserts humans will live again. Another version of the story tells that the moon sent the hare with the message about life to humanity, but the hare gave the wrong message—the one asserting death would be forever—and as punishment the moon struck the hare. Bleek, Wilhelm Heinrich Immanuel, *Hottentot Fables and Tales* (London: Trubner, 1864), 69–73. Variants found in Bleek, W.H.I., and L. C. Lloyd, *Specimens of Bushman Folklore* (London: George Allen, 1911), 57–65; and in Schapera, I., *The Khoisan Peoples of South Africa* (London: George Routledge & Sons, 1930), 357–358. A possible variant may be found among the Chitimacha people native to the Americas; see Swanton, John R., "Some Chitimacha Myths and Beliefs," *Journal of American Folk-Lore* 30, No. 118, Oct.–Nov. (1917): 476.
11. Broomell, Anna Pettit, ed., *The Children's Story Garden* (Philadelphia and London: J. B. Lippincott, 1920), 65–69.

12. "Folk-lore Scrapbook," *Journal of American Folk-Lore* 11, No. 118, Oct.–Nov. (1917): 301.
13. Crane, Thomas Frederick, ed. *The Exempla of Jacques De Vitry* (London: David Nutt, 1890), 137.
14. Variations of this story are common among many European sources (including Russia), and there are two Slavic versions, including one with two brothers as the main characters. Often it is the twelve months that are encountered rather than the four seasons, and in European sources the heroine is generally a stepdaughter who has been granted an impossible task by her unkind stepmother and stepsister. However, in today's society where so many children live with "step" relatives, it seems unwise to perpetuate negative stereotypes. Therefore, the story has been presented here as simply the tale of two sisters. Mabie, Hamilton Wright, Edward Everett Hale, and William Byron Forbush, eds., *The Young Folks Treasury: Myths and Legendary Heroes,* Volume 2 (New York: University Society, 1919), 150–156. See variant in same volume, pp. 147–150. Wiggin, Kate Douglas, and Nora Archibald Smith, *Tales of Laughter* (New York: Doubleday, 1908), 20–24.
15. Swainson, Charles, *The Folk Lore of British Birds* (London: Elliot Stock, 1886), 17.
16. Broomell, Anna Pettit, ed., *The Children's Story Garden* (Philadelphia and London: J. B. Lippincott, 1920), 208–209.
17. Swainson, Charles, *The Folk Lore of British Birds* (London: Elliot Stock, 1886), 16. Native American variant: Cresswell, J. R., "Notes and Queries," *Journal of American Folk-Lore* 36, No. 142, Oct.–Dec. (1923): 406.
18. Chidley, Howard J., *Fifty-two Story Talks* (New York: Hodder & Stroughton, George H. Doran, 1914), 89–90. Variants: Clark, Galen, *Indians of the Yosemite Valley and Vicinity* (Yosemite Valley, Calif.: Galen Clark, 1904), 92–95; and Cooper, Frederic Taber, *An Argosy of Fables* (New York: Frederick A. Stokes, 1921), 470–471.
19. Lowe, Samuel E., and Viola E. Jacobson, *Fifty Famous Stories* (Racine, Wisc.: Whitman Publishing, 1920), unnumbered pages.
20. Lummis, Charles F., *The Man Who Married the Moon* (New York: Century, 1894), 169–177.
21. Milne, Mrs. Leslie, *Shans at Home* (London: John Murray, 1910), 271–272.
22. Nuttall, Zelia, "A Note on Ancient Mexican Folk-Lore," *Journal of American Folk-Lore* 8, No. 29, April–June (1895): 128–129.
23. The character of Anansi in the story must be an import to Guyana from Africa. Penard, A. P., and T. E. Penard, "Surinam Folk-Tales," *Journal of American Folk-Lore* 30, No. 106, April–June (1917): 248–250.
24. The Karok home is near the Klamath River in California. Judson, Katharine Berry, ed. *Myths and Legends of California and the Old Southwest* (Chicago: A. O. McClurg, 1912), 51–52.
25. Mabie, Hamilton Wright, Edward Everett Hale, and William Byron Forbush, eds., *The Young Folks Treasury: Myths and Legendary Heroes,* Volume 2 (New York: University Society, 1919), 528–529.
26. Swainson, Charles, *The Folk Lore of British Birds* (London: Elliot Stock, 1886), 15.
27. Bryant, Sara Cone, *How to Tell Stories to Children* (Boston and New York: Houghton, Mifflin, 1905), 179–181. Bryant's source was "Gleanings in Buddha-Fields," by Lafcadio Hearn.
28. As the proverbs remind us, don't judge a book by its cover or a bird by its feathers. Gaster, M., *Rumanian Bird and Beast Stories* (London: Sidgwick & Jackson, 1915), 151–152.
29. *Fables of Aesop* (New York: A. L. Burt, 1890), 92–93.
30. Harper, Wilhelmina, *Fillmore Folk Tales* (New York: Harcourt, Brace, 1922), 45–53.
31. In ancient days the Arabs were known as Ishmaelites because they trace their heritage from Abraham's eldest son, Ishmael. Garnett, Richard, Leon Vallee, and Alois Brandl, eds., *The Universal Anthology* (London: Clarke, 1899), 329.
32. The Santal Parganas are a Munda tribe, a branch of a group that may have entered India from the northeast and came to inhabit the eastern outskirts of the Chutia Nagpore plateau. This story has been shortened and adapted. At the end of the original was this quote: "It is said that what you give away in this world, you will get back in the next; there you will get good wages for what you have done in this life." Bompas, Cecil Henry, trans., *Folklore of the Santal Parganas* (London: David Nutt, 1909), 240–241.
33. This is part of the Jataka tales of Buddhism. The justice of the first king who meets and overcomes opposition by the equal measures of the same is judged less righteous than the king who overcomes evil by the opposite goodness. Jacobs, Joseph, *Indian Fairy Tales* (London: David Nutt, 1892), 127–131.
34. Sellers, Charles, *Tales from the Lands of Nuts and Grapes: Spanish and Portuguese Folklore* (London: Field & Tuer, Leadenhall Press, 1888), 26–33.
35. Milne, Mrs. Leslie, *Shans at Home* (London: John Murray, 1910), 229.
36. Crane, Thomas Frederick, *The Exempla of Jacques De Vitry* (London: David Nutt, 1890), 162–163. Variant by Jean La Fontaine: Cooper, Frederic Taber, *An Argosy of Fables* (New York: Frederick A. Stokes, 1921), 339–341.
37. Curry, Charles Madison, and Erle Elsworth Clippinger, eds. *Children's Literature* (New York: Rand McNally, 1921), 174–175.

38. Basden, G. T., *Among the Ibos of Nigeria* (Philadelphia: J. B. Lippincott, 1921), 280–281.
39. Cooper, Frederic Taber, *An Argosy of Fables* (New York: Frederick A. Stokes, 1921), 268.
40. Bundy, Richard C., "Folk Tales from Liberia," *Journal of American Folk-Lore* 33, No. 125, July–Sept. (1919): 426.
41. Lowe, Samuel E., and Viola E. Jacobson, *Fifty Famous Stories* (Racine, Wisc.: Whitman Publishing, 1920), unnumbered pages.
42. Davis, F. Hadland, *Myths and Legends: Japan* (Boston: David D. Nickerson, ca. 1918), 182–186.
43. Gaster, M., *Rumanian Bird and Beast Stories* (London: Sidgwick and Jackson, 1915), 263–266.
44. Boas, Franz, "Notes on Mexican Folk-lore," *Journal of American Folk-Lore* 25, No. 97, July–Sept. (1912): 215–217.

6
Wisdom & Foolishness

1. Also see notes on "The Raja Who Went to Heaven." Bompas, Cecil Henry, trans., *Folklore of the Santal Parganas* (London: David Nutt, 1909), 370.
2. This story is inspired by folk motifs in a variety of cultures. In Japan there is the stonecutter, Hofus, who is turned by a kindly fairy into the sun, a cloud, the wind, a mountain, then finally—because a stonecutter chips away at his heart—returned to his own self. Tales with similar sequences (such as the mouse bride who seeks to be married to the sky, cloud, wind, etc.) can be found in different parts of Asia, India (among the Santal Parganas), Africa, and so on. Another way to tell the story is to tell the naming of the cat: sun, cloud, wind, wall, mouse, cat, with various friends or relatives suggesting which is stronger. See "The Story of Long-Legs" for a similar type of progression but with a different point to the story. Whereas the original story uses a mouse as the protagonist and potential bride, the humor of a cat marrying a mouse is irresistible for most listeners. Rinder, Frank, *Old-World Japan* (London: George Allen, 1895), 183–187; Knatchbull, Wyndham, trans., *Kalila and Dimna* or *The Fables of Bidpai* (Oxford and London: W. Baxter, for J. Parker and Messrs. Longman, Hurst, Rees, Orme, and Brown, 1819), 243–246; Cooper, Frederic Taber, *An Argosy of Fables* (New York: Frederick A. Stokes, 1921), 209–211. French variant: Wiggin, Kate Douglas, and Nora Archibald Smith, *Tales of Laughter* (New York: Doubleday, 1908), 3–5.
3. Adapted from a story of the Santal Parganas in India. See notes on "The Raja Who Went to Heaven." Bompas, Cecil Henry, trans., *Folklore of the Santal Parganas* (London: David Nutt, 1909), 372–373.
4. *Fables of Aesop* (New York: A. L. Burt, 1890), 241.
5. *Fables of Aesop* (New York: A. L. Burt, 1890), 157.
6. Curry, Charles Madison, and Erle Elsworth Clippinger, eds., *Children's Literature* (New York: Rand McNally, 1921), 280–281.
7. *The Poetical Works of John Godfrey Saxe* (Boston and New York: Houghton, Mifflin, 1887), 165–166.
8. Hanauer, James Edward, *Folk-Lore of the Holy Land* (London: Duckworth, 1907), 141.
9. Cooper, Frederic Taber, *An Argosy of Fables* (New York: Frederick A. Stokes, 1921), 267.
10. Swainson, Charles, *The Folk Lore of British Birds* (London: Elliot Stock, 1886), 108.
11. *Fables of Aesop* (New York: A. L. Burt, 1890), 326.
12. Gaster, M., *Rumanian Bird and Beast Stories* (London: Sidgwick and Jackson, 1915), 325–326.
13. Drouse, W. H., *The Talking Thrush* (New York: E. P. Dutton; London: J. M. Dent, 1899), 36–38. Variants: Crane, Thomas Frederick, ed. *The Exempla of Jacques De Vitry* (London: David Nutt, 1890), 144; Wilson, Epiphanius, *Turkish Literature* (New York: P. F. Collier & Son, 1901), 19–20.
14. In some versions of the story, the legs carried the stag away, but the horns became entangled in the brush, trapping the stag for the hunters. *Fables of Aesop* (New York: A. L. Burt, 1890), 15.
15. Swainson, Charles, *The Folk Lore of British Birds* (London: Elliot Stock, 1886), 107.
16. The ancient kingdom of Abyssinia (Ethiopia) believed its royal line and its original faith stemmed from the visit paid to Solomon by the Queen of Sheba. *The Poetical Works of John Godfrey Saxe* (Boston and New York: Houghton, Mifflin, 1887), 138–139.
17. *Fables of Aesop* (New York: A. L. Burt, 1890), 68.
18. This story is similar to a fable often attributed to Aesop. The story might be useful to launch a discussion of dangers in the modern world. Mechling, Wm. H., "Stories from Tuxtepec, Oaxaca," *Journal of American Folk-Lore* 25, No. 97, July–Sept. (1912): 203.
19. "Animal Stories from the Muskhogean Indians," *Journal of American Folk-Lore* 26, No. 101, July–Sept. (1913): 204; Swanton, John R., *Myths and Tales of the Southeastern Indians* (Washington, D.C.: U.S. Government Printing Office, 1929), 254.

20. See notes on "A Man from Gotham." Field, John Edward, *The Myth of the Pent Cuckoo* (London: Elliot Stock, 1913), 8.
21. Von Schiefner, F. Anton, and W.R.S. Ralston, trans., *Tibetan Tales* (London: Trubner, 1882), 353.
22. Ruskin, Edward A., *Mongo Proverbs and Fables* (Bongandanga: Congo Balolo Mission Press, 1921), 81.
23. Stories have been told for centuries about the wise men or wise fools of Gotham, and as such they became a proverbial title for anyone charged with folly. When Washington Irving caricatured the wisdom of the people of New York, he called the city by the satirical name of Gotham. Field, John Edward, *The Myth of the Pent Cuckoo* (London: Elliot Stock, 1913), 3–4.
24. This story might be used in connection with talking about drugs and drug pushers, who seem to promise much, but only entrap the one who closes eyes and brain. Barker, W. H., and Cecilia Sinclair, *West African Folk-Tales* (London: George G. Harrap, 1917), 29–31.
25. *Fables of Aesop* (New York: A. L. Burt, 1890), 27–28.
26. *Fables of Aesop* (New York: A. L. Burt, 1890), 100–101. Variant: *The Works of Lyof N. Tolstoi* (New York: Thomas Y. Crowell, 1899), 160.
27. *Fables of Aesop* (New York: A. L. Burt, 1890), 211–212.
28. *The Poetical Works of John Godfrey Saxe* (Boston and New York: Houghton, Mifflin, 1887), 144–145.
29. *Fables of Aesop* (New York: A. L. Burt, 1890), 72.
30. Curry, Charles Madison, and Erle Elsworth Clippinger, *Children's Literature* (New York: Rand McNally, 1921), 288–289.
31. Schwab, George, "Bulu Folk-Tales," *Journal of American Folk-Lore* 27, No. 105, July–Sept. (1914): 268–269.
32. Dennys, N. B., *The Folk-Lore of China* (London: Trachner, 1876), 150.
33. Mathew, John, *Two Representative Tribes of Queensland* (London: Adelphe Terrace, 1910), 186.
34. *Fables of Aesop* (New York: A. L. Burt, 1890), 52.
35. Krug, Adolph N., "Bulu Tales from Kamerun, West Africa," *Journal of American Folk-Lore* 25, No. 96, April–June (1912): 123.
36. *Fables of Aesop* (New York: A. L. Burt, 1890), 288–289.
37. Crane, Thomas Frederick, ed. *The Exempla of Jacques De Vitry* (London: David Nutt, 1890), 148.
38. Cooper, Frederic Taber, *An Argosy of Fables* (New York: Frederick A. Stokes, 1921), 438–440.
39. *Fables of Aesop* (New York: A. L. Burt, 1890), 266–267.
40. *Fables of Aesop* (New York: A. L. Burt, 1890), 187–188. Variant: Eliot, Charles W., ed., *The Harvard Classics: Folk-Lore and Fable,* Volume 17 (New York: P. F. Collier & Son, 1909), 45.
41. Basden, G. T., *Among the Ibos of Nigeria* (Philadelphia: J. B. Lippincott, 1921), 273.
42. *Fables of Aesop* (New York: A. L. Burt, 1890), 195–196.
43. Ruskin, Edward A., *Mongo Proverbs and Fables* (Congo Belge: Congo Balolo Mission Press, 1921), 83.
44. Grundtvig, Svend, E. T. Kristensen, and Ingvor Bondesen, *Danish Fairy and Folk Tales*, J. Christian Bay, trans. (New York and London: Harper and Bros., 1899), 1–3.
45. *Fables of Aesop* (New York: A. L. Burt, 1890), 24–25.
46. Dennys, N. B., *The Folk-Lore of China* (London: Trachner, 1876), 151. Variant: Jones, William, *History and Mystery of Precious Stones* (London: Richard Bentley and Son, 1880), 220.
47. This story can be found in the diary of Abraham dela Pryme, p. 220, under date November 10, 1699 (Surtees Society). Hartland, Edwin Sydney, *English Folk and Fairy Tales* (London: W. Scott, 1890), 76–77.
48. *Fables of Aesop* (New York: A. L. Burt, 1890), 61–62.
49. Bulfinch, Thomas, *The Age of Fable* (Boston: S. W. Tilton, 1881), 190–191.
50. Wilson, Epiphanius, *Turkish Literature* (New York: P. F. Collier & Son, 1901), 20.
51. The original story from one source had Anansi dying because he was blind and didn't know where to swim to shore. This ending may be hard for many listeners to take, and the story can easily be concluded by saying the men picked him up after he got tired. In any case, this folktale will be a thought-provoking discussion starter on several subjects. Courtesy and gratitude may be the most immediate theme that comes to mind. However, deeper themes should be considered—for example, the frustration of the handicapped or of the aging with failing faculties, facing the loss of independence, and sometimes the loss of dignity and a sense of self-worth. Another important subject for discussion is the stress and concerns of the caregivers who are responsible for the elderly or infirm. As a contextual note on this story and the manner in which it ends with Anansi's death, it should be remembered that Anansi is a special figure in African folktales and more than one story of his death is told. He is a trickster, murderer, and thief, and he is selfish and unkind even to his family. In this context, his fate at the hands of his caregivers may have seemed appropriate to those who first heard the story. Source: Barker, W. H., and Cecilia Sinclair, *West African Folk-Tales* (London: George G. Harrap, 1917), 73–75.